LISTENING IN CLASSROOMS

WITHDRAWN

LISTENING IN CLASSROOMS

◆ ◆ ◆

Mary M. McCaslin
University of Arizona

Thomas L. Good
University of Arizona

HarperCollinsCollegePublishers

Acquisitions Editor: Chris Jennison
Project Coordination: York Production Services
Cover Design: Wendy Ann Fredericks
Cover Photo: Will & Deni McIntyre/Tony Stone Images
Art Studio: York Production Services
Manufacturing Manager: Hilda Koparanian
Electronic Page Makeup: R.R. Donnelley and Sons Company, Inc.
Printer and Binder: R.R. Donnelley and Sons Company, Inc.
Cover Printer: Color-Imetry Corp.

Listening in Classrooms, First Edition

Library of Congress Cataloging-in-Publication Data
McCaslin, Mary M.
Listening in classrooms/Mary M. McCaslin, Thomas L. Good.—1st ed.
p. cm.
Includes bibliographical references and index.
ISBN 0-673-46881-X
1. Teacher-student relationships. 2. Communication in education. 3. Listening. 4. Group work
in education. 5. Students—Interviews. 6. Home and school. I. Good, Thomas L., 1943-. II.
Title.

LB1033.M34 1996
371.1'023-dc20   95-41088
                                                                                  CIP

95 96 97 98 9 8 7 6 5 4 3 2 1

Dedication

*This book is dedicated to our parents and friends,
James A. McCaslin and Shirley A. McCaslin*

BRIEF CONTENTS

CONTENTS

PREFACE

The relationships among teacher, students, and the opportunities available to them are complicated, challenging, and fundamental. Relationships, in our view, are the stuff of classrooms; relationships bond the aspirations with the realizations of schooling. In this book we develop one model that illuminates the relationship between teacher and student, and how opportunities—other persons and objects—directly (e.g., classmates, tasks) and less directly (e.g., family, nonschool events) influence that relationship. We term our model of teacher-student relationship "co-regulation" to emphasize the supportive, scaffolding role that teachers engage with students, who are themselves actively mediating their experiences.

The ultimate goal of co-regulation may well be student self-regulation; however, it is our position that students and teachers learn in classrooms together and, together, share responsibility for that learning. Students do not learn alone; they are not solely responsible for their learning, nor should they be required to "self-regulate" or "self-motivate" to compensate for or overcome inadequate instruction, materials, or opportunity. And teachers need to be more than subject-matter specialists or presenters of subject matter who teach particular content rather than students. Although an intellectual focus is important and knowledge of the subject matter basic, teachers must have the ability to care about students in ways that *demonstrate* their care.

Co-regulation is one means for demonstrating care. This text describes ways for teachers to communicate systematically and knowledgeably with students and to create structures that are supportive and transitional. We term these transitional structures "scaffolds." These scaffolds enable students to learn about learning—social and academic—so that they might get better at it and come to understand and value who they are as learners, social beings, and human beings.

Our model of co-regulation provides one way to think about how and when teachers might set specific goals to influence particular student processes (e.g., motivation, self-evaluation). The book is rich with examples and illustrations of goals that teachers may have when they listen to students.

Co-regulated learning first distinguishes teacher scaffolding from student processes. In this way specific linkages can be considered between what a teacher wishes to discuss (and influence) and how students might mediate that conversation. Second, co-regulated learning differentiates among motivation, enactment, and evaluation, as processes within students and as features of classroom learning and teacher supportive scaffolding. Although motivation (e.g., goal setting), enactment strategies (e.g., seeing through and following through), and self-evaluation (of progress that informs the achievement and viability of goals), are clearly interdependent and mutually informative processes, we believe that distinguishing among them helps identify and influence student dynamics.

We titled this book *Listening in Classrooms* because we believe that listening is basic to the teacher-student relationship. It is our thesis that understanding co-regulation dynamics leads to meaningful conversation between teachers and students wherein teachers talk with students as well as listen, support, and teach them. We believe that listening conveys and promotes more than trust, although trust is certainly a critical feature of healthy and helpful relationships. Within a model of co-regulation, listening is also a powerful instructional tool that can deepen and strengthen student motivation, enactment, and evaluation. Listening is strategic; listening is learned. One aspect of learning to listen to students is learning what it is like to be a student. Chapters 2 and 4 explore the experience of being a student and being in the company of students in small group work.

The text presents ways in which teachers can structure conversations and interviews with students to support students' academic and social learning. The focus of the text is on conversations with students about their experiences in the classroom. Classroom walls, however, do not block non-classroom experiences. Students can and will bring the non-school with them to the classroom. It is all part of being a student. We address this reality specifically in two chapters: Chapter 5 covers the ethical considerations of listening to students, and Chapter 6 focuses on listening to parents.

In short, our goals for this book are interdependent. We hope to provide one useful way for thinking about the relationship among teacher, student, and opportunity—co-regulation—and to illustrate one useful instructional tool—meaningful, deliberate listening—to promote and empower that relationship.

ACKNOWLEDGMENTS

The ideas in this book have evolved over the past decade and have benefitted from the participation of many persons. The authors have had the good fortune to learn with challenging and caring students and colleagues. We would like to acknowledge and thank the students at Bryn Mawr College whose rigorous thinking and lively support in the early stages of these ideas influenced much of what was to follow. Special thanks to Abbie Segal-Andrews, Susan

Burggraf, Usha Balamore, Stephanie Berg, Tina Blythe, Giulia Cox, Ruth Curran, Eleanor DiMarino-Linnen, Nedra Fetterman, Ray Fields, Barbara Glazier, Eunice King, Tamera Murdock and Elissa Roman. At the University of Missouri-Columbia two students, DeWayne Mason and Catherine Mulryan, were especially helpful in discussing issues of teaching and learning. More recently, we have been able to bring our thinking to the seminar tables at the University of Arizona. We thank participating students, the critical eye of Elisa Thompson and creative challenge of Catherine Seraphim, in particular.

Many colleagues have stimulated and encouraged us along the way. We thank Phyllis Blumenfeld, Lyn Corno, and Bernard Weiner in particular for their good friendship, humor, and critique. The insights of Ursula Casanova, Abbie Segal-Andrews, and Glenda Wilkes strengthened the chapter on listening to parents. We are indebted to Jo Ann Santoro for her assistance, good thinking, and patience with manuscript preparation and revision. Much of the work described in this book was supported, in part, by a Spencer Post-doctoral Fellowship to McCaslin (pka Rohakemper), the Bryn Mawr College Junior Leave Program, and National Science Foundation Grant #TPE–895517 to both authors.

This book would not have been completed without the continuing support and challenge of our editor and friend, Chris Jennison, who believes in the value of focused books and emerging ideas. Thanks Chris.

Finally, we wish to mention two most special students in our lives, Kate Good and Molly Good, who have taught us much about the importance of listening in classrooms.

LISTENING IN CLASSROOMS

◆ ◆ ◆

A MODEL FOR TEACHER–STUDENT CONVERSATIONS: CO–REGULATED LEARNING

Conversation, Co-Regulation, and the Informal Curriculum
Questions and Suggested Activities for Chapter 1

In this book we explore the potential of talking with and listening to students when teachers want to better assess student *learning* (a task of the "formal" curriculum) and when teachers want to better understand student *experience* of the classroom (a task of the "informal" curriculum). In this chapter we introduce our argument for the value of having conversations and interviews with students. We suggest that teachers listen to students as learners, individuals, and as social beings. Classroom events are inherently complex, ambiguous, and subject to different perspectives and multiple interpretations. Interviews and conversations between teachers and students (and teachers and parents) can promote the realization of both academic and personal goals that teachers hold for the students in their classrooms.

We illustrate the potential power of teacher-student conversations to enhance student learning (the attainment of formal curriculum expectations) through a proposed model of *co-regulation*. Our model of co-regulation, which we examine at length, is based on the concept of *relationship*. Relationships connect teacher, students, and opportunities. Co-regulation is the process by which teachers, through their relationships with students and the opportunities they provide them, support and "scaffold" adaptive student learning. Just as teachers learn more about student learning and motivation by discussing it with them, so too do students learn more about their own learning and motivation when they try to articulate their understanding within the context of teacher structure (questions) and support.

Students negotiate more than the intended, formal curriculum of subject-matter expectations when they learn in classrooms. They also navigate the often unintended (and unattended) informal curriculum of "things that matter" other than mastery of assigned subjects: Am I a good friend? an honest student? Students more and less learn this informal curriculum; the nature of their learning has important consequences for students themselves and those with whom they interact. Negotiating the informal curriculum affects not only academic performance (and, thus, attainment of formal curriculum goals) but also students' general dispositions and coping strategies, which in turn affect a wide arena of interpersonal action and intrapersonal (inner) dynamics (e.g., willingness to cooperate, respect for diversity in people and ideas, response to conflict).

Students confront multiple and competing goals within and between the formal and informal curricula. They need to learn how to identify and coordinate among them if they are to resolve conflicts and make progress. We will argue that the informal curriculum needs to become explicit and include the deliberate recognition of goal conflict and teaching of what we call "goal coordination" (Dodge, Asher, & Parkhurst, 1989; McCaslin & Good, 1996). We think mindful conversation and planned interviews with students are important ways to model, teach, and learn these goal identification and coordination strategies. We also illustrate the importance of conversations and interviews so that teachers and students simply better understand themselves and one another.

In summary, we maintain that listening to students is important for academic, affective, and social reasons. Our intent in writing this book is to provide useful tools that teachers might use to help them attain the goals they hold for students in their classrooms. Our "tool kit" contains an array of instruments and models that we hope will have general power and service. We judge a tool's value by its usefulness in the everydayness of classrooms and its place within the existing teacher role. However, a tool must be selected in order for it to be potentially useful, and selection rests on perceived need and appropriateness. This, then, is where we begin.

We focus on why we think listening to students is a feasible and worthy goal in the first place. Teachers are nearly overwhelmed by multiple and competing expectations for their time, talents, and energy. We certainly are asking teachers to stretch if not strain their own arsenal of goal-coordination strategies. In this chapter we make our case for listening to students. We describe how listening to students fits within the teacher role and provide a model of co-regulation that connects student mediation and teacher listening. We suggest that listening to and discussing concerns with students aid their attainment of formal curriculum standards *and* personal/social growth. Distinctions between the formal and informal curriculum are necessarily difficult to make because they mutually influence and inform each other. Indeed, our model of co-regulation illustrates just this point.

Finally, although there are other tools available to obtain information about student knowledge and affect in general (e.g., questionnaires), we think classroom conversations with individual students (or small groups of students) are uniquely suited to understanding and supporting students' intellectual progress and affective world. We also believe that, through deliberate conversation, student self-knowledge is enhanced as teachers actively mediate and influence students' experiences and their interpretation of them. In short, conversations with students, in our perspective, serve a purpose larger than the conversation itself. Conversations, like questions, help *structure and mediate* student self-knowledge even as they enhance teacher understanding of student experience. In our view, then, conversations are deliberate and fundamental learning opportunities for teachers and students. We return to this point in Chapter 3, especially.

◆ AMBIGUITY OF PERFORMANCE AND BEHAVIOR

Classroom events are inherently ambiguous; thus, they are open to multiple and competing interpretations. One way to organize these events is to impose a framework that might lend predictability—or at least interpretability—to the stream of complex and ambiguous activity that characterizes "life in classrooms" (Jackson, 1968; Jackson, Boostrom, & Hansen, 1993). We find a three-part framework useful to differentiate the "presses" of teaching and learning that confront teachers *and* students: instruction, management, and assessment. These three presses are interdependent. For example, one way that a teacher might minimize management concerns is by controlling the delivery and increasing the pace of instruction. Indeed, this type of "managed instruction" has been advocated for the less-advantaged, presumed nonmotivated learner. Basically, the idea is to keep things moving so these students don't have time to get off track or "off task." (See Rosenshine and Stevens, 1986, for more complete discussion.)

Weinert and Helmke (1987), noting the management advantages of fast-paced instruction, however, also found that students in these classrooms experienced *increased performance anxiety* when required to demonstrate their learning. Increased student anxiety clearly interferes with both teachers and students attaining their goals. Importantly, these dynamics are not apparent. Based on observation alone, teachers are likely to draw inappropriate conclusions about and, thus, respond inappropriately to students. That is, teachers are likely to infer that students' low performance is due to students' lack of motivation (one of the rationales for this form of managed instruction in the first place), rather than due to the students' very desire to demonstrate learning. Without knowledge of student anxiety, teachers' potential strategies (e.g., increase the pace, strengthen accountability) with these students likely exacerbate the situation.

Instruction, management, and assessment, then, are interdependent features of the formal curriculum that affect student experience in classrooms, teachers' beliefs about and perceptions of those experiences, and teachers' subsequent strategies with students. Teacher strategies with students directly and indirectly affect student beliefs and performance. It would be nice if these dynamics were straightforward, but they are not. Ambiguity is one key reason for engaging students in conversations and interviews. Teachers confront ambiguity and need to decipher student behavior in order to respond strategically in even the most routine and well-patterned classroom procedures.

Consider, for example, student hand raising. Which students raise their hands frequently because they are unsure and are trying to clarify their understanding? Which ones raise their hands because they are confident and want to show teacher and peers how they have mastered material? Who just wants to participate? avoid surprises? One of the authors learned early that in some classes she was less likely to be called on if her hand was raised than if it was not. Careful observation and record keeping over time might help the teacher to make these decisions; however, a simple conversation might be an easier, more efficient, and efficacious way to interpret student actions. Discussions can also help students articulate and better understand their own motivation and interests as well as communicate with their teacher.

◆ DEMANDS OF THE TEACHER ROLE

Teachers are not dispassionate researchers; they have the responsibility of designing and maintaining interactions in the pursuit of student learning. Consider that even researchers, who can sit in classrooms and reflect upon what is happening (without such responsibility), often have difficulty in understanding and determining the significance of particular actions. (For extensive coverage of this concern, see Good & Brophy, 1994.) If researchers have difficulty, it seems apparent that teachers, who have many responsibilities other than observing and interpreting student behavior, might have difficulty in understanding classroom events without additional information.

Jackson, Boostram, and Hansen (1993), a group of university researchers, describe the problem in their work this way:

> But what we were discovering as classroom observers was that often, the more we looked, the more puzzling the situation became and, consequently, the more unreliable were our conclusions about the situation in general. Contrary to what we had previously learned, repeated observations seemed to breed doubt rather than certainty. (pp. 235–236)

Jackson and colleagues stressed that the more they looked and reflected upon what they had seen and heard, they became both more aware of the difficult complexity of classroom life and more respectful of teachers and their ability to deal with such difficult complexity.

Furthermore, although a viable research goal may be to (merely) *interpret* classroom events, teachers are not allowed the distance and relative passivity of bystanders. Teachers *influence* classroom events, and through the opportunities they design and the interactions they have with students, teachers actively participate in student learning and experience. We maintain that *teachers are coparticipants in and co-regulators of student learning and experience*. Thus, resolving ambiguity is no small matter.

The role of teacher, then, requires teachers to actively seek and act on information about student learning of the formal curriculum. Student learning and motivation to learn are ambiguous phenomena that we infer from student activity and performance. Students and teachers judge and are judged by student performance. Indeed, there are times when judgment of teachers and students based on student test performance seems like a national sport (Good, 1996; McCaslin & Good, 1992). Thus, student performance seems an especially important facet of the formal curriculum for teachers to get smarter about. We suggest that a model of co-regulation, which we now present, informs: 1) how students' motivational and learning processes might mediate their performance, and 2) how teachers might influence those mediational processes through their relationships with students and the kinds of opportunities and supportive structures they provide them.

First, we describe the proposed student mediational processes. Second, we suggest how teachers might influence them with specific examples of teacher scaffolding conversations with students. Co-regulation is all about student mediation and teacher scaffolding, *taken together* (this model and discussion is adapted from McCaslin & Good, 1996).

❖ A MODEL OF CO-REGULATED LEARNING

We suggest that students seek a certain standard of excellence in their negotiation of the formal curriculum. Standards include setting, pursuing, and evaluating goals and their attainment. We may set standards for students, but as any teacher will remind us, students do not necessarily accept them. It also is not unusual for students to set goals for themselves that differ from what we might wish for them. For example, some students set unrealistically high goals, given their present capabilities. Others may select unchallenging, readily attainable goals—perhaps because they fear failure, believe *fast* means *smart*, or just don't care. Others may remain passive; they will work on what is required (to avoid trouble) with little personal investment, one way or another (see, for example, Brantlinger, 1993).

In our view, how students negotiate classroom standards—the accountability demands of the formal curriculum—is open to teacher influence through modeling, instruction, and instructional opportunities like tasks and tests. One way teachers can influence how students set, pursue, and evaluate goals is through conversations around student engagement of informative tasks. Deliberate conversation about task performance is one way to enhance the *co-regulation*, or mutual influence, between teacher and students in the setting and attainment of a standard of excellence.

Conversations (versus monologues, sermons, or lectures) convey a sense of "we-ness." Student learning is not an individual struggle, goals are not set in isolation, persistence is not only about "how long" but about "in what way" and "for what purpose." Negotiation of standards, in this perspective, is a responsibility that teachers and students share. Co-regulated learning replaces an exclusive focus on the teacher *or* students (or their parents) who are more or less willing and/or able to learn. Co-regulated learning integrates the social supports of the classroom with the opportunities it affords.

Figures 1.1, 1.2, and 1.3 depict three broadly defined interdependent domains of co-regulation—motivation, enactment, and evaluation—and how teachers might scaffold student mediation within each domain through the design of instruction and opportunity. Taken together, we think the full model of co-regulated learning (see Figure 1.4) meaningfully organizes how students negotiate standards, that is, how they transform the expectations and supports of the formal curriculum as represented by teacher, tasks, and tests. We define what we mean by each mediational domain.

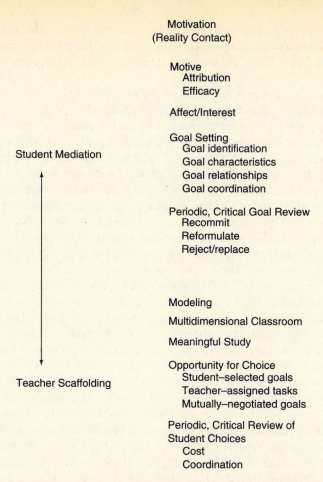

Motivation
(Reality Contact)

Motive
    Attribution
    Efficacy

Affect/Interest

Goal Setting
    Goal identification
    Goal characteristics
    Goal relationships
    Goal coordination

Periodic, Critical Goal Review
    Recommit
    Reformulate
    Reject/replace

Modeling

Multidimensional Classroom

Meaningful Study

Opportunity for Choice
    Student–selected goals
    Teacher–assigned tasks
    Mutually–negotiated goals

Periodic, Critical Review of
Student Choices
    Cost
    Coordination

Student Mediation

Teacher Scaffolding

FIGURE 1.1 A Partial Model of Co-Regulated Learning: Motivation

◆ MOTIVATION

Motivation, as we mean it here, refers to motives and goal setting, coordination, and review. *Motive* includes both the looking back, the "why" behind our own or another's performance, and the looking forward, the "what next" that influences how we understand ourselves in relation to a future task. Thus, motive incorporates both the attributions we make for—the reasons behind—our performance (e.g., because of ability, anxiety, effort, fear, help, hindrance, interest, luck, task difficulty) and our sense of efficacy—our expectations—about how we will perform in the future (see Weiner, 1992, for extended discussion of attribution theory; Bandura, 1986, for extended discussion of social learning theory and the enhancement of self-efficacy).

    Goal setting includes individual goal(s), their interrelation, and their coordination (see Dodge et al., 1989; McCaslin & Good, 1996, for extended discussion). Individual goals can be considered by features like their difficulty (e.g., moderately difficult versus easy), specificity (e.g., finish first versus do well), and psychological distance (e.g., do well today versus be a physician when I grow up).

Relationships among goals need consideration. For example, multiple goals can be compatible in that they complement each other (e.g., you can go to class and to the pep rally), are instrumental to each other (e.g., your ticket to the pep rally is to do well in class; doing well today promotes being a physician later), or compensate for each other (e.g., you participate in the pep rally to offset minimal participation during small group in class). And, of course, goals can be incompatible. Attainment of one goal can interfere with another (e.g., working swing shift to maintain employment and completing daily homework assignments). Goals can negate each other (e.g., attending a late-night party with friends the day before a morning exam). Finally, goals can be independent of each other; thus, they neither interfere nor overlap. Each takes up psychological space, personal time, and energy.

Students have multiple goals. Multiple goals call for identification of individual goals and the relationships among them, and *goal-coordination* strategies. Students learn goal-coordination strategies when they learn, for example, to prioritize, modify, substitute, abandon, or defer goals. Thus, students learn to get the homework done before television, decide to "do well enough" or "satisfice" (Simon, 1969) on an assignment to allow time with friends, join a research project to combine school work with social life, or quit the team because there is not enough time for practice *and* work—but maybe next year.

In short, motivation is all about knowledge of oneself and one's goals: considering where one is in relation to where one wants to be, knowing how hard it is to be in more than one place at a time, and coping with the stress of choice. We include personal interest, affect, and desires in motivation, and note that personal goals can reflect both "intrinsic" (because I want to learn more) and "extrinsic" (so I can go out to recess with my friends) motives. *We do not claim*, as others have (e.g., Deci & Ryan, 1985; Harter, 1981; Nolen, 1988), that one is inherently better than another (i.e., that intrinsic motivation is, by definition, better than extrinsic motivation). Rather, we would hope that classrooms are designed so that students can enjoy and optimize multiple sources of motivation. For example, multipli-motivated students complete assignments because they want to learn *and* they want what results—to go to recess with their friends. Uni-motivated students might only value the learning or only engage in learning because it is required in order to be with valued friends.

Just as we do not consider a single source of motivation optimal or promote an absolute hierarchy of goodness among sources of motivation, we do not believe that classrooms should be only about compatible goals. Indeed, we think learning how to coordinate goals requires the opportunity—the need—to coordinate among them. Neither "having it all" nor "having none" is particularly useful preparation for coping with the reality of choice, and the conflicts of choice, that are part of life. Nor do we think a classroom designed for the single-minded pursuit of a single goal is an optimal situation. We think this is one of the more important lessons of biology: organisms can be singularly oversuited to a particular environment such that even minor changes in context bring about their demise. The world is simply too interdependent and changing for singlemindedness to be a realistic, productive, or mentally healthy model (see also Dodge et al., 1989).

We believe that teachers should promote students' *periodic, critical goal review*. Periodic, critical goal review both teaches and allows students to reassess the value and feasibility of their goals, in their own terms and in relation to the stated goals or standards of the curriculum. Goal review should also promote and teach students how to decide to recommit, reformulate, or reject (and replace) their goals.

This constellation of context, self, and other in students' setting, pursuit, and coordination of their goals, then, is what we mean by *student motivation*. We do not consider motivation a personal variable, one that resides only in the student. Nor do we look solely to the environment. In our conception, motivation is a shared, co-regulated variable which emerges through the integration of the student with the personal and task resources within the context of the classroom. Students clearly bring more than their physical selves to this formulation. Just how students integrate messages from family and friends about who and what they are and want will be explored in Chapters 2 and 6.

◆ ENACTMENT

Enactment is not about choice, it is about the seeing through and following through on choices that have been made (or, as we will see, required). The enactment phase protects and promotes the goals set in the motivation phase. If motivation is a sort of "reality contact" (that is, the setting of reasonable goals given capabilities and the situation), enactment is the arena of "reality testing." Enactment is all about *resource management*; resources are to be found within oneself and within the classroom setting (Corno & Mandinach, 1983; Corno & Rohrkemper, 1985).

Enactment strategies include control over the self and control over the persons (e.g., teachers, peers) and physical resources of the classroom. Control over the self refers to self-modification that might alter or mediate affect, volitional, and cognitive strategies. For example, a student can take a deep breath when feeling anxious; try harder on a difficult task; recognize frustration and change detrimental inner speech before tears; review procedures, revise expectations, and approach a task with a different plan.

Control over other resources—interpersonal and physical—in classrooms includes such modifications as asking teacher or peers for help, changing seats to avoid distraction, and checking a different book if the current explanation is unclear (see Corno, 1992; Corno & Rohrkemper, 1985; Rohrkemper & Corno, 1988, for more complete examples). In our view, enactment strate-

Enactment
(Reality Testing)

Strategic Resource Management
    Management of self
      self–involved
        affect
        volition
      task–involved
        cognitive and
        metacognitive
        strategies;
        goal refinement

Student Mediation

    Management of others
      assistance
      assertion
      equity
    Management of objects
      modification of tasks,
      time, space, location

Strategic Progress Checks
    Interim assessment of
    momentum, purpose, direction

Instructional Opportunities
    Student self–management
      self–involved
        drafts
        time lines
        reinforcements
      task–involved
        algorithmic, heuristic, and
        "executive" strategies
    Management of others
      norms for peer:
      assistance

Teacher Scaffolding

      mobility
      conversation
      norms for teacher:
        availability
      conversation
    Management of objects
      task structure,
      complexity and difficulty;
      malleability of classroom features

Strategic Progress Checks
    Interim progress reports
    Accountability

FIGURE 1.2 A Partial Model of Co-Regulated Learning: Enactment

gies for seeing through and following through are learned through interpersonal supports and constructive opportunities. We look to teachers and tasks that both *promote and require* the development of enactive strategies.

Finally, we include the notion of *progress* in our definition of enactment. Without progress there is simply activity. Thus, we take issue with conceptions of students who are believed "mastery-oriented" because they will not quit in the face of repetitive or overwhelming failure. Compulsivity is not necessarily a virtue. Similarly, students are not by definition "helpless" because they quit when they do not experience progress. Rather, knowing when to cut one's losses and recognizing when one cannot do it alone is part of what we consider "adaptive learning" (McCaslin, 1990; McCaslin Rohrkemper, 1989; Rohrkemper & Corno, 1988; cf., Diener & Dweck, 1978). Implicit in this conception is the notion of periodic, critical goal review described previously. Prolonged enactment without progress or without pleasure suggests that it is time to pull up and reconsider.

Relationships Between Enactment and Motivation   In short, enactment is the mindfulness that incorporates what we think of as perseverance with a sense of malleability and the strategic capability to make progress toward one's goal—and, if not one's *own* goal, then that imposed by another.

Enactment without motivation is clearly possible; indeed, much of schooling is about the pursuit of goals prescribed by others. In this case, students are known by their "volition" rather than by their "motivation" (see Corno, 1992, Heckhausen, 1991, for discussion of volition). Students are doing as required; their motivation is actually a moot point. The students' job is to *bear down* and get it done. Too much volitional striving in the absence of motivation, strategic engagement without periodic goal review (reflecting on "Why am I doing this? What am I looking for? What do I want?") has been hypothesized as the stuff of alienation and diffusion of responsibility (McCaslin, 1990; McCaslin & Good, 1992, 1996). Sheer volition can be costly (see also, Kelman & Hamilton, 1989).

Motivation without enactment is also possible. Needs and wishes are not always acted on. "If only I had . . ." is an all-too-common lament. Goals, even if set and "objectively" realistic, are not always attained—witness New Year's resolutions. The self-defeat of lack of organization, procrastination, and simply not knowing how to marshall resources—one's own or others', to follow through on intentions are as common as they are frustrating and painful. Motivation unrealized has little to recommend it.

In our view, an optimal learner is one who is motivational *and* volitional. Our optimal learner knows how to set and pursue goals and, when goal setting is not feasible, knows how to transform assigned tasks to make them more palatable, if not more personally meaningful. *Motivation with enactment* is usually preferable to either one without the other, but these dynamics are not as straightforward as they might seem at first glance. Let's consider how they might evolve.

Opportunity, Motivation, and Enactment Mediating, or transforming, assigned tasks to make them more attractive and/or accessible is an important skill because life is not always about choice; sometimes it is simply about work (see also Corno, 1992; Corno & Kanfer, 1993) and doing as told. This is certainly true of many classrooms. Choice is not always possible; indeed, we argue that choice is not always desirable. Allowing students the "choice" to learn to read or not, for example, is simply untenable. Similarly students are not allowed to choose to hurt themselves, each another, or the teacher. Other limitations of sheer choice are more subtle, however, and are often overlooked in the pursuit of student interest to enhance student intrinsic motivation (e.g., Clifford, 1991; Deci & Ryan, 1985; Nolen, 1988).

Nash (1979, as reported in Fennema, 1987), for example, found that across the school years (grades 2–12), students perceive certain intellectual capabilities as feminine and others as masculine. Students of both genders believed that girls' abilities are in verbal and social skills and boys' are in spatial and mechanical domains. With puberty, students of both genders added mathematics and science to the "male" list. Students acted on these beliefs when given the opportunity to choose tasks. First, students chose tasks for their believed gender-appropriateness. Second, Nash found that not only did task choice channel student learning opportunities in stereotypic ways, but that students persisted longer and valued their successes more if they were associated with gender-appropriate tasks. Yikes! Choice may foster motivation, but it may also foster detrimental self-fulfilling prophecies. It is not clear that choice, by definition, promotes optimal learning.

We suggest that teachers can only be *assured* that students will choose what is "good for them" when the choices offered are all good for them. Determining the array of opportunity is the responsibility of the teacher; extending the option of choice beyond the array is also the teacher's call. In our view, in optimal classrooms, teachers provide opportunities for educative choice and are clear when choice is not an option. Teachers also allow opportunities for students to negotiate within an assigned task so that teacher and student *share* aspects of the negotiated goal. Each is important; the issue is one of *proportion*. Students who only pursue what "interests" them may be learning bad habits of self-indulgence and narcissism. Students who only experience "getting what they want" through protracted after-the-fact negotiation may be learning cynical habits of manipulation. And students who only do as they are told may be learning dangerous habits of self-denial and obedience (Kelman & Hamilton, 1989). Again, the issue is one of appropriateness and proportion.

Through the interplay of opportunity, instruction, and development, students learn about setting goals, pursuing assigned tasks, and transforming assigned tasks into shared goals. Through these opportunities, students learn how to make informed choices. As students are able to assume more responsibility for their choices—that is, they understand the implications of their decisions—then increasing opportunities for more informed choice makes sense. In each instance—choice, nonchoice, and shared or "negotiated" choice—teachers support and scaffold (co-regulate) student enactment strategies to at-

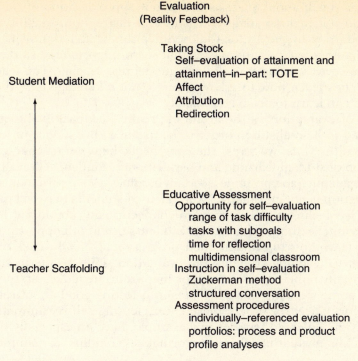

Evaluation
(Reality Feedback)

Taking Stock
    Self–evaluation of attainment and
    attainment–in–part: TOTE
    Affect
    Attribution
    Redirection

Student Mediation

Teacher Scaffolding

Educative Assessment
    Opportunity for self–evaluation
        range of task difficulty
        tasks with subgoals
        time for reflection
        multidimensional classroom
    Instruction in self–evaluation
        Zuckerman method
        structured conversation
    Assessment procedures
        individually–referenced evaluation
        portfolios: process and product
        profile analyses

FIGURE 1.3 A Partial Model of Co-Regulated Learning: Evaluation

tain progress toward a self-selected, other-assigned, or negotiated shared goal. In each instance, however, responsibility for student attainment is shared.

◆ EVALUATION

A third feature of student mediation, and thus, of co-regulated learning, is the opportunity for self-evaluation. Evaluation usually occurs after completing a task, but it can occur along the way *if* the task provides the opportunity. We think of evaluation as a sort of "taking stock," testing where one is against a standard one is trying to achieve. Miller, Galanter, & Pribram (1960) described this sort of taking stock as a "TOTE unit." TOTE stands for Test-Operate-Test-Exit in the information-processing tradition. The student first tests if she is where she wants to be, if she has met her standard. If so, she is done and exits. If not, she operates—that is, she does something she expects will take her closer to her goal. She then tests again: is she there? If so, she exits; if not she acts again, and so on, until the standard is met, the cycle complete. Upon attaining the standard they seek, students may go on to another task or, as Heckhausen (1991) describes, "linger a while with the pleasant feeling" (p. 187). They have earned a feeling of satisfaction and pride (Weiner, 1986).

Admittedly, the TOTE unit is not an ideal model of self-evaluation by individuals who feel, as well as think, about what they do (Vygotsky, 1978). Self-evaluation is as much about *affect* as it is about approximation of *standards*. TOTE units do not include anxiety, frustration, distraction, inability to approach a standard strategically, or the modification or abandonment of that standard, to name a few missing pieces that seem important in student self-evaluation. However, we find it useful as a model that teachers can teach students so that they learn how to assess change (not *all* change is in the right direction) and can learn to do so realistically.

We think of evaluation as the arena of "reality feedback." Student self-appraisals need to be realistic in order to be useful in the service of learning and mental health. Thus, we stress the *congruence* between teacher and student evaluation of student learning and performance. Student self-evaluations also need to be adaptive and promote a certain hardiness. We return to this point.

Self-evaluation is not automatic. Even talented students may feel more relief (or negative feelings) after an exam than curiosity about the level or causes of their intellectual performance. Students need both opportunity and instruction to learn how to evaluate their progress realistically. Lack of deliberate attention to teaching students self-evaluation skills results in students who are essentially nonreflective about, or inappropriate judges of, their own learning. For some students this translates into feeling good about relatively mediocre performance; for others there is unrelenting self-recrimination for lack of perfection. Talented females, for example, have an especially difficult time realistically evaluating their performance (Phillips & Zimmerman, 1990).

Opportunity   Learning to self-evaluate, like learning to set, coordinate, and pursue goals, requires opportunity. Thus, students profit from exposure to a range of task difficulty. They cannot learn about not knowing, incomplete understanding, and/or mastery without confronting the full array of challenge. Steady exposure to tasks that are much too difficult or too easy is not an appropriate vehicle for learning self-evaluation (or much else, see Rohrkemper & Corno, 1988), unless the goal is to locate one's boundaries. We suggest that it is much more educative to provide students opportunities that sample the spectrum, with primary emphasis on tasks of moderate difficulty (Atkinson, 1964; Clifford, 1991; McCaslin, 1991; McCaslin Rohrkemper, 1989; Rohrkemper, 1986; Rohrkemper & Corno, 1988).

Opportunity for evaluation includes tasks that consist of subgoals or other markers of understandings-in-part or incomplete learning. Opportunity also includes time, because evaluation takes time. Perhaps this is one reason students in fast-paced classrooms (the managed instruction described previously) are more anxious when taking tests: they haven't had a chance to learn—to evaluate—whether they know the material. Evaluation for them will occur *after* the test and likely only by the teacher.

Instruction   Instruction in evaluation can be both direct and indirect. Direct instruction might look like the processes described by Zuckerman (1994), a

Russian educator. She describes student self-evaluation as "self-appraisal" and defines it as the ability to differentiate one's knowledge, partial knowledge, and ignorance "in a manner that is as optimistic as possible, perceiving in areas of ignorance and inability not evidence of their weakness and helplessness, but prospects of improvement" (p. 410).

Zuckerman's curriculum, "Introduction to School Life" is designed to change students' private perceptions of personal deficiency into active, interpersonal opportunities. The goal is that, through realistic self-evaluation, students will replace self-recriminations of "Why can't I do this?" that do not promote improvement with "What do I need?" plans for action. Realistic self-evaluation is systematically taught to students as early as first grade. Briefly, students are asked to evaluate their performance. Their evaluations are compared with their teacher's evaluation. If the evaluations match, *independent of the level of attainment*, students are praised for appropriate self-evaluation. Overevaluation and underevaluation are confronted and discussed as teachers ask the individual students questions designed to make them more aware of the relationship between their progress and the performance criteria.

Indirect instruction can occur through the evaluation systems that teachers use to assess student learning in their classrooms. Krampen (1987), who studied teachers in Germany, found, for example, that students can profit from assessment procedures that help students focus on themselves in relation to the subject matter (individually oriented) rather than focus on themselves in relation to others (social comparison), or sheer subject matter acquisition (criterion-referenced mastery assessment, like current approaches to outcome-based education).

A focus on "self in relation to subject matter" is a focus on one's own progress, on how much progress one has made. Teachers in Krampen's study fostered student focus on self in relation to subject matter through individually oriented feedback that compared a student's present performance with her/his own past performance. Students of all levels of ability whose teachers provided this type of feedback improved more than students whose teachers provided social-comparison feedback (e.g., "in comparison to the other students . . . ") or simple mastery feedback (e.g., "you have achieved 8 of 10 objectives . . . ").

In addition, in comparison to students whose teachers provided social comparison or simple mastery feedback, students exposed to self in relation to subject matter, or individually oriented feedback, held positive expectations for continued improvement. Finally, over the long term, these students also decreased in test anxiety. Research by Ames and colleagues (e.g., Ames, 1992) in the United States generally support these results. Individually oriented feedback improves student performance, self-appraisal, and expectations for future learning. We suspect this happens in part because individually oriented feedback scaffolds student learning to self-evaluate. Teachers who provide individually oriented feedback on learning progress also are more likely to support the *processes* of learning rather than only the products. In this way, they help students learn how to evaluate progress toward a goal.

In sum, teachers can help students learn to self-evaluate through the kinds of task opportunities they provide, active instruction in how to realistically evaluate one's work, and assessment of student learning that focuses the student on her/his individual progress (rather than as compared to how others are doing or how much more there is to learn).

Finally, we hypothesize that realistic self-evaluation functions as an important motivational tool because it empowers the student by integrating realistic goal setting (motivation), seeing through and following through on one's commitments (enactment), with level of attainment and its consequences. Thus, the three features of our model of student mediation and co-regulated learning are mutually informative for the student and the teacher who co-regulates these processes through classroom opportunities and personal support.

Student Self-Evaluation and Teacher Support Earlier we mentioned that in addition to being realistic, student self-evaluation needs to be adaptive. We suggest that teaching students realistic self-appraisal will not always be comfortable. If a student has failed, for example, the failure needs to be verified without undoing the student—and that is not an easy thing. We find Zuckerman's (1994) work helpful here.

Recall that Zuckerman's focus was to help students recognize that partial learning and ignorance are cues that signal the need for additional resources, one's own and others'. Thus, realistic self-evaluation goes hand in hand with enactment strategies. Teacher and student agree that the student has not yet achieved a desired standard of performance. This agreement signals the need for strategic behavior, which is the primary focus of the conversation. It is important to pull students away from negative attributions (e.g., of low ability) and detrimental self-talk (or "inner speech" [Vygotsky, 1962; 1978]) when they fail to meet a goal and to bring them into a future, next-step, action perspective (Kuhl, 1985; Rohrkemper, 1986). Negative self-talk ("It doesn't matter how much I try") inhibits learning. It is useful to focus students instead on future plans ("I am going to work on this a different way. This time . . . ").

It goes without saying that if failure is pervasive and eminent, or if failure is uninformative, it has little to recommend it. Indeed, we would argue that mindless or overwhelming failure has no place in the classroom (see also, Covington, 1992; and Rohrkemper & Corno, 1988). In cases of such uninformative failure, realistic self-evaluation calls for critical goal review: whatever is desired (or demanded) is costing too much and, even if one pays the high price, one is still not likely to acquire it. In the meantime, other more feasible goals are left unexamined. Goal modification or substitution seem the options for teacher and student to explore. In our view, realistic and adaptive self-evaluation is a critical skill for learning and for mental health.

As this discussion illustrates, our model of co-regulated learning situates the teacher *with* the student; the teacher actively scaffolds and supports the development of student mediation in each of three interdependent domains. Figure 1.4 displays the full model of co-regulated learning. The co-regulation

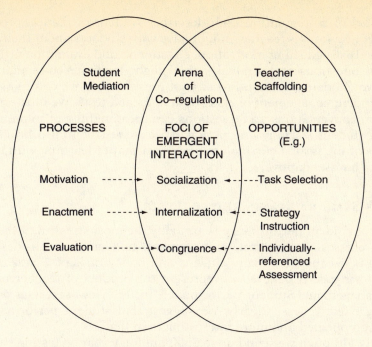

FIGURE 1.4 A Model of Co-Regulation: Student Mediation, Teacher Scaffolding, and Foci of Emergent Interaction

model in Figure 1.4 illustrates our hypotheses about the arena of higher psychological processes that teachers and students "share." Thus, students' interdependent mediational domains of motivation, enactment and evaluation are in emergent interaction with teacher scaffolding via specific opportunities—tasks, instruction, and assessment—within the context of the teacher-student relationship. Each influences the other. We have tentatively labeled the focus of each emergent interaction to highlight what we believe are the relative teacher priorities that guide teacher scaffolding.

We now turn our attention to illustrative examples of how *deliberate conversations* with students might also scaffold and enhance specific features of student mediation of performance expectations.

❖ CONVERSATION, CO-REGULATION, AND STUDENT ASSESSMENT

We have emphasized throughout our discussion that deliberate conversation is an important part of co-regulating students' learning. Although the ultimate goal may be that students learn to self-regulate in ever-increasing arenas, coregulation is the process by which the teacher scaffolds and supports that learning through her/his relationships with students.

Our model of co-regulation both describes student mediation processes and guides conversations teachers might have with students about their learning progress. Distinguishing motivation, enactment, and evaluation organizes the kinds of questions and strategies that might facilitate co-regulation of (and improve) student learning. For ease of presentation, we confine our examples to student engagement of classroom tasks and tests. We illustrate how co-regulation conversations and questions can meaningfully promote the assessment of student learning and performance. Assessment also bridges the expectations of the formal curriculum of subject-matter learning with the development of hardy, adaptive, learners.

◆ Assessment as Symbol: Standardized Tests

Assessment of student performance is arguably the most stressful of the three curriculum presses—instruction, management, and assessment—described earlier. This is because, for many citizens and policy makers, assessment of student performance is believed to represent the product of teacher instruction and management. Student performance, in this view, serves as a proxy for teaching effectiveness. Clearly, we suggest that student performance is both more complicated and more interesting than that.

Ironically, although we spend up to $500 million a year on testing students in the United States, we seldom ask students what they think, believe, or feel about things that matter—to us and/or to them. As McCaslin and Good (1992, 1996) have noted, society's unquestioning belief in standardized testing is very expensive and often counterproductive. In our standardized-testing agenda, we primarily "ask" students what they know—and some contend that even this focus on limited, factual-knowledge assessment is done poorly (e.g., Good, 1996; Mitchell, 1992). We believe that assessment has the potential to reveal both student knowledge of subject matter and of things that matter. We believe this potential is yet to be realized, and we suggest that if this potential is *ever* to be realized it will be because teacher-designed tasks and tests set the standard and led the way (witness student portfolios).

◆ Assessment as Real: Classroom Tasks and Tests

Relatively traditional aspects of classroom life—like classroom tasks and tests as compared with standardized tests—often go unexamined; they are like the very air teachers and students breathe. However, the everydayness and pervasiveness of these performance vehicles is one reason to be mindful of students' understanding of them. Further, the potential cumulative effects of everyday tasks and tests are all the more reason to deliberately construe them as opportunities for students to better understand themselves as learners. As we have argued, everyday tasks and tests can be one way for students to learn (and teachers to assess) a certain hardiness and adaptiveness, in addition to level of mastery of subject matter.

How, then, might teachers make tasks and tests more informative? We have already discussed issues of opportunity, instruction, and feedback in students learning to self-evaluate. We now focus on the types of questions teachers might want to ask students so that both teachers and students may be more aware of how students mediate assessment opportunities. We consider these questions part of the supportive scaffolding that co-regulates student mediation.

◆ **MOTIVATIONAL SCAFFOLDING**

One area that teachers may want to explore is the *why* behind student performance goals. Often, researchers and teachers *assume* they know what kinds of tasks students prefer and, thus, why they select or how they modify them. We provide a detailed example to illustrate our point: if you want to understand students' mediation and motivation, asking them is a useful start.

Doyle (1983) for a decade argued persuasively that students seek to reduce risk and ambiguity in classroom tasks and spend their energies "dummying down" the curriculum rather than learning it. Doyle's arguments struck a chord for many (the authors included) and were essentially unchallenged. Ray Fields (1990), an educator and school psychologist, however, thought otherwise. Rather than assuming students wanted to reduce risk and ambiguity, he decided to conduct research to test the assertion. In part, Fields wanted to explore students' perceptions about the relationship between perceived risk and ambiguity. He suspected that it was not additive (i.e., more ambiguity = more risk), as Doyle asserted. Fields found that, not only did students not want to reduce ambiguity, they wanted to *increase* it. Increased ambiguity for these students meant *decreased* risk. Thus, for these students, risk and ambiguity were inversely, not additively, related—the opposite of the prevailing wisdom.

Consider this typical scenario. The teacher calls on a student with a relatively "low-level" factual question: "Who was the first to sign the Declaration of Independence?" The student pauses; the teacher assumes she/he does not know the answer and moves on. Ambiguity is very low (it is a straightforward question), but the risk is high: there is one, single right answer, and either you know it (now) or you don't. Compare this with a teacher-asked, higher-level question that requires integration or analysis: "In what ways has the concept of "independence" evolved in our country since the Declaration of Independence?" Ambiguity is high (it is a complex question), but the risk is low: there are multiple reasonable responses and answers-in-part, thus the bandwidth of acceptable responses is greater. Importantly, student pauses in responding to higher-level, complex questions are more apt to be interpreted as thoughtfulness, not lack of knowledge or avoidance.

Fields's study, with elementary-school students, indicated that students understood these dynamics and preferred to take their chances with ambiguity. Low-level, unambiguous questions were the most threatening; if the answer was not known, the student could not attempt an answer-in-part. Ironically, students who are believed less talented and less motivated to learn are especially likely to be asked low-level questions. Given the perceived threat of such questions, rather than helping these students to display competence (as intended), low-level questions may well exacerbate the problem.

Fields's study teaches us that students understand that ambiguous questions provide more time and more space to think and more generous evaluation. Such insights give a whole new perspective to current trends across the curriculum to increase emphasis on problem solving and creativity rather than recall (e.g., National Council of Teachers of English; National Council of Teachers of Mathematics). Students may mediate these curricular goals in unexpected ways—certainly if our expectations are that they will resist such ambiguous opportunities.

Motives as Cues and Tools   In short, understanding student motivation matters. Let's consider types of questions that may be useful to pose when considering motivation and assessment. If a teacher were interested in student interest, for example, she/he might ask questions that explore both the level of interest the student brings *to* the task and ways in which the student may *transform* tasks to make them more interesting. In these questions, the teacher scaffolds how to identify one's motivation and how to make it work for you by making less-interesting tasks more motivating. We suggest that this type of conversation, illustrated here, can help students become more adaptive by learning how to modify opportunities to optimize their motivation and learning.

Scaffolding the Functions of Interest

Do you like the unit we have been studying? How come? (Why not?)
    What about _____ interests (bores) you?
Do you think that when you like something or find it interesting it is easier to
    learn? Is it easier to remember?
Are there ways that you can try to make work more interesting or fun for you?
    What are some of the things you do?
    Does that seem to help you learn?
    Why do you suppose that is?
    Have you ever tried _____ ?
    Etc.

Taking Charge of Personal Beliefs, Emotion, and Action   Teachers may also wish to understand, even as they help students understand, students' beliefs about themselves as learners and how this might influence their attitudes toward, expectations about, and strategies with tasks, both new and familiar. That is, teachers may want to make student attributional judgments and self-efficacy beliefs explicit so that together, teacher and students can discuss the veracity of students' beliefs and identify internal cues that may enhance students' control over their learning. (An example of such a conversation is presented at the top of page 21.)

Scaffolding the Relations Among Beliefs, Emotion, and Action

Do you ever think about how well you are doing in school?

How well do you think you are doing?

How is it different for different subjects?

Why do you suppose that is?

Do you think it's because of _____ for all of your subjects? How come (why not)?

If you are doing (well/okay/poorly) in _____ now, how do you think you'll do on the unit we start next week, the one on _____ ? How come?

What about in _____ ? Why do you suppose that is?

Sometimes when I don't expect to do very well, I get *upset and mad* when I'm stuck and I give up sooner. But if I think I can do an assignment, I'll keep at it longer. Even if I get confused, I don't get so *frustrated*. I just stay calm and think about it, and I might ask for help if I need it.

How about you? How does it go for you when you are not sure you can do an assignment?

I think lots of people feel that way. If they think they can't do an assignment, they probably feel frustrated when they get stuck.

When we feel frustrated it's time to try something different. If you don't know how to help yourself think of a different way, then you *do know* it's time to ask someone else for help.

Who would you want to ask for help if I were busy and couldn't help you right away? How come? etc.

Our primary emphasis in this example is to scaffold a *profile* of student ability (Cohen, 1986). In this way, the teacher has already engaged the student in *relative* personal judgments which can then be used to challenge pervasive negative beliefs and attributional judgments (or inappropriately pervasive positive beliefs and attributions) and identify strengths to bring to weaker areas. Notice the first step is to determine a student's beliefs about how well he/she is doing. This forms the basic foundation for conversations that foster and mediate realistic self-appraisal.

The last segment of the example presented above focuses on validating and labeling emotion, and teaching how emotion can function as a cue to transform the self and task by building on strengths (one's own and others'). Notice that emotions are recognized and accepted, the focus for change is the *response* to emotion. The model we use in this example is based upon work by Weiner and colleagues (1986; 1992) which indicates that cognition (here, expectations for success and recognition of current difficulty) leads to emotion (frustration in this example), which results in behavior (here, give up).

In this conversation, the teacher is setting the stage for continued discussion of how our beliefs influence the way we feel and how our feelings influence the way we act—and that we can *take charge* of how we respond to emotion. Indeed, in this example, the teacher is conveying that the student is *responsible* for taking charge of emotion by managing available resources. The teacher also scaffolds strategies for resource management so that the student has a plan for future needs. This framework allows systematic teacher mediation and scaffolding at several intervention points and anticipates the linkages between motivation and enactment in personal processes.

Negotiating Shared Goals: Student Choice and Goal Coordination   Finally, we provide one example of a conversation that scaffolds identification of a student's individual goals, their relationships, and coordination (see below). The desire to do something one finds important, and to strive to do it well, is a motivational orientation we would wish for all students. This vignette illustrates how student attempts to make tasks relevant may well increase the complexity of goal coordination and require teacher scaffolding and support.

The assignment is to complete a research project that demonstrates the ability to use library resources, conduct research, integrate several sources, and write and present to the class an informative report of what was learned. The specific topic is to be negotiated between the teacher and each student. Mike, a high school sophomore, wants to do his project on divorce. His teacher knows that his parents have separated.

Let's assume that Mike tells his teacher he wants to study divorce because "it is important to him". With some exploration, his teacher learns that Mike wants to do his project on divorce because: 1) he has to do a project on something, 2) he wants to learn more about what it might be like if his parents divorce, and 3) he thinks his friends will be more comfortable and helpful if he can talk about it. From his perspective, Mike has multiple, compatible goals. He believes that a project on divorce, which is personally quite meaningful, will be instrumental to meeting teacher expectations and provide a forum for awkward conversations with friends. In Mike's view, this project is perfect.

Negotiation of Choice in Assignments: Scaffolding Multiple Responsibilities

Mike, I can see that you have thought through the pluses of choosing to do your project on divorce, and I can understand why you would want to pursue this. Your parents' decisions affect you directly.

However, it's time to consider some of the possible minuses. Let's start with how *you* feel.

One way to think about feelings is to think about how intense they are. Intense feelings sometimes make it difficult to stop, step back, and think.

How do you plan to structure your project?

Whose perspective do you want to focus on? parents (mother, father)? children (you)? relatives? friends?

Knowing how you feel, what are some things you might assume about that perspective?

What kinds of questions and resources might you use to see whether your assumptions are correct?

How might you develop that focus so that your project meets the assignment requirements?

What are some self-checks that will help you keep on track?

Another way to think about divorce is to consider *all* the people it affects. How many people are affected in your family if your parents get divorced?

Different people have different perspectives, beliefs, and feelings about divorce. Families also differ in how much they like to keep things private, just among themselves or with close friends.

How about your family? Has your family told other people about the possibility of divorce?

Have you thought about discussing your project topic with your family? How might you get a conversation started?

How might you approach this project so that members of your family feel okay about their privacy?

Let's think about your presentation in front of the class. Think through the kinds of examples and questions that respect your feelings *and* your family's feelings about others discussing divorce with you for a class assignment. What might you anticipate? Would you want questions about how friends might help you?

I would like you to think some on these concerns. Let's meet again on Thursday to settle on a plan.

The scaffolding shown above illustrates an attempt to help Mike view his project from a perspective other than his own. The teacher's concern is that Mike think through the possibility of incompatible goals. The first focus both accepts and challenges Mike's adolescent egocentrism and attends to the possibility of intrapersonal conflict. Specifically, the teacher draws Mike's attention to the possibility of incompatible personal goals: pursuing an emotional and personally painful topic while negotiating the dispassionate research and self-presentation demands of the assignment. The second focus also accepts and challenges Mike's focus on himself by raising the possibility of interpersonal conflict with his family over privacy.

◆ ENACTMENT SCAFFOLDING

We provide three quite different examples of enactment interviews designed to help students keep on track. The first example focuses on strategic task management, the second examines student knowledge of an intellectual skill (reading), and the third assesses student conceptual understanding in a specific lesson (fractions). For the first example, we continue with the assigned research project. We have illustrated how conversation can help students better identify and coordinate multiple personal goals that may not be readily apparent. Recall that within each negotiated topic (shared goal), however, the structure and expectations for the project are standard for all students. Thus, successful completion of the project is also about strategic enactment to meet a standard *set for* students (see example below). Recall that part of the conversation between Mike and his teacher was to reaffirm that Mike's primary responsibility was to meet the expectations of the assignment rather than the personal goals he negotiated within that assignment. These expectations are not open to student choice, although students always have the option to settle for less and experience associated consequences.

Strategic Task Management   Several tasks are embedded in the research project assignment. Thus, students as a group will profit from conversations that help identify individual tasks (assigned goals), their relative difficulty and timing given a student's profile of abilities, and strategies to enhance their completion. The example below also illustrates that setting expectations does not imply a lack of concern for the individuals who are expected to meet them. It also again models a profile of ability.

Scaffolding Personal Mediation of Tasks

There are several steps in doing a project like this. Some steps will be more difficult than others.

Which steps do you generally think will be the most difficult? Why?

Not everyone will find the same steps the hardest. This is because we are all different in which things we feel more confident and competent about doing.

Usually, things that are harder for us or that we worry about take more time.

For example, some of you find it hard to write. You'll need to budget extra time to allow enough time for thinking and revision.

Some of you are uncomfortable using the library. You may need to set aside time to get to know your way around and whom to ask for what materials.

Most of us get nervous when we make a presentation. How might you prepare for that part of the project?

It's a good idea to think about what are your strong points and not-so-strong points, so that you set your priorities and have enough time to complete each part of the project. Each part is important; I will grade each part.

This rather lengthy example has illustrated how teachers might help students both negotiate an assigned task to make it personally meaningful (e.g., for Mike) and strategically plan their work to make it academically informative and successful (for everyone). Generic examples such as this are useful tools that teachers can bring to a wide array of task assignments, particularly those that consist of an interdependent series of subtasks and/or those that allow for student negotiation. Through this kind of interview the teacher scaffolds for students how to educatively negotiate, organize, and pursue tasks in light of one's own profile of abilities.

Other types of enactment interviews that teachers may want to pursue with students are those that examine students' general knowledge of and cognitive strategies within a subject area (e.g., "What is the scientific method?") or students' specific understanding of a concept within a lesson (e.g., "What is the structure of species classification?"). We provide an example of each type of interview. Both interviews focus on what we call *enactment processes*. The first explores student beliefs and knowledge about reading; the second focuses specifically on student understanding of a fraction lesson in mathematics.

Reading Comprehension   The first example is the "Reading Comprehension Interview" by Karen Wixson, Anita Bosky, M. Nina Yochum, and Donna Alvermann presented below. Wixson and Lipson (1991) also include this interview in their text, *Assessment and Instruction in Reading Disability*. These authors argue (and we agree) that interviewing students can enhance assessment of their knowledge of and motivation to read. Wixson and Lipson divided their questions into those designed to "examine students' knowledge and beliefs about the functions of reading, the goals and purposes of reading, self-appraisal and goal-setting, and the skills and strategies necessary for skilled performance" (p. 99).

Reading Comprehension Interview

Name: Date:
Classroom teacher: Reading level:
                              Grade:

Directions: Introduce the procedure by explaining that you are interested in finding out what children think about various reading activities. Tell the student that he or she will be asked questions about his/her reading, that there are no right or wrong answers, and that you are only interested in knowing what s/he thinks. Tell the student that if s/he does not know how to answer a question s/he should say so and you will go on to the next one.

General probes such as "Can you tell more about that?" or "Anything else?" may be used. Keep in mind that the interview is an informal diagnostic measure and you should feel free to probe to elicit useful information.

1. What hobbies or interests do you have that you like to read about?
2. **a.** How often do you read in school?
   b. How often do you read at home?
3. What school subjects do you like to read about?

Introduce reading and social studies books.

Directions: For this section use the child's classroom basal reader and a content area textbook (social studies, science, etc.). Place these texts in front of the student. Ask each question twice, once with reference to the basal reader and once with reference to the content area textbook. Randomly vary the order of presentation (basal content). As each question is asked, open the appropriate text in front of the student to help provide a point of reference for the question.

4. **a.** What is the most important reason for reading this kind of material?
   b. Why does your teacher want you to read this book?
5. **a.** Who's the best reader you know in ____ ?
   b. What does he/she do that makes him/her such a good reader?

6. **a.** How good are *you* at reading this kind of material?
   b. How do you know?
7. What do you have to do to get a good grade in ____ in your class?
8. **a.** If the teacher told you to remember the information in this story/chapter, what would be the best way to do this?
   b. Have you ever tried ____ ?
9. **a.** If your teacher told you to find the answers to the questions in this book, what would be the best way to do this? Why?
   b. Have you ever tried ____ ?
10. **a.** What is the hardest part about answering questions like the ones in this book?
   b. Does that make you do anything differently?

Introduce at least two comprehension worksheets.

Directions: Present the worksheets to the child and ask questions 11 and 12. Present the worksheets to the child and ask questions 11 and 12. Ask the child to complete portions of each worksheet. Then ask questions 13 and 14. Next, show the child a worksheet designed to simulate the work of another child. Then ask question 15.

11. Why would your teacher want you to do worksheets like these (for what purpose)?
12. What would your teacher say you must do to get a good mark on worksheets like these? (What does your teacher look for?)

Ask the child to complete portions of at least two worksheets.

13. Did you do this one differently from the way you did that one? How or in what way?
14. Did you have to work harder on one of these worksheets than the other? (Does one make you think more?)

Present the simulated worksheet.

15. **a.** Look over this worksheet. If you were the teacher, what kind of mark would you give the worksheet? Why?
16. **b.** If you were the teacher, what would you ask this person to do differently next time?

SUMMARY SHEET

What does the child perceive as the goal or purpose of classroom reading activities? (see questions 4 and 11)

Basal reader:
Content textbook:
Reading worksheets:

What criteria does the child use to evaluate his/her reading performance? (questions 5, 8, 7, 12, and 15)

Basal reader:
Content textbook:
Reading worksheets:

What strategies does the child indicate s/he uses when engaging in different comprehension activities? (questions 8, 9, 10, 13, and 14)

Remembering information
    Basal reader:
    Content textbook:
    Reading worksheets:

Answering questions
    Basal reader:
    Content textbook:
    Reading worksheets:

"Reading Comprehension Interview," from *An Interview for Assessing Students' Perceptions of Classroom Reading Tasks* by Karen K. Wixson, Anita B. Bosky, M. Nina Yochum, and Donna E. Alvermann. Reprinted with permission of Karen Wixson and the International Reading Association.

Research by Wixson and colleagues indicates that many students believe that the goals of reading are to not make mistakes reading aloud and to remember what was read word by word. Such beliefs likely affect detrimentally student enactment strategies in reading. The interview reprinted above seems a useful tool to get underneath such self-defeating beliefs. It is designed to be used with classroom materials so that the teacher can understand and mediate students' unique constructions. In our view, this is a promising window for teacher intervention and supportive scaffolding.

The reading comprehension interview might be longer than is feasible for each student who can benefit from participation. It may also require materials that are not used in a teacher's curriculum. Thus, teachers may want to prioritize their goals in conducting a reading comprehension interview and, like all the other examples in this book, use it as a model from which to draw. We find that revision is often easier than starting from scratch.

Fractions as Concept, Algorithm, and Leftovers   Our final example of interviews and conversations that focus on and scaffold enactment processes is part of a mathematics curriculum and teacher professional-development project sponsored by the National Science Foundation (Good, McCaslin, & Reys, 1990). As part of their participation in the project, teachers of students in grades three through five interviewed students in their mathematics classrooms about their understanding and experiences in cooperative-learning groups and about their understanding of specific lesson concepts. The interview reproduced here occurs between a teacher and student who are discussing student understanding of the concept of fractions and how they can be compared. It differs from the two previous examples in its specificity and interest in relatively immediate (same-day) assessment of student learning of a lesson. Like the reading comprehension example, this interview includes written and manipulative materials from the lesson. Students had completed worksheets and a test prior to the interview.

We like this interview because it illustrates for us the importance of interviewing students—even as briefly as described here. Teachers using this interview found that their students seemed to learn through the conversation. And teachers were surprised to learn about the limitations of student written performance as a proxy for student problem-solving strategies and understanding of concepts! Teachers compared student test performance with their interviews on the identical material. In nearly every case, teachers reported they had *overestimated* how much students understood and, we would add, *underestimated* how much students were instead describing manipulatives and concrete examples. We suspect this is not an isolated case. Interviewing students about their enactment knowledge and strategies instructs as it assesses, for both student and teacher. We think it has much to recommend it.

Scaffolding Fractional Understanding

Teacher:	Thank you. Okay, number 2. John—[laughs] John and Nick each ordered a small pizza. John asked the pizza maker to cut his into three slices, and Nick had his cut into four slices. Each boy ate two slices. Who ate the most pizza, John or Nick?
John:	Nick.
Teacher:	Why?
John:	Nick ordered . . .
Teacher:	Yeah, you can read along if you want with me.
John:	Which one are we on, this one?
Teacher:	Yeah, Number 2.
John:	[pause] It's Nick because he ordered four slices and John ordered three.
Teacher:	No, they both ordered a whole pizza. John . . .
John:	A small pizza?
Teacher:	Yeah—had his cut into three pieces and Nick had his cut into four. Both of the boys—out of this whole pizza . . .
John:	John ate more.
Teacher:	Why? How do you know?
John:	Because he ate a lower number.
Teacher:	Which means what?
John:	That if Nick had—Nick ordered—he had his for four slices and he only ate two. Then he would have two left over; and then John would have one left over.
Teacher:	All right.
John:	So John ate more.
Teacher:	Okay. Because why—compare thirds to fourths. What does that mean?
John:	Hmm . . . three is lower than four.
Teacher:	Which means?
John:	That John ate more.

Teacher:	That part of the pizza, thirds are . . .
John:	Fourths.
Teacher:	Bigger than . . .
John:	Yeah.
Teacher:	Fourths.
John:	Fourths.
Teacher:	Okay. All right, let's look at Number—you can hold that—Number three. Bob ate 3/8 of his pizza, Cheri ate 1/4 of hers, and Michael ate 1/2 of his. Who ate the most?
John:	Michael.
Teacher:	Okay. The least?
John:	Hmm, Bob.
Teacher:	How much was eaten in all?
John:	5/8. Wait . . . 5/16, 17.
Teacher:	How did you get that?
John:	I added them all.
Teacher:	But where did 16ths come from? Why did you use 16ths?
John:	Well . . . well, I added up the denominator and the other denominators, but it should be 4/8 . . . shouldn't it?
Teacher:	I don't know, tell me why. How did you get it? Do you want to write them down?
John:	No, I know the answer. It's 5/8.
Teacher:	Well, tell me how you got 5/8.
John:	Well, you take the higher number and then you add the two numerators and it'll be . . .

◆ SELF–EVALUATION SCAFFOLDING

We have already discussed how tasks, time, active instruction, and assessment policies might afford student self-evaluation. Here we provide a few examples of the types of questions that help teachers assess the extent to which these opportunities are actually *realized*. These questions are designed to encourage students to evaluate their performance realistically *and* to consider their performance as a function of task expectations, preparation, actual performance, and self-perception. In this way, the teacher integrates students' self-evaluation of their performance products with the processes by which they are obtained. We want students to feel in control of, rather than privately labeled by, their performance.

In the Scaffolding the Intellectual Dynamics of Preparation and Performance example presented on page 30, the teacher scaffolds student self-evaluation with questions that include self-perception, because we consider students' attributional knowledge (e.g., Weiner, 1986, 1992) an important predictor of their preparation (both study behavior and mental "set") and their (re)constructions of learning/performance experiences (the "story" they take with them to their next task). Thus, we consider attributional ascriptions the stuff of future expectations and autobiography. In both time frames, we maintain that students' attributional understanding of their performance is an important feature of their present self-evaluation and a predictor of their future study plans.

Expectations, Preparation, and Performance The question series presented below concerns student performance on a classroom test; however, the model is easily adapted to structuring retrospective evaluation of task performance. Notice that this example is from a postperformance perspective, although it could be modified for a sort of in-progress report on tasks with multiple steps and phases. In this latter instance, it would be useful to integrate enactment scaffolding with self-evaluation. Similarly, assessment of student portfolios seems an especially fruitful opportunity to encourage realistic in-process as well as end-product self-evaluation.

Scaffolding the Intellectual Dynamics of Preparation and Performance

Was the test what you expected? (what did you expect?)
How did you prepare for this test?
Now that you have taken a test like this, will you change how you prepare next
    time? In what ways (why not)?
How confident are you of your performance?
Which questions do you think you answered most completely?
    Why do you think so? How were the others different?
    Do you think I will agree with your assessment? Why (not)?

After the initial conversation, as depicted above, the teacher may want to evaluate immediately student performance and assess the congruence between the student's self-evaluation and the teacher's own. For younger students or those whose self-evaluations are often unrealistic, a type of "talk-aloud" item-by-item evaluation while the student's self-report is still fresh may be especially beneficial. For older or more self-aware students, briefly noting at a later time the degree of agreement between teacher and student evaluation likely provides sufficient reality feedback. In either case—immediate or delayed feedback—Zuckerman (1994) teaches us that it is the degree of congruence between evaluations that is stressed and rewarded, not the absolute level of performance. That is the stuff of other self-evaluation conversations, focused on the individual student's progress in learning the subject matter (Krampen, 1987).

Self–Perception and Personal Power The first conversation presented on page 31 focuses on the affective dynamics of preparation and performance, and closes on student self-perception and its implications for future performance. Our focus in this conversation shifts attention to the affective dimension of self-evaluation. The second example concludes the conversation on self-evaluation by integrating the student's intellectual and affective report.

Scaffolding the Affective Dynamics of Preparation and Performance

Are you satisfied with your performance? What had you hoped for?

How did you feel before you started the test? Sometimes it is harder (easier) to concentrate when you feel ____.

Was it like that for you?

Did you do anything (say anything to yourself) while you were taking the test? (If so, What? Did it help you keep on track? Why do you think it helped [did not help]?)

How did you feel when you finished the test? Is that how you usually feel when you finish a test? How come?

Do you ever say anything to yourself when you feel like that? (If so, What do you say? Does that make it easier to get ready for the next test? How come [why not])?

Integrative Scaffolding of Affect and Intellect

Let's think about this for a minute, you mentioned that you prepared ____ for the test and you expected it to be like ____. Before you started the test, you felt ____, and when you finished you felt ____.

Is that how it usually goes for you?

Do you think it *has* to be that way?

Is there anything you could do next time so that you will have a better (good) sense of how much you have learned, be ready, and feel more confident (keep feeling confident) about taking a test?

That seems like a reasonable plan to me. I'd like you to practice doing ____ on our next assignment, then we will touch base again.

◆ **SUMMARY**

Earlier, we proposed that the co-regulation model of teacher and student processes is a useful way to think about how students negotiate and mediate classroom learning expectations. We now propose that it is also a useful model to guide thinking about how to *influence* and *scaffold* those processes. In our view, teacher questions and conversations with students function on two levels: 1) the apparent topic or surface feature of the conversation (e.g., considering family privacy, understanding fractions) and 2) the structure that undergirds student mediation processes (e.g., goal coordination, abstraction from concrete examples). Both levels of co-regulation optimally function as scaffolds—that is, they are *temporary supports*. The ultimate goal of co-regulation is student self-regulation *within contexts that can support that independence* (we return to this point in Chapter 6). Thus, teachers should expect their conversations with students to evolve as students confront and cope with new challenges to their developing mediational and regulatory abilities, within the supportive context of the classroom.

❖ CONVERSATION, CO-REGULATION, AND THE INFORMAL CURRICULUM

Much of our concern in the remainder of this book is directed to what we call the *informal curriculum*, by which we mean those experiences that are not deliberately planned and promoted in the school curriculum but that occur nonetheless. Elsewhere we defined the informal curriculum this way: "The informal curriculum is not official; thus, it is not prescribed, orchestrated, nor monitored. Yet, we argue, it is the stuff of schooling; the continuous, albeit uncoordinated, stream of momentary experiences that students aggregate and internalize with varying degrees of awareness, protest, and satisfaction" (McCaslin & Good 1996). Concern with the informal curriculum is not new (e.g., Dewey, 1938) and it persists (e.g., Brantlinger, 1993; Jackson, Boostrom, & Hansen, 1993).

As educators, we feel that teachers need to consider students' affective lives as well as their subject-matter knowledge. Other educators have expressed similar positions. For example, Noddings (1992) asserts that schools need to do more than help students to develop their capacity for intellectual work and to deal with the world of ideas:

> Teenage pregnancies nearly doubled between 1965 and 1985; the teen suicide rate has doubled in the same period of time; teenage drinking takes a horrible toll in drunk driving accidents and dulled sensibilities; children take guns to school; and homicide is the leading cause of death among minority teens; a disgraceful number of children live in poverty; and still, many school people and public officials insist that the job of the schools is to increase academic rigor. In direct opposition, I will argue that the first job of the schools is to care for our children. (p. xiv)

Noddings's position may seem a bit extreme. It is important to understand that she was, in part, responding to the then (and now) predominant *zeitgeist* of subject-matter acquisition and competitive student tests scores as *the* function of schools. This narrow focus continues, and we think it has serious consequences. Conceptions of student as expert, and expert test taker, have unidimensionalized how policy makers view schools and narrowed how teachers are prepared in our colleges of education for the realities of students in classrooms. Extreme distortions of this sort often call for extreme responses, if the responses are to be heard.

Thus, we do not agree with Noddings that schools must choose or prioritize between teaching and caring for students. This is because we do not believe that the intellectual and affective are independent processes and goals. Rather, in our view, the affective and intellectual are interdependent in classroom learning. Students think thoughts and feel emotions; they also feel that they know the material and think that they are afraid. We do agree with Noddings, however, that schools must care about students. We believe that co-regulation of students' mediation—their motivation, enactment, and evaluation—of themselves in relation to learning and to a standard of excellence empowers students in fundamental ways, ways that *demonstrate* our care. Thus, although we now focus on what traditionally has been the affective aspect of schooling, we simply have shifted relative emphasis within an interdependent context; we have not left one for the other.

❖ QUESTIONS AND SUGGESTED ACTIVITIES FOR CHAPTER 1

1. The authors stress that teachers need to listen to students as learners, individuals, and as social beings. What does this imply? Do you think that your teachers listened to you more as a learner or an individual or as a social being? Why do you feel this way?

2. The authors note that students confront multiple and competing goals within and between the formal and informal curricula. From your own experience, generate three or four instances where this has occurred in your own learning. Compare you list with those of classmates.

3. The authors argue that the complexity of the classroom (multiple interpretations of the same behavior) make it important for teachers to take time for conversations with students. To what extent do you think that students want such conversations to take place with their teachers? That is, is it possible that some students would prefer their behavior and their intentions to remain ambiguous? Cite a couple of examples where students might want to maintain an ambiguous situation.

4. The authors present a model of co-regulated learning in Chapter 1. In your own words, how would you describe a model of co-regulated learning to a peer who has not read the book. Is it a useful perspective? Why or why not?

5. In your own words, differentiate *enactment* and *motivation*.

6. In their model of co-regulation, the authors stress the need for periodic, critical goal review. Thinking back on your experience in high school, did any teacher ever encourage you to review your goals (e.g., essay topics, etc.)? Did any teacher make you feel comfortable in reformulating goals or rejecting them? Did this happen in some subjects more than others? Why?

7. The authors argue that teachers tend to encourage (at least implicitly) the importance of goal setting and goal accomplishment and tend not to include goal review as part of the process. Do you agree with their assessment in terms of your own experience? Why do you think this is?

8. How would you define *self-evaluation?* What is the role of self-evaluation in a model of co-regulated learning? To what extent, as a student, did you receive both the opportunity and instruction in how to evaluate your progress realistically? In terms of self-evaluation, why do the authors emphasize providing primarily tasks of moderate difficulty?

9. The authors argue that it is important to scaffold a "profile of student ability." How does this contrast with an orientation that calls some students bright and others less talented? What are the advantages and disadvantages of a profile approach?

10. Think about the grade level that you plan to teach and decide how you would scaffold goal coordination. If you wanted students in your class to become better at coordinating goals, outline your plan for how you would attempt to help students develop appropriate dispositions and abilities to do this. We will discuss goal coordination more thoroughly in Chapter 2; keep your plan for further development.

❖ REFERENCES

Ames, C. (1992). Classrooms: Goals, structures, and student motivation. *Journal of Educational Psychology, 84,* 261–271.

Atkinson, J. (1964). *An introduction to motivation.* Princeton, NJ: Van Nostrand.

Bandura, A. (1986). *Social foundations of thought and action: A social cognitive theory.* Englewood Cliffs, NJ: Prentice-Hall.

Brantlinger, E. (1993). *The politics of social class in secondary school: Views of affluent and impoverished youth.* New York: Teachers College Press.

Clifford, M. (1991). Risk-taking: Empirical and educational considerations. *Educational Psychologist, 26,* 263–298.

Cohen, E. (1986). *Designing group work: Strategies for the heterogeneous classroom.* New York: Teachers College Press.

Corno, L. (1992). Encouraging students to take responsibility for learning and performance. *Elementary School Journal, 93,* 69–83.

Corno L., & Kanfer, R. (1993). The role of volition in learning and performance. In L. Darling-Hammond (Ed.), *Review of research in education* (vol. 19, pp. 3–43). Washington, DC: American Educational Research Association.

Corno, L., & Mandinach, E. (1983). The role of cognitive engagement in classroom learning and motivation. *Educational Psychologist, 18,* 88–108.

Corno, L., & Rohrkemper, M. (1985). Self-regulated learning. In R. Ames & C. Ames (Eds.), *Research on motivation in education* (vol. 2, pp. 53–90). Orlando, FL: Academic Press.

Covington, M. (1992). *Making the grade: A self-worth perspective on motivation and school reform.* Cambridge: Cambridge University Press.

Deci, E., & Ryan, R. (1985). *Intrinsic motivation in self-determination in human behavior.* New York: Plenum.

Dewey, J. (1938). *Experience and education.* New York: Collier Books.

Diener, D., & Dweck, C. (1978). An analysis of learned helplessness: Continuous changes in performance, strategy, and achievement cognitions following failure. *Journal of Personality and Social Psychology, 36,* 451–462.

Dodge, K., Asher, S., & Parkhurst, J. (1989). Social life as a goal-coordination task. In C. Ames & R. Ames (Eds.), *Research on motivation in education: Vol. 3. Goals and cognition* (pp. 107–135). New York: Academic Press.

Doyle, W. (1983). Academic work. *Review of Educational Research, 53,* 159–200.

Fennema, E. (1987). Sex-related differences in education: Myths, realities, and interventions. In V. Richardson-Koehler (Ed.), *Educators' handbook: A research perspective* (pp. 329–347). White Plains, NY: Longman.

Fields, R. (1990). *Classroom tasks, children's control perceptions, and their relation to inner speech.* Unpublished doctoral dissertation, Bryn Mawr College, Bryn Mawr, PA.

Good, T. (1996). Teaching effects and teacher evaluation. In J. Sikula, T. Buttery, & E. Guyton (Eds.), *Handbook of research on teacher education* (2nd ed.). New York: Macmillan.

Good, T., & Brophy, J. (1994). *Looking in classrooms* (6th ed.). New York: HarperCollins.

Good, T., McCaslin, M., & Reys, B. (1990). *Enhancing teacher professionalism through collaborative curriculum development in mathematics.* National Science Foundation Grant TPE–8955171.

Harter, S. (1981). A new self-report scale of intrinsic versus extrinsic orientation in the classroom: Motivational and informational components. *Developmental Psychology, 17,* 300–312.

Heckhausen, H. (1991). *Motivation and action.* (P. Leppmann, Trans.). Berlin Heidelberg, Germany: Springer-Verlag.

Jackson, P. (1968). *Life in classrooms.* New York: Holt, Rinehart, & Winston.

Jackson, P., Boostrom, R., & Hansen, D. (1993). *The moral life of schools.* San Francisco: Jossey-Bass.

Kelman, H., & Hamilton, V. (1989). *Crimes of obedience: Toward a social psychology of authority and responsibility.* New Haven, CT: Yale University Press.

Krampen, G. (1987). Differential effects of teacher comments. *Journal of Educational Psychology, 79*(2), 137–146.

Kuhl, J. (1985). Volitional mediators of cognition-behavior consistency: Self-regulatory processes and action versus state orientation. In J. Kuhl & J. Beckmann (Eds.), *Action control: From cognition to behavior* (pp. 101–128). Berlin: Springer-Verlag.

McCaslin, M. (1990). Motivated literacy. In J. Zutell & S. McCormick (Eds.), *Literacy theory and research: Analysis for multiple paradigms.* Chicago: NRC.

McCaslin, M., & Good, T. (1992). Compliant cognition: The misalliance of management and instructional goals in current school reform. *Educational Researcher, 21,* 4–17.

McCaslin, M., & Good, T. (1996). The informal curriculum. In D. Berliner & R. Calfee (Eds.), *The handbook of educational psychology.* New York: Macmillan.

McCaslin Rohrkemper, M. (1989). Self-regulated learning and academic achievement: A Vygotskian view. In B. Zimmerman & D. Schunk (Eds.), *Self-regulated learning and academic achievement: Theory, research, and practice* (pp. 143-168). New York: Springer-Verlag.

Miller, G., Galanter, E., & Pribram, K. (1960). *Plans and the structure of behavior.* New York: Holt.

Mitchell, R. (1992). *Testing for learning*. New York: Free Press.

Noddings, N. (1992). *The challenge to care in schools*. New York: Teachers College Press.

Nolen, S. (1988). Reasons for studying: Motivational orientations and study strategies. *Cognition and Instruction, 5*, 269–287.

Phillips, D., & Zimmerman, M. (1990). The developmental course of perceived competence and incompetence among competent children. In R. Sternberg & J. Kolligian, Jr. (Eds.), *Competence considered* (pp. 41–66). New Haven, CT: Yale University Press.

Rohrkemper, M. (1986). The functions of inner speech in elementary school students' problem-solving behavior. *American Educational Research Journal, 23*, 303–313.

Rohrkemper, M., & Corno, L. (1988). Success and failure on classroom tasks: Adaptive learning and classroom teaching. *Elementary School Journal, 88*, 297–312.

Rosenshine, B., & Stevens, R. (1986). Teaching functions. In M. Wittrock (Ed.), *Handbook of research on teaching* (3rd ed., pp. 376–391). New York: Macmillan.

Simon, H. (1969). *The sciences of the artificial*. Cambridge, MA: MIT Press.

Vygotsky, L. (1962). *Thought and language*. Cambridge, MA: MIT Press.

Vygotsky, L. (1978). *Mind and society: The development of higher psychological processes*. Cambridge, MA: Harvard University Press.

Weiner, B. (1986). *An attributional theory of motivation and emotion*. New York: Springer-Verlag.

Weiner, B. (1992). *Human motivation: Metaphors, theories, and research*. Newbury Park, CA: Sage.

Weinert, F., & Helmke, A. (1987). Compensatory effects of student self-concept and instructional quality on academic achievement. In F. Halisch & J. Kuhl (Eds.), *Motivation, intention, and volition* (pp. 233–248). Berlin: Springer-Verlag.

Wixson K., & Lipson, M. (1991). *Assessment and instruction in reading disability*. New York: HarperCollins.

Zuckerman, G. (1994). A pilot study of a ten-day course in cooperative learning for beginning Russian first graders. *Elementary School Journal, 94*, 405–420.

BEING A STUDENT

Theoretical Representations of Children
Societal Beliefs
 Constructions of Children
 Constructions of Student
  Language Minority Students
  Student Gender, Race, and Ethnicity
  Students in Poorly Funded Schools
 Summary
Classroom as Context
 Student Friendships
 Students as Classmates
  Why Go to School?
  Beliefs About Ability
  Beliefs About Ability and Virtue
  Coping With the Stress of Achievement
  Rejecting Achievement
 Summary
"Being a Student": Nora
 Family Social/Instructional Environment
 School Social/Instructional Environment
 Classroom Social/Instructional Environment
  Teacher
  Peers
 Goal Setting and Coordination
 Emergent Interaction and Goal Coordination
Goal Coordination as a Basic Task and Opportunity
 Some Basic Considerations
  A Brief Review of Goal Characteristics
  Goal Relationships

In this chapter we present one conception of what it means to be a student. In the framework we have described thus far, students pursue multiple tasks (assigned by others), goals (set by themselves), and shared goals (negotiated tasks) as they actively engage the demands of classroom learning. As we discussed in Chapter 1, one essential capability for students is to learn to identify and coordinate among tasks, goals, and shared goals. We term this *acquired* disposition and capability *goal coordination* (see also, Dodge, Asher, & Parkhurst, 1989) and consider it a basic *task of* and *skill for* learning in classrooms. In our model of co-regulated learning (see Figure 1.4), we stressed the dynamic relationship among teacher supportive scaffolding, provision of opportunity, and student mediation processes of motivation, enactment, and evaluation. Together, teacher and students learn in classrooms.

In this chapter we stress that a student is more than a learner of subject matter. Students participate in classrooms with others who are friends, rivals, and acquaintances. Students and classmates (and teacher) have beliefs about themselves, one another, and the dynamics of learning that are part of the essence of classrooms and being a student. Students also have lives outside the classroom that do not stop at the classroom door. Classmates, coaches, families, and teachers (to name a few) are social resources—or strains—that can facilitate classroom learning or render it problematic. Similarly, society's beliefs about "student" and the characteristics s/he brings to school advantage some students and disadvantage others. Taken together, these social (re)sources provide an uneven mix for the student to call upon, so that students are best known by their particular *integration* of strengths and vulnerabilities. Our goal in this chapter is to provide one lens for thinking about students as those who influence and integrate (re)sources in the classroom. First, we provide a rather broad and sketchy map of the terrain we consider especially informative; second, we provide a detailed case to illustrate the map's potential; third, we consider how teachers might actively understand, influence, and scaffold students' integration of multiple resources through helping students to identify and coordinate multiple goals.

❖ THEORETICAL REPRESENTATIONS OF CHILDREN

Educational texts often describe school-aged students in terms of *stage theories* about children. We distinguish "children" from "students" because stage theory approaches tend to think about and study children as individuals who, even so, are best known by "universal" features of children at their (st)age. Thus, stage theories of child development are devoid of individual differences (how children might differ within a stage) and context (the settings children negotiate). For stage theorists, children are children no matter where they are found or who they are with: home, school, day care, summer camp, movie theaters. There is much this research and theoretical work can offer that helps us think about what a theory of "student" might look like—where we might extend, where we might differ.

For example, stage theory approaches suggest that we think of students as engaged in different stages of cognitive development (e.g., Flavell, 1985; Piaget, 1983) and personality development (e.g., Erikson, 1968; Freud, 1953–1974; Sullivan, 1953), especially as related to issues of industry and identity. Thus, students in grades two to four are often known by their concrete operational thinking (after Piaget), period of latency (after Freud), and their feelings of industry versus inferiority (after Erikson). Adolescents, in comparison, are described by the presence or absence of formal operational thinking in their mastery of learning (after Piaget), their genital stage (after Freud), and their emerging sense of identity versus role diffusion (after Erikson).

Stage approaches are also dominant in research on children's moral judgment (e.g., Gilligan, 1982; Kohlberg, 1969; Rest, 1986), which is closely linked with work on perspective taking, social cognition, and altruism (e.g., Damon, 1981; Eisenberg, 1982; Flavell & Ross, 1981; Furth, 1980; Selman, 1980). These abilities and dispositions are linked via development and socialization. That is, a student must have the cognitive ability to "decenter" from her/himself (after Piaget) to take the perspective of another, which allows as well an understanding of how another might feel or what s/he might need (which can vary due to different socialization practices). How and whether a student might act on that knowledge is then a viable social cognitive question.

Finally, perspective taking and altruism are linked to the developmental study of children's friendship (e.g., Asher & Gottman, 1981; Asher & Parker, 1989; Berndt & Perry, 1990; Sullivan, 1953), a point to which we return. Notice that within each of these developmental approaches, differences among students who differ in age (*stage* in the theories; typically *grade* in research practice), loosely defined, are explored. It is typical for stage theories to describe and judge younger students to be less sophisticated than older students throughout. The bandwidth of variation is tied to differences between developmental milestones or stages, not to individual differences within a developmental stage. Thus, in these approaches, we know students by their stage placement, not by their differences within a stage or by their transition between stages. In our view, stage descriptions provide useful hypotheses to bring to understanding how students integrate the multiple sources of influence on who they are, who they are with, what they do, what happens to them, and what that means in the classroom.

Children are also known by their personality and dispositions—by how they differ. Some of these characteristics are particularly suited to the classroom and being a student (e.g., achievement motivation). However, much research on achievement motivation is often generalized *to* the classroom rather than conducted within it. For example, Atkinson's (1964) work on individual need and choice of task difficulty is based on tasks that are novel to the classroom (e.g., ring-toss games) and some would argue choice in itself is novel to classrooms (e.g., Nolen, 1988). More recent work on achievement motivation, however, is very much involved in the classroom and the student experience (e.g., Ames, 1992; Covington, 1992) and has much to offer as we explore what it might be like *being* a student. We return to this work in considerable detail.

Extant research and theory then, helps us derive hypotheses about students who differ in general ways via development and disposition. Taken together, we can start to form interesting development/individual-difference interaction questions, like how might aggressive, concrete-operational students tolerate ambiguity? We can also extend the personal-construct hypotheses to include setting and experience: How might aggressive, concrete-operational students tolerate ambiguity in small-group learning? There are considerable theoretical and research contributions to help us derive just such questions.

Understandings of children are also influenced by theories about experiences that might happen to them. For example, theories about stress, resilience, and adaptation seem particularly relevant for extrapolation to understanding students. Some children experience extreme sources of stress—for example, abuse by a caretaker or death of a parent. More children experience the stress of parental divorce or death of a pet. Many children are hungry and poor. Children bring these stressors into the classroom. And classrooms, due to their social configuration and accountability demands, are themselves sources of stress.

For example, Sears and Milburn (1990), describe common sources of stress for children. Based upon work by Elkind (1982) and Sears and Navin (1983), they list 25 stressors, *18* of which are directly related to schooling. In alphabetical order, they are: anxiety about going to school, bullies, changing schools, conflict with teacher, competitive culture, difficulty with classmates, failing an exam, failing marks at school, failing to make an athletic team, giving oral reports or speeches in front of the class, lack of parental interest in achievements, learning disorders, not being able to complete homework assignments, older siblings setting school expectations too high, parental pressure to achieve, peer teasing about glasses and such, special recognition for outstanding performance (e.g., honor roll), and worry about taking tests (p. 225).

Finally, abundant theoretical and empirical work has been conducted on how to influence children's learning and behavior directly—behaviorism, for example (e.g., Skinner, 1953)—and less directly, cognitive behavioral theories, for example (e.g., Bandura, 1986). These studies have been very important in helping teachers design effective classrooms and tasks, and instruction, evaluation, and reward systems. They have also transformed teachers' beliefs about teaching to include notions of themselves as models who have expectations and who need to monitor self-fulfilling prophecy effects (e.g., Good & Brophy, 1994) in their own behavior and in classroom system processes. As a result, teachers learn to focus on themselves—their perceptions and behavior—and their settings in relation to student perception and behavior, looking for patterns that although subtle are pervasive. As teachers we learn, for example, to question ourselves and monitor the questions we ask; taking care that all students are likely to be asked to check the equipment, take notes for the group.

Extant theoretical and empirical work with children (and to the extent available, students) can do much to increase teacher facility with thinking about how students might change throughout the school years, how students might differ from one another, what kinds of experiences are apt to be part of their schooling (directly and less so), and how teachers might think about their own role in students' lives. Our purpose in this chapter, however, is to complicate these understandings as we try to comprehend what it might be like to *be* a student in today's classrooms. One complication comes from societal beliefs about children and students and how they vary. Academic theoretical understandings of children do not always match societal beliefs. Thus, teachers are often confronted by a considerable mismatch between the constructs about children and education at the university and those in their community and school. The former, as we have seen, tend toward a rather benign secular humanism, and the latter are often conflicting, negative, and reactive. Popular culture is just as important as "high" culture in understanding what it is to be a student. As we now describe, it certainly makes it more complicated.

❖ SOCIETAL BELIEFS

◆ CONSTRUCTIONS OF CHILDREN

Children are what we make of them. *We* refers to those who have children, those who interact with children, those who provide for children, and the larger society to which children belong. As we have noted, *we* also includes those who study children. Within the academic world, for example, Borstelmann (1983) notes:

> Binet's daughters exemplified individual differences in mental and personal styles, Watson's children were proper behaviorist products, Piaget's infants were active constructionists, and Skinner's daughter dwelt happily in the baby box. Thus, children of behavioral scientists are not only their fathers' biological progeny but their cultural inventions. (p. 34)

Our understanding of "children" is influenced by our definitions of and expectations for them in both the academy and in the culture. These do not always match; however, conflicting definitions and expectations have been with us for some time. Historically, there has been a lack of consensus among people of the same era about what a child is; the lack of consensus continues, although the specific arguments change with time and place. This is because definitions of children are culturally embedded.

Societies construct images of children that incorporate beliefs about changing and stable aspects of human development, their openness to influence, and thus the role of society in those processes (see McCaslin & Good, 1992, 1993, for extended discussion). Thus, as Borstelmann (1983) notes, societal constructions of children reflect societal beliefs about human nature and *adults*, and the world we create for ourselves and our children and within which we all live.

Constructions of children historically have vacillated and continue to do so. Children have been and are perceived as deficits (e.g., crosses to bear, missed opportunities, financial drains), as responsibilities (e.g., requiring commitment, control, guidance, instruction), and as assets who are instrumental to parental or societal needs (e.g., economic resources, marital or parental self-justifications, "second chances"). McCaslin and Good (1993) describe modern ambivalence this way:

> Our popular culture is replete with discordant messages about children. Children kill children. Children fear children. Each day 135,000 children take a gun to school (Haycock, 1990). Children are having children. Every day 2,740 adolescents get pregnant (Haycock, 1990). Minority children especially face huge problems. Reston (1991) notes, "Though there is a developing black middle class, almost half of the black teenagers in Chicago fail to graduate from high school; in Washington, D.C., four times as many blacks are jailed as graduated from the public schools" (p. 460). "Hurried children" are the measure of their parents' success, engaged in adult pressures in pre-school (Elkind, 1982). "Latchkey" children assume responsibility for home, sibling, and self-care. Working children are exploited by employers and required to work long and late hours" (p. 246).

Children take drugs ("When I Grow Up," 1990). Children drink. National survey data suggest that more than half of the nation's junior- and senior-high-school students drink alcohol; many "binge" (five or more drinks in a row), reportedly to reduce stress. Data released by Antonia Novella (former Surgeon General in the Bush administration) describe *8 million* 7th- through 12th-grade students who drink—weekly; *5.4 million* who binge "on occasion"; and 454,000 who binge *at least once a week* ("454,000 U.S. Teens," 1991). There is no reason to believe that these numbers have decreased in the interim.

Consider the variation in these messages; note how implications for the treatment of children varies with each. Throughout history, like today, good management practices have been measured by frequency and/or severity of punishment *and* by the absence of punishment; by submission to authority *and* by assuming authority. As our definitions of children and child rearing fluctuate, so too do our beliefs about the standards by which children are held responsible and by whom. Changing family structures and changing school boundaries (which, some argue, are due to the changes in "family") blur the identification of who is responsible for children's upbringing.

For example, our culture is immersed (some might say drowning) in arguments over children's sexuality that directly pit school against family: Is sex education a preventive or incentive? Can it ever be void of value? Is the home or the school ultimately responsible for who receives it? Who is to blame for children's promiscuity, pregnancy, sexually transmitted diseases? Who is going to pay for it? What should happen to the children (and their children)? As we write, Congress is debating its "Contract with America," which includes severe cuts in supports for unwed adolescent mothers and their children. It seems that cultural debates over responsibility for and by children will certainly escalate and certainly involve the schools—in the education of pregnant adolescents, soon-to-be-fathers, and ultimately, their children.

We take the position that the multiple facets of society share the responsibility for building and maintaining an infrastructure (e.g., health care, nutrition, safety) that supports children. Currently, children are the poorest Americans; the fastest-growing segment of the homeless population is families with children (Haycock, 1990). And poverty is not a static problem; it increases yearly. According to the U.S. Census Bureau, the number of people described as "poor" in 1990 increased by *2.1 million* within one year (De Parle, 1991). Natriello, McDill, and Pallas (1990) estimate that the number of educationally disadvantaged children will increase by 33 percent between 1987 and 2020.

How the popular culture thinks of and treats its children has profound effects on how we think of and treat our students. As citizens, we know that poor children are hungry children. As educators, we know that children do not learn as well when they are hungry. As educators and citizens, we know that many of our elected Representatives seek to reduce, if not remove, school breakfast and lunch programs. The effects of such a reduction will directly influence the classroom, the students who try to learn there, and the children who go home hungry.

Teachers are part of the supportive safety net for children; however, they are *only* a part of it. Our focus on teachers is meant to help them meet their goals with students by providing a framework within which to consider the coordination of teacher and student goals and the strategies to pursue them. In no way do we mean to suggest that teachers—because of their proximity to and time with students—are or ought to be the sole or even primary providers of the safety net for children. As we have said throughout, it is our position that we *all* share in that responsibility. However, we know that in some instances, teachers *are* the sole providers of essential, supportive safety nets for children (Rose, 1989).

◆ CONSTRUCTIONS OF STUDENT

Society also holds conceptions of "student" that are important to consider when imagining what it might be like to be a student. Society endorses general beliefs about students' commitment to achievement and excellence: They have none. Students as a group are portrayed as self-indulgent and irresponsible individuals who could do better on cross-national test comparisons if only they would (e.g., Tomlinson, 1993). Beliefs about students are linked to beliefs about economic and national security. The popular culture does not seem to trust students to do what is "best" for the culture.

Within these general beliefs, students are also differentiated by certain characteristics—namely, their language, race/ethnicity, gender, and economic resources. Students themselves are not immune to the beliefs that often accompany these categories (nor are teachers). Students often have varied expectations for themselves and one another based upon these characteristics; societal beliefs can permeate classrooms in ways that are not particularly educative.

Language Minority Students Students speak many different languages and represent many different cultural groups. This diversity brings with it vastly different arrays of student prior experience and knowledge and its recognition in the classroom. Students vary widely in their ability to communicate in English, and we know that the potential of many gifted students is not recognized and developed in schools because their language is believed to be a barrier rather than a cherished resource.

Minicucci and Olsen (1992) argue that one of the most underserved student groups in the U.S. school population is that of language minority students at the secondary level. Faltis (1993) argues that many bilingual and immigrant students who enter public secondary schools in the United States have exceedingly difficult, and sometimes frightening, experiences:

> These students enter a world in which the opposing forces of docility and individual responsibility are constant goals. They enter a world in which the pressures to succeed are unrelentless and omnipresent. At the same time, because of their limited proficiency in English, expectations for failure strike these students hard and often. In secondary school, learning subject-matter content is given priority over teaching students, at a time when students' social, emotional, health, and individual needs are arguably the greatest. (p. 1)

These students can face unrelenting pressures; they need strategic help—supportive scaffolding—to learn how to cope with them (see Chapter 1). Further, seemingly minor events that can undo students (e.g., dropping one's lunch tray) can be especially traumatic for limited-English-speaking students. It seems useful, as a starting point, to ensure that they (and all students) have basic if/then strategies so that they do not sweat "the small stuff" (e.g., what to do if they lose a book, forget their lunch money, cannot open their locker, leave their gym clothes at home, do not understand).

Student Gender, Race, and Ethnicity It is beyond the scope of this chapter to review societal expectations or societal issues associated with student gender, race, ethnicity, or economic status. However, we know that problems with gender discrimination and harassment continue to permeate school settings (American Association of University Women, 1992, 1993; Noddings, 1992; Sadker, Sadker, & Klein, 1991). Further, we know that schools in the United States remain largely segregated (Hacker, 1992). African-American, Hispanic, and other language minority children attend segregated schools or, as we have noted, are segregated because of language barriers within a school. Further, these students confront racial devaluation in classrooms because images of color are stigmatized in our culture and these preconceptions come to school. Steele (1992), writing of the African-American experience in school asserts:

> These images do something else as well, something especially pernicious in the classroom. They set up a jeopardy of double evaluation for blacks, a jeopardy that does not apply to whites. Like anyone, blacks risk devaluation for a particular incompetence, such as a failed test or a flubbed pronunciation. But they further risk that such performances will confirm the broader, racial inferiority they are suspected of. Thus, from the first grade through graduate school, blacks have the extra fear that in the eyes of those around them their full humanity could fall with a poor answer or a mistaken stroke of the pen.
>
> Moreover, because these images are conditioned in all of us, collectively held, they can spawn racial devaluation in all of us, not just in the strongly prejudiced. (pp. 72, 74)

Teacher-student conversations about dynamics of race, ethnicity, gender, and economic status seem invaluable for estimating the health of a school culture, in all schools. Students need to be able to discuss issues such as harassment; cliques; opportunities based on race/ethnicity, gender, and economic status; and peer attitudes in class and in the hallways that make it difficult for some students to show initiative (see, for example, Brantlinger, 1993). Society sets low expectations for people based upon category membership; teachers, if not thoughtful and reflective and willing to engage the task, risk replicating and allowing students to replicate negative expectations for some students. All students should be able to *assume* their acceptance in the collective academic goals of the classroom.

Students in Poorly Funded Schools   School financing formulas can create inverse relationships between level of need and actual funding. Thus, the schools that are in the most need of funding—both for basic functioning and to compensate in part for the consequences of poverty—receive the least funds. It is the unfortunate case that in our society the correlation among income, race, and ethnicity ensures that most minority students attend underfunded schools, often located in dangerous places.

It may be especially important in underfunded schools with limited equipment for the school to maintain safe early and/or late class periods that extend the availability of extant school resources. Increased opportunities to interact with limited resources are one way to expose more students to work with computers and scientific experiments, and thus to give them at least a chance to imagine careers in technology and science. School facilities that are safe and available for community activities seem especially important for schools serving neighborhoods that are less advantaged in terms of material resources.

◆ **SUMMARY**

Societal beliefs about and attitudes toward children and students differ from the theoretical constructs of the academy. Societal beliefs about children and students are part of the fabric of classrooms that contribute in significant ways to what it means to "be" a student. Taken together, academic and societal constructions of children and students can help us better understand the student experience and frame questions to improve that understanding. One way to facilitate this integration is to develop a framework to describe classrooms that affords the dynamic interplay of societal beliefs, educational goals, and developing learners. We use the term *social/instructional environment* to describe our integrative framework for classroom contexts.

❖ CLASSROOM AS CONTEXT

We use the term *social/instructional environment* (abbreviated as SIE) to describe the functions of contexts. In our view, contexts are more than places or settings in which people happen to be at a particular time; rather, contexts also afford and directly promote instruction and socialization (McCaslin Rohrkemper, 1989; Rohrkemper & Bershon, 1984). For example, we know that which classroom a student is in matters in ways more subtle and pervasive than we often describe. Classrooms are contexts that are more than a specific instructional approach or subject or room number. They are also places in which intentional and incidental instruction and learning about things that matter is pervasive. Students learn, for example, about tolerance for ambiguity, recognition and negotiation of conflict, personal and class pride and responsibility. They learn from teachers, events, and one another.

Contexts then, ever so subtly, continuously teach and socialize. We term functional contexts *social/instructional environments* to help us stay mindful of their critical role for students who are coming to understand themselves and their relations to others and to opportunities. The socialization aspect of SIE is especially important to consider. If students are motivated to set and pursue goals, we want to influence the goals they set: where do they, when do they, how might they learn what they value? We will return to this question.

Just as classrooms are SIEs so, too, are other functional contexts in students' lives: families, friends, neighborhoods, churches, clubs, and so on. Each is a SIE that affords and provides instruction and socialization. Each is a SIE that influences who we are: what we value, what we learn, what we do. Notice as well the potential range of interrelation of SIEs from mutually compatible to competitive opposites. Friends, for example, can mediate family influence, for good (Sullivan, 1953) or ill (Erikson, 1968). Family influence on friends changes over time; school's influence on family *and* friends changes over time.

Friends in young childhood are often selected by parents—perhaps they are relatives or members of the neighborhood or church. With schooling comes a new set of adult influences beyond the family (who have not been selected by them) and a new pool of potential friends (who also have not been selected by the family). With school, then, comes considerable "sharing" of the child/student across home and school (and other families), which results in a blurring of boundaries and responsibilities that make many families and schools uncomfortable. Multiple social/instructional environments also create coordination tasks for students—some easier than others.

For example, as students progress through school, the structures of schooling change. In middle school/junior high, the primary teacher is replaced by multiple teachers who become structurally more dispassionate, typically interacting with more than a hundred students each day. Classmates become the constant influence in students' school lives. It seems few parents, educators, or researchers are satisfied with the middle-school or junior-high-school transition and its unfortunate timing with student biological and social development (e.g., Eccles, Midgley, Wigfield, Buchanan, Reuman, Flanagan, & MacIver 1993; Mergendoller, 1993; Simmons and Blyth, 1987). The middle-school/junior-high transition is a good example of what we mean by the *function of contexts:* something larger and more pervasive and subtle than class schedules, lockers, and extracurricular activities permeates middle school and junior high. Their very contexts, for better or worse, afford much more.

In brief, we think of classrooms as embedded social/instructional environments that integrate the physical presence of teachers, peers, tasks, and tests (as examined in Chapter 1) with the less-direct, yet pervasive, influences of home (explored in Chapter 6), school (e.g., previous grades, beliefs about "next year" [Fetterman, 1990]), and other SIEs in students' lives. As if that is not complicated enough, the multiple and dynamic sources of influence that comprise classroom settings interact with learners who are themselves evolving as biological and social beings. Students' biological and social development are interdependent and ever-present aspects of classroom SIEs, but they are especially apparent when comparing classroom coordination tasks of young students with early adolescent students.

For example, second-grade students are apt to be comfortable in their bodies and have basic biological control, although an occasional "accident" would not be unheard of. Second graders likely experience little if any dissonance as social beings; they are able to maintain simultaneously self-perceptions of "good boy," "good student," and "good friend" without concern for contradiction. These constructs mostly overlap for young children—that is, good boys are good students and good boys are good friends. Neither the SIE of home or school is apt to afford or require distinction among them. Neither do friends. Thus, for second-graders, it is okay to compete with friends to *be* a good student and a good boy. School-imposed consequences (rewards) are relatively small and do not threaten the young student's belief system. That is, the rewards that young students win through competition typically are concrete (e.g., stickers, pretzels, ribbons), contained (i.e., they tend to be specific to the competition), and temporary (due to the young student's sense of time ["that was yesterday"] and to the consumable or faddish nature of the reward itself).

Consider how this scenario might differ for a sixth-grade boy, Joe, in the midst of puberty, who is not always able to stand up and speak out. He cannot count on his body anymore. To add to the ambiguity, his social development is in flux. Popularity is one thing, friendship quite another. Joe is well liked by his classmates, but his "chum" (Sullivan, 1953) does not do as well as Joe in school. Tracking starts next year in the junior high. Joe's sister says junior high is a big school, students change classes when the bell rings, and teachers are different each hour. She says it's fun—lots of new kids—but it can be lonely and hard, especially at first. Joe likely experiences considerable dissonance among being a good: 1) friend ("If I keep working hard, we won't be in the same classes next year"), 2) student ("If I quit working it's not fair to my teacher"), 3) son ("If I don't try, my parents will be disappointed and angry"), and 4) person ("Is withholding effort to stay in the class with my friend selfish? dishonest?").

Negotiating multiple influences and goals, within evolving contexts and one's own changing body, understanding, expertise, and needs is a difficult task. It is also what being a student is all about; the task itself changes with development and changes in SIE expectations. The third-grader is praised for asking teacher how to spell a word; the fourth-grader is chastised to "look it up." We call this reciprocal process of mediation and internalization *emergent interaction*, after Wertsch and Stone (1985) to highlight that both students and the SIEs of their lives change and influence each other.

Emergent interaction helps us stay mindful that students are actively involved in the processes that influence them. Further, how students mediate the objectively same influence varies, for example, with their development. This is readily apparent when you consider the success of a management attempt to influence classmates with an "ILTW" (*"I Like The Way* Nicole is all ready to start . . . "). First-grade students, hearing classmate Nicole praised for being ready, bustle to be the next one ready and noted. Compare that success with the dismal failure of ILTWs in sixth grade: the audience rolls their eyes at the blatant attempt to control; Nicole, the target, glares at being used.

Students actively mediate their experiences even as they are learning more sophisticated mediational strategies and filters. Students, children, are co-constructors of their lives. Thus, in our view, with the exception of extreme and destructive SIEs, students are not passive victims of the social/instructional environments of their lives; nor are they the sole architects of their experience. Students and those who would influence them share that responsibility. Our approach is located within a Vygotskian (1962; 1978) or co-constructivist framework (Bruner, 1990; Wertsch, 1985), broadly defined.

Finally, in our perspective, students are an essential, emergent feature of the SIE of classrooms. So are the goals they pursue. Some goals that students pursue (or abandon) are self-imposed; some are imposed by others. For example, a student may want to do "well enough" in school, but *really want* ("gotta have it") stereo equipment. A part-time job allows the student responsibly to earn and save enough money to purchase a CD player. The job also competes with school preparation, both in terms of getting homework done and simply getting up in the morning and being alert in school. The goal of earning and purchasing a CD player is a priority; the student plans to postpone and "catch up" later in school. What appears as a lack of motivation in school is actually an issue of self-imposed goal coordination and prioritization. Parents reading this example may also worry about future goal-coordination strategies. They are likely thinking about the quality of their son's future study time—homework done to *that* music—that most certainly will follow purchase of the CD player (not to mention the musical quality of the parents' own evenings!).

Another student may want to be on the swim team; her parents may want her to make the honor roll. Practice lasts 2 hours each night after school; time for homework is not as easily scheduled. Parents believe that their daughter cannot achieve both goals; they value academics, and the honor roll is more readily attainable without sports. Quitting the swim team does not reflect the student's priority; achieving honor-roll status is not her primary goal, but it is evident in her behavior, nonetheless. Unlike the swim coach's and her teammates' belief, she is not a quitter; she is obedient.

Identifying and coordinating among goals is a major task whose features, as we have noted, likely change with the developing student and the dynamic social/instructional environment of classrooms. We assert that teachers *and* students are involved in students learning how to set, coordinate, pursue, and evaluate classroom goals so that students can better meet their aspirations in the classroom and beyond. Our focus here is on the classroom. Although we focus primarily on classroom participants, we wish again to stress that, in our view, teachers, parents, students/children, and the broader society *share* the responsibility of student goal achievement and the enhancement of adaptive learning.

In sum, classrooms are functional contexts—social/instructional environments—that are in emergent interaction with students, who bring more than their developing biology through the door. Just as classrooms are not sheltered from societal beliefs about children and students—indeed, unless mindful, classrooms can replicate those beliefs—they also are not independent of other, immediate SIEs in students' lives, like families and friends. We discuss students' families in Chapter 6; here we describe the dynamics of student friendship as it affects the classroom.

◆ STUDENT FRIENDSHIPS

There are considerable differences among children in how well they are liked and by how many. Consistent with work by Parker and Asher (1993; Asher & Parker, 1989) and Eder (1985), we distinguish among acceptance, friendship, and popularity. We will argue that in childhood, acceptance is essential, friendship is one of its riches, and popularity isn't all it is cracked up to be.

Some level of peer acceptance is a key mental health variable for children. Peer acceptance is about more than the experience of childhood, it is also about future outcomes. Asher and Parker (1988) describe a review of 40 studies on early peer adjustment, acceptance, and later behavior. They found:

> low acceptance was most consistently predictive of later dropping out [of school]. In study after study, children identified as low in peer acceptance dropped out at rates 2, 3, and even 8 times as high as other children. In percentage terms, on average, about 25% of low-accepted elementary school children

dropped out later compared to about 8% of other children. By contrast, aggressiveness was most consistently predictive of later criminality. Studies with measures of aggressiveness indicated that aggressive boys and girls were, on average, nearly 5 times more likely than other boys and girls to be involved in later crime, and in some studies these rates rose to 8 or 10 times more likely. In percentage terms, on average, 33% of all aggressive children were later involved in juvenile or adult crimes, compared to about 10% of nonaggressive children. (p. 18)

Asher and Parker conclude that children with peer relation problems should be considered "at risk." They suggest remediation be directed to helping these students gain acceptance and learn how to form and keep friendships, versus "be popular." They note that, in terms of a personal sense of well-being, there are few differences between average-acceptance children and popular children. Indeed, Eder (1985) notes that popularity and friendship are not only different, sometimes they can be antagonistic. In an ethnographic study of middle-school girls, Eder found that the popular girls were *not liked.* Popularity is not about friendship, it is about status. We will focus our remaining comments on student friendships and how these relationships might mediate students' experience in the classroom.

Friendships have been termed *reliable alliances* (Weiss, 1974, as reported in Asher & Parker, 1988). Reliable alliance refers to the security and strength that comes with knowing that another can be counted on; another is loyal. Berndt and colleagues (e.g., Berndt & Perry, 1990) have studied issues of loyalty in children's friendship. Loyalty in children means such things as not telling on each other and sticking up for each other. Loyalty in friendship is especially important in preadolescent children and among girls. With age, children begin to include "not compete with" as a condition of loyalty. Changing beliefs about loyalty and friendship likely have important implications for classroom evaluation procedures, particularly those based upon social comparison, as previously described. Just as an "ILTW" has the opposite of the intended effect with older students, so too might some motivational techniques designed to imitate the competition of sports.

Gender likely plays a part in this as well. Organized competition in the classroom is, on the average, more compatible with boys' approach to relationships than it is with the typical social relationships of girls. Daniels-Beirness (in Asher & Parker, 1988) describes gender differences in the boundaries children place on group belongingness. Boys form groups that are fairly large and hierarchically organized; girls tend to form dyads and focus on equality within the relationship. Boys' groups also are more open to new friendships; girls' groups are not. We suspect these differences mediate teacher attempts to "motivate" students through both competitive gamelike activities *and* the construction of small cooperative groups. In both instructional formats, students' relationships with one another and their beliefs about those relationships become inherent features of the learning.

But how do these relationships begin? How do children's relationships move from acquaintance to best friend ("chum")? Why do others not evolve? Duck (1988) notes that "relationships do not just begin on their own" (p. 99) and examines how open communication and appropriate disclosure promote them. Duck further suggests that competence in relationships is strategic and includes elements of "getting noticed in the right, promising ways," continuing with skills in conversation, communication about self, and increasingly, relational knowledge of the other's needs (p. 99).

Sullivan (1953) is perhaps the earliest and best-known theorist to focus on children's friendships—especially those of preadolescents. Sullivan maintained that preadolescent friendship with a "chum" is a key collaborative, intimate relationship for children that serves as a model for later intimate, romantic relationships. Through valuing the chum, the child learns to value her/himself. Sullivan so believed in the power of chum relations that he maintained that it is possible for these relationships to substitute and counter maladaptive parent-child relationships. Chums validate one's interests and fears and support feelings of self-worth within a context of self-disclosure. And chums provide affection. Sullivan's chums are even more essential than the "reliable alliance" described by Weiss or the strategic communication discussed by Duck. There is loyalty *and* love. There is also practice. Sullivan describes the hours chums spend trying out what they think and feel and believe as an important vehicle for learning who they are and what that means.

Clearly, friendships are an important part of life; chums are a special gift. Students who have friendships that matter are likely more able to adapt to the daily stresses that are part of classroom life. They are not alone; they have a peer who values them and who watches out for them; just as they value and keep watch. They also have an intimate who is part of their mediation of events: a peer "co-regulator" who helps figure things out and try things out.

Students who are without friends are often the target of teacher (and parent) attempts to "find them one." That is beyond a teacher's power. One student cannot be made to like another; however, students can be taught skills that will make them more likable (e.g., how to take turns, show an interest in what someone else is doing, negotiate conflict, assert needs). Teachers can also ensure that children without friends are not mistreated in word or deed by their classmates. We suspect teachers are well aware of all of the above. Student friendships are fundamental features of classroom life; dealing with peer relationships is an on-going task of teaching. Teacher concern for the student who is rejected by peers or so withdrawn as to not even approach peers is well documented (e.g., Brophy & McCaslin, 1992), even in an era of subject-matter learning and test scores.

Conversations with students about peer relationships are important—not only for their alleged topic ("How do you think Ann feels when you treat her that way?") but also because they structure student mediation of social events, their "social cognition." Such conversations are important opportunities to scaffold the social norms and attributional rules that guide much of our interpersonal judgments and behavior (e.g., Weiner, 1986, 1992). Scaffolding in the social realm is especially needed because social events are so ambiguous ("Did she mean to knock my book?" "Why did he look at me *that* way?"). Rohrkemper (1984, 1985) found that how teachers scaffold interpersonal rules have important effects on students' capacity for interpreting and responding to their own and others' behavior and emotion. Across the elementary grades, students better understand their teacher and each other when teachers help students learn notions of control, intention, and responsibility, and their relation to others' perception, feelings, and behavior. This is especially the case for younger students who are often confused by interpersonal events.

Another feature of student social cognition that we consider an important feature of classroom SIEs—and thus, what it means to be a student—are the set of emergent beliefs students hold about the function of ability and achievement in classroom learning and what those beliefs mean for oneself and others. It is all part of being a classmate and having classmates.

◆ **STUDENTS AS CLASSMATES**

Students come to school with a host of strengths and difficulties that present resources and problems—not only for themselves but also for their classmates (and teachers). As we have described, students differ in their strategic ability to set, pursue, coordinate, and attain goals. They arrive with different beliefs about who they are, who they are becoming, and what that means. Students have different personalities, dispositions, and strategies for coping with classroom demands and conflicts. They also have different expectations about schooling and "what works."

Why Go to School?   Some students come to school because it is relatively safe and warm and they serve food. Some come to learn; some come because it would not occur to them to do otherwise. Some students attend school for the purpose of participating in sports; some to avoid sanctions of the law (Covington, Guthrie, Webb, & Pipho, 1990). Other students come to school because it is the vehicle for acculturation to which their families aspire. Cusick (1973) describes students for whom high school is just a place to "hang out"; Brown (1993) describes it in terms of the cliques—who hangs with whom. Others have likened it to a "shopping mall" (Powell, Farrar, & Cohen, 1985). In short, students' reasons for attending school are as varied as their expectations, especially as they move through the grades and school structures. Their reasons for attending school are not as focused as the culture or the school would like; but they are there.

Beliefs About Ability   Students also hold varied beliefs about ability. Ability has been described as incremental (it changes) and fixed (it is stable) (e.g., Dweck, 1986). Incremental beliefs promote effort; fixed beliefs do not. Younger students typically hold incremental ability beliefs; older students maintain a more fixed perspective (e.g., Stipek, 1986). This does not appear to be a strictly developmental phenomenon, based solely upon cognitive development. The multidimensionality of classrooms affects students' beliefs about ability (e.g., Rosenholtz & Simpson, 1984). So, apparently do evaluation procedures.

In Chapter 1 we described individually referenced evaluation systems (Krampen, 1987) that promote student effort and self-efficacy. This may well occur because individually referenced evaluation promotes an incremental and profile view of one's abilities ("I can get smarter, learn more, if I try"). We suspect evaluation as represented on report cards also plays a role. In the middle elementary-school years, many schools replace vague ratings of "satisfactory" or "needs improvement" with more precise comparative letter grades ("A–," "C+" etc.). More-exact grades are concomitant with a comments checklist describing student effort ("needs to work harder") and conduct ("gets along [too!] well with others"). Thus, students' developing cognitive abilities co-occur with structural changes in information; development of beliefs about ability and socialization of those beliefs are likely codetermined. Development and socialization are in emergent interaction; they go hand in hand.

Others have found that teachers' beliefs about the nature of ability affect the evaluation systems they use with students, and thus, student beliefs. Teachers who believe ability is incremental typically use individually referenced evaluation; those who believe ability is fixed are more apt to use social comparison evaluation procedures (how the student is doing relative to others) (e.g., Rheinberg, 1980, as discussed in Heckhausen, 1991). In addition to these two profiles, we suspect that some teachers who adhere to an incremental belief in ability nonetheless incorporate social-comparison information in their feedback to students, likely in the belief that it boosts motivation. Rohrkemper and Bershon (1984), for example, found that, by fourth grade, students wanted social comparison information more than knowledge of individual progress—they found it more motivating and informative. We are unaware of research that explicitly examines the co-occurence of these types of teacher evaluation on students' beliefs about the incremental or fixed nature of ability, but it seems a particularly interesting question to pursue as both levels of information seem important in setting realistic yet optimistic goals.

Teachers also influence student beliefs about ability through their management systems. Ames (1992) and colleagues have found that classroom reward systems that foster competition result in student attributions that reflect a fixed view of their ability ("I am smart"; "I am dumb"). Covington (1992) and colleagues also view the classroom as a public and competitive arena where students develop strategies to save face and save pride. Ironically, these face-saving—self-handicapping—strategies interfere with incremental conceptions of ability that likely would protect feelings of "self-worth" (Covington, 1992).

Specifically, Covington and colleagues have examined how students come to "dual classify" (Piaget, 1983) ability and effort (i.e., think of ability in relation to effort, possibly an *inverse* relation) and what that means for classroom behavior. Covington describes the increasing cognitive sophistication of preadolescent students who are able to coordinate and evaluate amount of effort with amount of ability, with the result: *the less effort expended, the more the underlying ability*. Ouch! The opposite of teacher expectations for effortful, successful student behavior. We will see this belief in action when we discuss how students cope with the stress of achievement and again, when we describe how one sixth-grade girl, Nora, coordinates her effort with ability as she negotiates learning in her classroom. We think Covington's insights do much to help us better understand what it is like to be a student.

Beliefs About Ability and Virtue   Beliefs about ability can also relate to beliefs about "goodness." That is, "smart" students are often believed to be better *persons* than the less smart. Smart students are often the recipients of special privileges (e.g., choice of assignments) and leadership and tutorial roles in the classroom, such that a caste system emerges among students. Smart students' special status is supported by teacher *and* peers (McCaslin & Good, 1996; McCaslin & Murdock, 1991; Weinstein, 1993; Weinstein, Marshall, Brattesani, & Middlestadt, 1982).

It is not only students who confound goodness with ability. Recent popular "best-sellers" like *The Bell Curve: Intelligence and Class Structure in American Life* (Herrnstein & Murray, 1994) have once again brought to the forefront implicit (and at times explicit), self-serving beliefs in our culture about ability, race, and "goodness" via economic deservedness. In brief, arguments of this sort maintain that members of certain racial groups are genetically superior (inferior) in intelligence, and that intelligence and economic advantage (disadvantage) are linked via genetic endowment (vs. societal beliefs or conditions). Therefore, the reasoning continues, economic status can be considered a "birthright."

In our view, books such as this serve as a societal Rorschach: they tell us much about the emotional and intellectual functioning of the audience and the authors, particularly given the limitations of inherently correlational research. We are not alone in our stance that such arguments are without merit and distract us from our commitments and our power as educators and citizens (e.g., Berliner & Biddle, 1995). Nonetheless, race and ability as a sort of "hierarchy of genetic goodness" are part of the popular culture of beliefs about ability that extend the racial devaluation described previously. These beliefs can permeate classrooms as they influence students and other participants. Such beliefs, in our view, need to be met head on in the classroom. Students are not valued for their ability nor their resources, they are valued for exercising their talents and their humanity.

Coping With the Stress of Achievement   We have described students who are under tremendous pressure to excel in school in order to make their best way for self and family. Students who feel pressure to succeed—whether self- or other-imposed—can display their anxiety in a variety of ways. Some simply shut down, paralyzed by fear of failure (e.g., Atkinson, 1964). These "failure syndrome" students do not even attempt a task. They passively wait for teacher help, the end of class, or the end of the day. They display helplessness and hopelessness. Other students who fear failure may opt to entertain (class clown) to distract self and others (and, hopefully, teacher) from their own personal achievement.

Other anxious students pursue perfection, often losing perspective, substituting relatively superficial detail for the basic task. Many teachers, for example, have coped with the perfectionist student who continually erases less-than-perfect penmanship, slowly retracing the letters. Often, the results are an incomplete writing assignment, a hole in the paper, clenched fists, and tears.

Much research has been conducted on students who cope with the stress of achievement by substituting social comparison for learning and by engaging in competitive "performance" rather than individual mastery (e.g., Ames, 1992; Dweck, 1986). Students also engage a variety of self-handicapping strategies (e.g., procrastination, absenteeism) to avoid displaying inadequacy (Covington, 1992). Covington has found that students who believe in a compensatory relationship between effort and ability would rather feel guilty about lack of effort than shame about perceived low ability. They cannot manipulate ability, but they can manipulate their effort. By withholding their effort, they can save their "self worth," that is, save their beliefs in their ability.

Covington and colleagues (Covington, 1992; Covington et al., 1990; Covington and Omelich, 1979) have described effort as the "double-edged sword" of classroom life. Consider: if a student is effortful and fails, her perceived self-worth is maximally vulnerable. In her view, even considerable effort could not compensate for her low ability. If the student withholds effort, however, her self-worth is relatively intact. A little effort is a necessary, but insufficient, condition for most tasks. Withholding effort, however, invites difficulties with the teacher. Brophy and McCaslin (1992; Brophy & Rohrkemper, 1981; Rohrkemper & Brophy, 1983) found that teachers perceive underachieving students (i.e., those who do not strive to their abilities, who could achieve but choose not to) as culpable for their behavior, and they respond with punishment. Rohrkemper (1984, 1985) found that students as early as the spring of their first-grade year understand this teacher perception/response pattern.

Students who engage self-handicapping strategies, then, apparently knowingly take the risk of teacher anger and punishment. Self-handicapping "works" in the short-run ("Who could do a 20-page report in a *single night*?" "How could *anyone* do well on a test if he missed four classes during that unit?" "If only I hadn't gone to the party last night, I could at least have been *awake* for the test this morning!"). As these examples illustrate, beliefs about ability are protected as the barriers to achievement are so "obvious" and so obviously not about individual ability. Unfortunately, they also are obviously short-term solutions with debilitating long-term effects: the student has not learned to cope with the anxiety of achievement demands *and* has not learned material upon which subsequent work will be based.

Rejecting Achievement   Some students, however, just seem not to care. They achieve below their abilities and believe they are doing well enough. Underachievement has long been a concern of classroom teachers. Underachievement is not considered a "syndrome"; thus, little attention is given to systematic research on these students or intervention strategies with them. Mostly, underachievers are blamed for their lack of motivation to meet their abilities, and/or classroom tasks are labeled as "irrelevant" and teachers "uninspiring" to explain the students' lack of motivation. In either case, underachievement is mostly viewed as a school-related, school-age problem.

Recent research, however, indicates that underachievement in school has a significant impact on future attitudes toward challenge and maintaining commitments. McCall (1994) considers underachievement a disposition that continues well into the adult years. He writes that underachievers who were followed up 13 years after high school "demonstrated less persistence in completing their college degrees, holding on to their jobs, and maintaining their marriages. . . . an underachieving diamond in the academic rough tends to stay in the rough" (p. 18). We suggest that it is useful to consider a chronic underachieving pattern within the co-regulation model of student mediation that was presented in Chapter 1. In particular, we refer to relatively undeveloped enactment and self-evaluation strategies. That is, independent of motivational dynamics, underachieving students may not know *how* to see a task through—they lack strategic volition (see Corno, 1992, for extended discussion)—and/or they may not know how to assess their progress *realistically*. Underachiever *motivation*, the typical focus of concern about underachievement, may well be a relatively minor point.

◆ SUMMARY

In short, students are essential features of the classroom SIE. Students' beliefs and relationships have important implications for what it means to be a student—for themselves and one another—now and in the future. The typical classroom includes the whole array of beliefs, preparation, motivation, and sociality among students in emergent interaction; it is part of the particular "context" of the social/instructional environment of a classroom. Students can be resources for, or drains on, themselves and each other—sometimes more than others.

Classroom SIEs are also fluid. Students enter for reading. Students leave for the gifted and talented program, remediation, band, in-school suspension. Each wonders what s/he missed. Families move in and out of school boundaries, some repeating the cycle throughout the year. Recent estimates indicate that 20 percent of elementary and secondary students transfer to new schools each year. Adjustment to the new school setting is particularly stressful; indeed, some research indicates a heightened vulnerability to failure, dropping out, and delinquent activities during this transition (Custer, 1994). Absent students, new students, and those returning at midyear—each with his/her own anxiety and coping style—add to the mix called "life in classrooms" (Jackson, 1968). Classrooms are social places by design and reality; thus, they are about more than academic learning, and *student* is not a generic term, as in the "student perception." As we have maintained throughout, this book is all about the "non-ability determinants" (Bandura, 1990) of students and their *experience* of classrooms. We now illustrate what we mean about the "experience" of being a student as compared with a theoretical or popular description of students. As you read, notice how both the academic and the societal lenses are integrated.

❖ "BEING A STUDENT": NORA

Earlier we described a student as a changing and developing person who pursues, and more or less successfully coordinates, multiple goals that include (with more or less priority) the management of learning requirements and accountability systems within the social setting of classrooms. We have sketched the many ways that students can be described as changing and developing and how differing social/instructional environments (SIEs) might influence and be influenced by those processes. We think the experience of being a student, however, is also all about coordinating goals, as we stressed in Chapter 1.

It seems useful now to ask about the potential sources of the goals to which students might aspire. We suspect that the sources that influence the setting of varied goals inform how students attempt to coordinate among them as well. We illustrate our hypothesis with an example, a sixth-grade, 12-year-old student, Nora (whose mother we will meet again in Chapter 6). The lengthy case study this account is based on ("A Case of Emergent Interaction") and other illustrative cases are available elsewhere for the interested reader (McCaslin, in progress; McCaslin Rohrkemper, 1989; McCaslin & Murdock, 1991). Here we focus on Nora's (fictional name) negotiation of expectations from multiple SIEs to illustrate our position: students negotiate multiple sources of influence as they come to set, seek, and coordinate goals. Goal pursuit, in turn, helps define "who they are."

◆ FAMILY SOCIAL/INSTRUCTIONAL ENVIRONMENT

Nora is from a working-class home in which everyone does her/his share: both parents have full-time jobs and the children (Nora and her two younger brothers) have their own home responsibilities. Nora's mother is actively involved in her children coming to understand what it means to be a member of their family: in this family everyone has multiple roles. Within her family, for example, Nora is a daughter, sister, and babysitter. Nora-the-babysitter has a different relationship with parents and siblings than when she is not in that role. What passes for bossy sister when the folks are home translates into responsible leadership when they are away.

All roles—within and outside the family—however, share certain maxims:

1. Life includes evaluation and boredom; learn to deal with each of them.
2. One way to "deal with it" is to become self-reliant. Everyone benefits from self-reliance: you can assess your own progress, experience satisfaction, and others can depend on you.

3.   The way we learn to be self-reliant is through being responsible—that is, by setting priorities and meeting our commitments.

Parents directly teach and model these family values. For example, Nora's parents focus on *effort and intention, not outcome,* in evaluating and consequating their children's behavior. Innate ability is not especially valued; instead, the value is on the striving. Further, striving—effort—does not have to be successful to be valued. Thus, achievement without effort is not noteworthy; complacency is definitely out. An essential task in this family, *effort* is defined as thinking through and following through; it is the first step in acting responsibly. Core family values are promoted by responsibility to self and commitment to others. These skills and dispositions are systematically scaffolded, supported, and taught, in part by increasing opportunities to display and develop them.

If you are now thinking how great it would be if all students lived in Nora's family, you are not alone! Nora is a member of a family who loves, values, and teaches her how to set her priorities and be "her own person." Nora's mother believes that one of Nora's strong points is "knowing who she is right now. . . . she doesn't care about the kids, being trendy. . . . You know, she doesn't need to go along with the tide" (McCaslin & Mudock, 1991, p. 242). In Nora's family, being "her own person" refers to self-reliance and dependability: you *are* your commitments. Most of us would see this as the kind of solid home support that facilitates life pursuit, accomplishment of and satisfaction with things that matter. That substantial support, however, does not necessarily obviate difficulties in Nora's "being" a student. Nora attends the neighborhood K–6 elementary school, and she adopts and adapts to other roles that are not always compatible with the rules of home (see, also McCaslin Rohrkemper, 1989).

◆ **SCHOOL SOCIAL/INSTRUCTIONAL ENVIRONMENT**

Nora is quite capable. Her file includes reports by school psychologists who are surprised by standardized test results: Nora seems a likely candidate for the "gifted and talented" program, yet her test performance with the school psychologist always falls short. Anecdotal reports describe Nora-the-third-grader saying she doesn't want to leave her classroom; Nora-the-fifth-grader saying she likes things the way they are. It appears the school would like Nora to display (and special education to promote) her considerable talents, but Nora is reluctant.

Indeed, the principal's stated goals for her school include *exceeding* the district-level goal of "one year's growth for every child." Growth is defined by scores on standardized achievement tests. Toward this end, the principal created a within-school reward system to motivate students to perform well on national standardized (normative) and city-mandated criterion tests. In reality, however, her vision is confined to the high-achieving/high-ability students. Only the select few profit from her incentive programs.

For example, students with the highest standardized test scores are selected (by the principal) as "class messengers" to the office and honored at assemblies. Sixth-grade students in the gifted and talented program are responsible for the schoolwide P.A. (public address) announcements after lunch. Interestingly, Nora and her mother both (independently) mentioned how "embarrassing" it is to have your name mentioned over the P.A. (as happens on students' birthdays). We suspect that one (more) reason Nora fails to place in the gifted and talented program is to avoid the "requirement" to speak over the P.A. (likely *not* the intended effect of the incentive program!).

In short, the principal values realized high ability as manifested in test performance. Effort by the highly able is especially valued. This contrasts with Nora's home, in which ability is not as highly valued as effort. Achievements (*if effortful*) are valued because of the commitment to strive and see something through, and evaluations by others are something to be endured because self-assessment of progress and *private* satisfactions (which Nora transforms into "tired and happy") are the key to self-reliance.

Home and school SIEs also differ in strategies used to influence the adoption of a goal. The school principal uses highly salient and pervasive status rewards. Nora's mother *never mentioned* the use of rewards as a viable strategy with children. Nora's mother prefers that, if necessary, the school praise her daughter privately and only if she has worked hard and done something extraordinary. There are substantial differences between the expectations and socialization strategies of home and school.

◆ CLASSROOM SOCIAL/INSTRUCTIONAL ENVIRONMENT

Teacher   Nora's teacher values successful, effortful, achievement; these are linked. The teacher adheres to an instructional model wherein tasks are believed appropriately sequenced and structured in a prerequisite skill hierarchy so that, *with effortful cognition*, students will succeed. In this instructional model, student successful performance represents student learning (see Rohrkemper & Corno, 1988, for extended discussion of instructional models and student success). In this classroom, then, effort is always expected. However, effort is linked to outcome; indeed, effort is *known by* the outcome. For example, if students fail, the teacher assumes that they did not try, not that they were not able or that the work was too hard.

It is appropriate, then, that Nora's teacher rewards the *product* of effort. Nora's teacher's conception of effort contrasts in one fundamental way with the conception of effort in Nora's home. In Nora's family, effort is required *independent* of the outcome; mother rewards the *process* of effort, not the effects. Thus, at home, Nora can evaluate her efforts by the value and intention that guide them. In contrast, in her classroom, the *outcome* of her effort must be known to understand its value.

In another way, however, Nora's mother and teacher are similar. Nora's teacher, like Nora's mother, also adheres to goals for students that contrast with school norms. The principal's schoolwide policies are based on the test score attainments of the highly able. Nora's teacher believes in the efforts (and, thus, achievements) of *everyone*.

Peers   Teachers do not solely control the SIE of classrooms; they share that power with students. These are sixth-graders; and for these sixth-grade students, popularity matters—a lot. The surest way to be popular is to be smart. Smart means fast. Fast means you didn't have to try. If you didn't have to try and you were fast, you must be *really smart*. As we described previously, by the sixth grade, students are well entrenched in a perception of competence that rests on a compensatory relationship between effort and ability. That is, they believe that the more effort expended, the less the available ability. Effort takes time; thus, effort is observable—others can know your ability.

Amount of student time on task is not only of interest to researchers and teachers! Students are quite aware of one another's relative efforts. One big difference between students and those who teach or study them, however, is that students are not apt to equate time on task—effort—with motivation, goodness, or opportunity to learn. Students are more apt to relate it to ability. Thus, a fourth distinct message emerges for Nora to negotiate in her setting and pursuit of learning goals. It comes from her classmates: effort is inversely related to ability. Classmates' beliefs are incompatible with teacher beliefs.

In this classroom, peers take the familiar ability-effort compensation argument a step further. For these students, ability is linked to personal worth and *popularity*. Popularity can get complicated; relative ability must be negotiated even among the "elite." But ability (defined by achievement with little effort) is, nonetheless, the only ticket to the game. Thus, although by a different route and with an inverse valence on effort, Nora's peers have re-created the principal's hierarchy. Indeed, for these students, P.A. announcements are one of the things that the popular kids do. Principal and peers define winners; mother and teacher define the "also rans."

◆ **GOAL SETTING AND COORDINATION**

It looks like Nora can't "have it all." She cannot simultaneously please home and school, teacher and peers—and she knows it. Repeated interviews with Nora about her self- and other-perceptions, observations of her classroom performance, and analysis of her classroom journal, reveal a 12-year-old who is struggling to negotiate among multiple expectations for her achievements: academically, personally, and socially. It does not come easily. Nora struggles with setting the multiple goals that are part of classroom life: to learn, to have friends, and to "be her own person."

On one level, Nora is aware of the differences in achievement expectations held for her. She knows how to please her parents and teacher, and she typically does. Nora shields knowledge of her considerable ability and maximizes perceptions of the "effort" in her achievements. Although Nora's mother may worry that learning comes "too easily to her"; her teacher does not. Nora's teacher considers Nora a moderate-ability/highly effortful student. In a real sense, Nora could not do better in the eyes of mother and teacher. She also knows how to avoid the embarrassing "perks" the principal provides without being too obvious about it—after all, the test data speak for themselves. Thus, Nora navigates adult achievement expectations and beliefs pretty well.

Negotiating social relationships with peers is more difficult for Nora, however—especially if friendships and popularity are to be coordinated with teacher and home expectations. Like the girls Eder (1985) studied, Nora's journal entries reveal a girl who is consumed with the other girls in her class: who has what; who wears what; who knows what and how fast; who likes what; who likes whom, when, and for how long. Unfortunately for Nora, the ticket to the popular clique is not the same as admission to her family. The two goals—being popular and being her own person—are antagonistic. Even though a priority over popularity, the goal to "be her own person" is difficult for Nora to pursue; she is very aware of the path not taken. Nora aspires to that self-reliant goal, but the getting there can be pretty tough.

Nora struggles with goal conflict on various levels. In one sense, she seems aware of the problem. For instance, when asked how the research interviews could be helpful to students, she suggests that the interviewer include ways for students to discuss the tensions between sociability ("being friends") and self-reliance ("being your own person") in small-group work.

In another sense, however, Nora appears unaware of her personal mediation of effort and its costs. She seems to have fused learning, morality, and modesty; and confused popularity, acceptance, and friendship. For example, one reason Nora does not believe it is possible to be "able and virtuous too" (Covington & Omelich, 1979) is that she does not believe it is possible to be a good student and be a good friend. The good students are snobs; they "think they are better" than everyone else.

◆ EMERGENT INTERACTION AND GOAL COORDINATION

Nora's recognition of multiple and competing SIE sources of influence on her goal setting and pursuit, and her attempted negotiation of them, are interactive with her own emergent developmental capabilities. Thus, Nora can recognize (and fantasize about) others' perceptions and expectations. She is able to "dual classify" effort and ability, ability and popularity. Nora has the metacognitive capability and time perspective that allow meaningful planning for and evaluation of "thinking through and following through"—the ethics of home.

She has discovered the phone as one possible point of integration between home and school, of effort and friendship. Nora gets calls from classmates who ask her to clarify homework assignments and test dates. She enjoys the calls, and classmates' phone requests validate her effortfulness in school (to a point!). Nora also is immersed in disentangling the tasks of friendship (intimacy) and popularity (status) that are part of being an early-adolescent female. In short, Nora is engaged in an early-adolescent struggle that involves forging emergent identity from multiple influences; the resolution of that struggle has enormous implications for her. Developmental stage theories (e.g., Marcia, 1980) would likely categorize Nora as a "foreclosed identity" (because she appears primarily to adhere to family beliefs about who she is and what that means as she negotiates other SIEs), or in "diffusion" (meaning she has not yet engaged the identity task in a meaningful way). In the identity literature, foreclosure and diffusion are considered less-healthy identities, because the individual did not explore and commit to other options. But Nora's struggle seems much more complicated (and mindful and healthy) than that. Further, Nora's "identity" is not just about Nora. It is about the messages in the multiple SIEs of her life and their relationship to one another. Multiple messages, like multiple goals, require mediation, identification, and coordination.

And then there's puberty. Nora and her classmates raise nervous questions: Do you have to take showers in gym in junior high? I hate my hair. I wish my parents would let me get contacts. Am I taller than you?

It's a pretty full plate.

This is what we mean by multiple sources of influence on negotiating, setting, pursuing, and coordinating goals. We think an understanding of these multiple sources is a useful framework for considering what it is like to *be* a student. Students negotiate multiple influences on who they are, who and what they ought to become, and how to get there. The magnitude of the task changes with students' emergent capabilities to appreciate it and with the steady increase in the sheer number of SIEs in students' lives. The first-grade student and the seventh-grade student have fundamentally different goal negotiation and coordination tasks, but nonetheless, each is engaged by and in it. We now reexamine our analysis of goal coordination (described briefly in Chapter 1) as one aspect of co-regulated learning. Our emphasis is on what it means to be a student within the social setting of the classroom and how teachers might facilitate student goal coordination within it.

❖ GOAL COORDINATION AS A BASIC TASK AND OPPORTUNITY

We have argued that when students navigate the classroom, they are coordinating more than the demands of the curriculum. Students' lives are complicated (Garbarino, Dubrow, Kostelny, & Pardo, 1992; Natriello, McDill, & Pallas, 1990); the complexity only increases with age. Pulls on students away from the classroom readily come to mind. As parents and teachers, we worry about the after-school activities that take precedence over assignments, the middle-level managers who do not respect their young employees, the seemingly magnetic attraction of the mall or the street. We recognize these extracurricular and extraschool attractions that compete for student goal setting and coordination, and their expense in terms of time, energy, and attention. It is our purpose here, however, to consider how teachers might streamline student goal conflicts *within* the classroom by creating opportunities for informative goal coordination.

◆ SOME BASIC CONSIDERATIONS

Recall the model of co-regulated learning described in Chapter 1. Here we briefly review characteristics of goals discussed previously and elaborate on ways to consider, teach, and promote goal relationships and goal coordination.

A Brief Review of Goal Characteristics   First, we remind readers that the goals a student has adopted are not obvious. As teachers, for example, you know that quietly working students are not necessarily motivated students. This observational error is compounded by the students who misbehave in ways visible to peers but not to the teacher (Spencer-Hall, 1981).

Second, students also can pursue goals for multiple, simultaneous reasons; for example, strategic study time is a way to: 1) learn, 2) not have to do it over, 3) please teacher and parents, and 4) ensure weekend privileges to boot. It is not particularly helpful to conceptualize students as the source of motivational traits (e.g., lazy, irresponsible, underachieving [e.g., Tomlinson, 1993], overstriving, or what have you).

Third, apparent strategies students engage can also be multifunctional. Consider effort. It may promote achievement, the presumed (i.e., preferred) goal. However, effort is also an effective impression-management strategy (at least for observing *adults*) and a fairly successful tool in grade-trade negotiation. We have all been confronted by the student who "deserves" a higher grade because s/he "really worked hard on this." Effort is also an acceptable way to avoid a task ("As long as I work on this task I can postpone, maybe even avoid, that one. I am not shirking responsibility; I am consumed by responsibility.").

Goal Relationships   The relationships among goals also are multidimensional. Dodge, Asher, and Parkhurst (1989) predict that the complexity among goals increases along several dimensions. Here we focus on three dimensions: the first two present intrapersonal dilemmas, the third presents an interpersonal dilemma. First, if multiple goals are pursued simultaneously, a time press makes it difficult to prioritize and to pursue them sequentially. Thus, *timing* increases the complexity among goals. This seems a straightforward observation. Simply recall your coordination task when preparing, performing, and merely enduring finals week of four-course semesters. Imagine how students with multiple teachers are confronted with this problem all the time—especially if teachers do not consult each other around homework, project, and test schedules. Junior-high students, who likely have not yet learned how to negotiate multiple, simultaneous goals, can easily receive three hours of homework on a night before a major test, in part because teachers are not aware of each other's intentions.

Second, goal coordination becomes more complex when multiple goals are *difficult* and require considerable personal investment and resources. It becomes more problematic to have enough energy to spread among difficult goals or to allocate enough energy for subsequent goals if they are sequential. Again, this is a straightforward observation but one that does not seem to influence practice. Recall the student who wanted to be on the swim team and who was expected to be on the honor roll. Her goals likely differ (even though status may be a feature of both), the motivational source differs (herself, her parents), strategies to obtain the goals differ (for example, personal pacing likely differs in sports and classroom learning), the goals are simultaneous (practice and meets, schoolwork and tests co-occur), and both are difficult. Imagine engaging mindful study after two hours of after-school swim practice at the end of an already long day.

Finally, personal goals can compete and clash with others' needs and interests, making them more difficult and costly to pursue because *conflict with others* is likely. Indeed, the intrapersonal negotiation of the two dimensions we have just described can create, or at least contribute to, this third interpersonal conflict. For example, families organize around children's hobbies and talents (Bloom, 1985). Our swimmer's family likely delayed meals, listened to the lap-by-lap replay, and attended Saturday meets to support the very accomplishments that were distracting their daughter from classroom performance—until her parents judged the goal-coordination task to be too costly. Swim practice and homework, the enactive strategies required to meet the standard of excellence set for each goal—the team (set by the swimmer) and the honor roll (set by the parents)—were creating interpersonal, family tension. Teachers likely accommodated both goal pursuits as well, adding to the conflict. Teachers typically give deadline extensions when performance events (e.g., concerts, games, meets) occur midweek; tests can be made up, assignments postponed. Extension of privileges to a subset of students can contribute to teacher-student and student-student conflict. This last dimension of multiple goals and interpersonal conflict is especially informative in classrooms, because the social aspects of classroom learning can often prompt goals that interfere with learning and with others. Recall Nora and the goal-coordination task she negotiates.

In sum, multiple goals are a part of life (thank goodness); indeed, single-mindedness is not a particularly healthy approach to life. A basic task for students is to learn to identify individual goals and their relationships. A basic task for teachers is to be mindful of the goal coordination tasks we create for students by setting multiple, simultaneous, and difficult requirements that can create conflicts within and among students.

We have noted that these processes are not necessarily open to observation, yet observation can form the basis of questions that can scaffold teacher conversations. Structured interview seems an important tool in learning about how students negotiate the classrooms teachers design so that goal co-ordination tasks present learning opportunities rather then uneducative failures. When teachers are aware of goal-coordination tasks, they can deliberately co-regulate students' learning how to identify individual goals and their relationships for the purpose of organizing and strategizing among them. One path toward this goal concerns identification of goal compatibility.

Goal Compatibility   We have described potential conflicts among goals that result from their timing, difficulty, and congruence with others' goals. Goal relationships also can be understood by their degree of inherent compatibility, independent of these dimensions, as we briefly noted in Chapter 1 (see, Argyle, Furnham, & Graham, 1981). For example, goals can be *compatible* in three different ways:

1.   They may be able to *compensate* for each other, as effort (to an extent) can compensate for ability.
2.   They can be *complementary*. For example, cooperative behavior complements cooperative learning.
3.   Compatible goals can be *instrumental*: study *now* helps college plans *later*.

Goals can also be largely *independent* of each other. For example, wanting to be on time for lunch so one can sit with friends is (usually) independent of wanting to do well on an upcoming math test. Finally, goals can be *incompatible* with each other in two ways:

1.   They might *interfere* with each other. In our previous example, the preadolescent let the goal "to be a good friend" interfere with his goal "to be a good student."
2.   Incompatible goals might *negate* one another. For example, if a student strives to perfect his game and to meet the no-pass/no-play academic criterion but is found with alcohol, he neither plays nor stays in school.

It should be apparent that prioritizing and choosing among independent and incompatible goals is essential if students are to meet any of their goals. Think of how much energy, time, and emotion is spent futilely because an individual does not realize that s/he cannot have her/his cake and eat it too, and as a result, achieves neither experience. Consider as well how this likely affects future goal-setting and risk-taking behavior (e.g., Rotter, 1966).

Goal-Coordination Strategies   Dodge and colleagues (1989) describe four strategies that might promote goal coordination, which are dependent on the relationship among the goals. We add two strategies to their list and order them on a continuum of inclusiveness, from greater inclusiveness to less. The six strategies are:

1.   *A single, integrative strategy:* Although this is the most efficient and inclusive strategy, the goals obviously need to be compatible (i.e., compensatory, complementary, or instrumental) for the strategy to be appropriate. Dodge notes that this strategy also requires a certain amount of skill. One example is the high-ability, highly focused student who is involved in the school yearbook and student government, has a part-time job at the local Quick Print, and hopes to attend college to study journalism. Her/his

parents could not be prouder. This student's achievement, belongingness, power, independence, and present and future career needs are met with a single broad, integrative strategy.

2. *Multiple, simultaneous strategies:* **Simultaneous strategies require goals to be compatible with or independent of each other and for some to be less difficult so that the student can "overlap" (Kounin, 1970), pursuing more than one thing at a time. This is easily observed in small-group work. Academically more-capable students are often able to meet the demands of the task, follow procedures, and catch up on the "chit-chat" with their group members. Thus, they follow the routines like "good" students, successfully complete the task like "smart" students, and maintain friendly banter like "popular" students.**

3. *Deferment strategies:* **Deferment strategies result when the student realizes that s/he can't "have it all" and prioritizes. Nonpriority goals are put on the back burner, they are not abandoned. As compared with integrative and simultaneous strategies, deferment means less gets done because less *can* get done. We suspect this is the initial reasoning as students begin to restrict their hobbies: piano is deferred for now to allow more time for flute and the school band; soccer takes priority over track, just for this year; a part-time job just this summer postpones time with family and friends.**

4. *Modification strategies:* **Goals or the criteria for their successful attainment are modified to make goals more compatible. Thus, like "satisficing" (Simon, 1969), students may decide that each and every paper in English does not have to be their best; it is important that some of their time be spent on science class, too. We think that learning to modify goals is a particularly important skill that teachers can help students to develop. Adolescents as well as first-graders can easily lose a sense of proportion in the goals they set and their abilities to meet them. Goal modification seems to have much in common with learning how to set appropriate-level (i.e., attainable) goals in the first place and is linked to periodic, critical goal review, which we will discuss later at length. Goal-setting strategies have received much attention in the psychology and education literatures (e.g., Bandura, 1986; Schunk, 1989), goal review and modification less so.**

5. *Goal substitution:* **By *substitution* we mean that one goal replaces another, original goal. Although goal substitution need not have a negative connotation, it is often offered as an explanation for student gang membership and general theories of "negative identity" (e.g., Erikson, 1968; Ogbu, 1992). That is, students who are unable to achieve belongingness in family or sense of place and recognition in school substitute membership and status in gangs to fulfill unmet needs. All of us have had "goal-substitution" experiences, however, and they typically are positive, involving more realistic aspirations. Consider the student who wants to be part of the school play: although stagefright and basic lack of talent may prohibit being cast in an acting role, scenery always needs painting. The production of a play includes the whole crew.**

6. *Goal abandonment:* By *goal abandonment* we mean to simply give up on a goal without deferring, modifying, or substituting another. In the specific instance, goal abandonment may be appropriate. For example, simply giving up and going home to regroup may help a student cope with temporary embarrassment. Giving up the goal to always be the best at whatever one does is probably a good idea—as long as it does not translate into giving up trying or giving up altogether.

We can think of many instances, however, where simple goal abandonment, in aggregation and in the long run, restricts important opportunities and, thus, the development of goal-setting, goal-coordination strategies, and a certain level of "hardiness." Consider the phenomenon of adolescent females' withdrawal from mathematics coursework and the subsequent effects on their career choice, adult level of attainment, and lifelong financial earnings. Except in extreme, inescapable situations, sheer withdrawal is not a viable life strategy.

◆ OPPORTUNITIES AND GOAL-COORDINATION TASKS

It is useful to consider the above strategies on a continuum where the single, integrative strategy is the most inclusive and abandonment is the most restrictive and limiting. It is also useful to consider the kinds of opportunities available to students and the goals they might pursue. It seems to us that most students, like most adults, do not live in present and future worlds that totally overlap. Thus, single integrative strategies typically are not a prevalent or viable option. Nor do we think this would be an optimal situation. Overadaptation to a specific context can heighten vulnerability to change.

Real problems occur when students live in incongruent or hostile worlds, possess limited skills, and pursue goals that are so incompatible or destructive that abandonment is the only strategy of choice—whether selected by self or imposed by another. The effects of such settings can be devastating, breeding destructive coping strategies as they disempower, disenfranchise, and destroy our young people. Some youth live in such worlds; goal identification and coordination are incredibly difficult, and sometimes impossible, tasks for them.

Most of us, however, do not live in totally discontinuous and destructive worlds—just like most of us do not live in totally harmonious, unidimensional ones. Thus, we suspect that teachers will mostly be helping students learn to identify individual goals and the relationships among them that will *allow and require* multiple simultaneous strategies or deferment, modification, and substitution strategies.

◆ PRESENCE OF MIND

Further, we think it is important for teachers to help students learn the difference between proximal (i.e., more immediate) goals and distal (i.e., more delayed) ones and their interrelation. We suspect that students can only feel real progress by attaining proximal goals (Bandura, 1986) and may well be undone by an exclusive, or even a primary, focus on distal ones—even if the student does have an orientation that integrates present and future. This is because distal goals are typically quite large (their sheer magnitude can be overwhelming), and the consequences of their nonattainment are also large and seemingly final.

Unfortunately, sometimes parents are so involved in their children "making it" through education that they evoke a frightening future if their child should not have a successful "everyday" present. Parents are not the only ones to do this. "They won't put up with *that* next year, let me tell you," is a fairly common teacher management technique, especially the year before a school transition such as junior high or graduate school. These "the future looms" statements do not help a student realize present or future goals—even if they are, in theory, compatible. It seems to us that these students (and their parents) would profit from teacher discussion of setting and coordinating proximal goals that are instrumental to a desired future, enactive strategies to promote their congruence, and self-evaluation strategies that are realistic and informative so that progress can be felt along the way.

Co-regulation, in other words, occurs in each phase of student mediation. This is an important consideration if student presence of mind is to promote a desired future. Recall Nora's family. Mother is quite involved in influencing the goals Nora seeks, yet she also directly teaches (and sometimes preaches) strategies for goal coordination (especially setting priorities), enactment, and self-evaluation. Compare this parent-child co-regulation and integration of the present with the future with the following interview excerpt of a father helping his sixth-grade son, Julio, "stay on track" in school (McCaslin & Murdock, 1991).

Father intensely believes in the power of schooling in America, and he intensely believes in his son. At the time of the interview, he is worried that his son does not pay attention in class (there had been one teacher call about an attitude problem in early spring semester). Father said it "was the first time we had any trouble all through school." He punished Julio with "no more outside or TV for the rest of the school year (approximately three months), study for two hours a night, and . . . extra homework (obtained from the teacher)" (p. 230). The interview takes place 4 weeks after the call (and into the punishment). Father reportedly tells Julio:

> . . . it's not like it used to be. Before you could have gotten a job, there was a lot of work available. Now if you don't have a diploma or college, you can hardly get a good paying job. . . . I told them if I had gone to college, I wouldn't be working like this, swing shifts, nights. . . . So I try to make him understand, by, even if I have to put myself on his part. I do so they can learn from it. . . . (p. 228)

Unfortunately, for both father and son, Julio is more likely learning that real goals are really big and far away and really easy to fail at today. Failure is a dead-end. Julio is not learning from his father (or anyone else) how to mediate his own motivation (goal-setting and coordination), enactment, and self-evaluation strategies. Julio's interviews and journal entries reveal a boy who does not know how to get from here to there but is totally committed to being "there." His teacher describes him as "one who endures" without a sense of progress; Julio feels relief more than satisfaction in the classroom. Julio likely believes his "everydayness" is more apt to block than to promote his future. He does not have a lot of room to move.

Julio is in the same classroom as Nora. Consider the different messages these students likely receive from home about school and how their families might differently mediate messages from school (e.g., trouble-shooting phone calls, report cards). Home learning also filters differently these students' class-room experiences. For instance, when asked how the research interviews could be helpful to students, Julio suggested that the interviewer instruct teachers not to yell at students when they ask for help, like his teacher does. (Recall that Nora's question concerned how to be friends and be your own person.) The interviewer was puzzled; Julio and Nora's teacher was observed to be very responsive to student requests for help—if requests were believed legitimate.

The subsequent interview with Julio's father indicates that in Julio's home, when the children are in trouble, parents speak slower and louder; slower and louder means you are about to "get it." In Julio's and Nora's classroom—which is fairly crowded; has bare floors, tall windows, and high ceilings; is located on a second floor, west corner (read "hot"—the windows need to be open a crack even in cold weather); overlooks a heavily-traveled street, and is across from a small manufacturing firm—the teacher assumes that students cannot hear when they ask a question. Thus, she speaks slower and louder *to help them*. Julio thinks his teacher is mad, that he is in trouble because he doesn't understand, and he gets upset; Julio likely does not profit from the intended help. Nora likely lets her mind wander to classmates; she already knows how to do it, she got it the first time.

How might these students understand each others' concerns? What dynamics would you expect if they were in a small work-group together? How might Julio negotiate the multiple messages from principal, teacher, and peers? Is he a contender? How are the messages of schooling congruent with his home? We will explore these issues in considerable detail in Chapters 4 and 5; here we preview the task.

◆ GOAL REVIEW

We have noted that goals exist in relation to other goals. Coordination among them is essential. Coordination can mean that some goals are not going to be met, especially if they are incompatible. The sheer magnitude of the goal-co-ordination task likely differs for students who differ in personal resources (including the co-regulation of home), dispositions, and opportunities (see McCaslin & Good, 1996, for consideration of these issues). Dodge, Asher, & Parkhurst (1989) note that personal competence does not necessarily mean that *original* goals have been met. Competence, according to these authors (and we agree), also involves recognizing insurmountable barriers to goal attainment. Making it to the NBA requires talent and a whole lot more; obtaining a professorship in molecular biology requires talent and a whole lot more. Dodge and colleagues (1989) define competence in goal coordination, then, as "the greatest possible satisfaction of needs and desires, given the circumstances" (p. 122).

In Chapter 1 we described *"periodic, critical goal review."* We consider this an important feature of goal competence. Periodic, critical goal review involves: 1) reassessing the value and feasibility of one's goals, and 2) deciding to recommit, reformulate, or reject/replace them. Unfortunately, the ability to change one's mind after thoughtful reflection is a form of intelligent and adaptive behavior that is seldom encouraged in school. This is a regrettable state of affairs; time and commitment should matter. Teachers can have considerable influence on students, helping them to realize that a thoughtful change of direction is likely better than passively or obsessively clinging to and playing out a bad decision.

❖ CLOSING COMMENTS

In this chapter, we have attempted to elaborate upon ways of knowing students so that we might better understand what it is to *be* a student. We have described students in terms of academic theories and societal beliefs. We have introduced the notion of functional context to convey the impact of multiple social/instructional environments (SIEs) on students' lives. We have maintained that students are actively involved in the processes that influence them. Students both contribute to and mediate their SIEs. Students' mediation is filtered through their own developmental capabilities. We termed this reciprocal internalization process *emergent interaction* (Wertsch & Stone, 1985) to highlight that both students and the SIEs of their lives change and influence each other. We have attempted to convey what it is like to *be* a student and how that might inform teacher co-regulation of student motivational processes—especially those involved in goal setting and coordination.

The setting of instrumental proximal (to distal) goals and the coordination of goals are no small matters. They are also learned. Classrooms, by their very nature, provide an important context for student learning about goals and their coordination, and for teacher learning about students. This is because classrooms are interpersonal environments that explicitly address intrapersonal learning. Students do and will care about things that matter: about the personal implications of knowing or not, of belonging or not, of having to choose. We need to learn how to talk with students about things that matter to them; things that matter to us. As long as classrooms are not tutorial settings, learning is not only *social in theory* (e.g., Bruner, 1990; Vygotsky, 1962; 1978; Wertsch, 1985), it is *social in reality* (e.g., Corno & Rohrkemper, 1985). (See also McCaslin & Good, 1996.) The processes of setting and coordinating goals are part of students' classroom reality; it seems they should be part of teachers' reality as well. These processes are all about what it is like to *be* a student.

❖ QUESTIONS AND SUGGESTED ACTIVITIES FOR CHAPTER 2

1. Think about these three grade levels: 1st grade, 6th grade, 12th grade. What are the different goal coordination issues that students might face at each level? What differences in goal coordination might male and female students face? What unique goal coordination issues are possibly faced by students whose ethnic group is a minority in the school?

2. What should a teacher do when her/his goal priorities differ with some of his/her students? To what extent should teachers help students to create or to value certain goals versus helping students obtain goals that they themselves have set? Give some examples to make your thinking clear (creating versus supporting versus changing goals).

3. What do the authors mean by the term *Social/Instructional Environment (SIE)*? Why is SIE important in viewing teacher-student conversations from a co-regulation perspective?

4. Think about the two high-school teachers you had that differed most in the SIE they helped to create. What were the four or five major dimensions that differentiated these two classrooms, and how did the different environments influence *how* and *what* you learned and how you felt about it?

5. Some students are less liked by their peers. Why is this? What can you do as a teacher to help a student who is not liked by peers?

6. Schools seem to pursue a linear approach to subject matter learning: finish the topic, move on to the next, and so forth. How might schools encourage more reflective actions? For example, should students sometimes rewrite papers and explore topics anew even though test performance was reasonable?

7. The authors argue that at times it is reasonable to abandon a goal. Is this realistic in school settings? Should students on occasion have the right to say, "I've lost interest in my report on Malcolm X—I want to start again and research the art of Spike Lee"? Under what circumstances might this be appropriate? If students are allowed to change topics, should they be given more time to complete the assignment? Why or why not?

8. The authors suggest that providing students with choice is good only if all choices are viable. Do you agree with this, or is it perhaps overstated—can one learn from a poor choice? Think about the specific role you have (or want) as a teacher (e.g., eighth-grade English) and list several ways that you could build appropriate choice into your curriculum.

9. What about conflicts between parents' and students' goals—how might teachers respond (e.g., the student wants to be a cheerleader, but the parent wants only "honor-roll" academic activities)?

10. A student visits you after school and complains that his friends have accused him of acting "white." The student laments, "Day after day, I am told this. I am tired of hearing it. I just want to be one of the guys." How would you respond? What would you say and do?

❖ REFERENCES

American Association of University Women. (1992). *AAUW report: How schools short-change girls: A study of major findings on girls in education.* Washington, DC: American Association of University Women Educational Foundation.

American Association of University Women. (1993). *Hostile hallways: The AAUW survey of sexual harassment in American schools.* Washington, DC: American Association of University Women Educational Foundation.

Ames, C. (1992). Achievement goals and the classroom motivational climate. In D. Schunk and J. Meece (Eds.), *Student perceptions in the classroom* (pp. 327–348). Hillsdale, NJ: Erlbaum.

Argyle, M., Furnham, A., & Graham, J. (1981). *Social situations.* New York: Cambridge University Press.

Asher, S., & Gottman, J. (1981). *The development of children's friendships.* New York: Cambridge University Press.

Asher, S., & Parker, J. (1988). Significance of peer relationship problems in childhood. In B. Schneider, G. Attili, J. Nadel, & R. Weissberg (Eds.), *Social competence in developmental perspective* (pp. 5–24). Dordrecht, The Netherlands: Kluwer.

Atkinson, J. (1964). *An introduction to motivation.* Princeton, NJ: Van Nostrand.

Bandura, A. (1986). *Social foundations of thought and action: A social cognitive theory.* Englewood Cliffs, NJ: Prentice-Hall.

Bandura, A. (1990). Conclusion: Reflections on nonability determinants of competence. In R. J. Sternberg & J. Kolligian, Jr., (Eds.), *Competence considered* (pp. 315–408). New Haven, CT: Yale University Press.

Berliner, D., & Biddle, B. (1995). *The manufactured crisis.* White Plains, NY: Longman.

Berndt, T., & Perry, T. (1990). Distinctive features and effects of early adolescent friendships. In R. Montemayor, G. Adams, & T. Gullotta (Eds.), *From childhood to adolescence: A transitional period?* (pp. 269–287). Newbury Park, CA: Sage Publications.

Bloom, B. (1985). *Developing talent in young people.* New York: Ballantine.

Borstelmann, L. (1983). Children before psychology: Ideas about children from antiquity to the late 1800s. In P. Mussen (Ed.), *Handbook of child psy-*

chology (4th ed.), Vol. 1: History, theory, and methods (p. 34). New York: Wiley.

Brantlinger, E. (1993). *The politics of social class in secondary school: Views of affluent and impoverished youth.* New York: Teachers College Press.

Brophy, J., & McCaslin, M. (1992). Teachers' reports of how they perceive and cope with problem students. *Elementary School Journal, 93,* 3–68.

Brophy, J., & Rohrkemper, M. (1981). The influence of problem ownership on teachers' perceptions of and strategies for coping with problem students. *Journal of Educational Psychology, 73,* 295–311.

Brown, B. (1993). School culture, social policies, and the academic motivation of U.S. students. In T. Tomlinson (Ed.), *Motivating students to learn: Overcoming barriers to high achievement* (pp. 63–98). Berkeley, CA: McCutchan.

Bruner, J. (1990). *Acts of meaning.* Cambridge: Harvard University Press.

Corno, L. (1992). Encouraging students to take responsibility for learning and performance. *Elementary School Journal, 93,* 69–83.

Corno, L., & Rohrkemper, M. (1985). Self-regulated learning. In R. Ames & C. Ames (Eds.), *Research on Motivation in Education* (Vol. 2, pp. 53–90). Orlando, FL: Academic Press.

Covington, M. (1992). *Making the grade: A self-worth perspective on motivation and school reform.* Cambridge: Cambridge University Press.

Covington, M., Guthrie, J., Webb, F., & Pipho, C. (1990, November). Carrots and sticks: The motivational and performance implications of incentive programs. Paper presented at *Hard work and higher expectations: A conference on student motivation.* Arlington, VA: U.S. Department of Education.

Covington, M., & Omelich, C. (1979). Effort: The double-edged sword in school achievement. *Journal of Educational Psychology, 71,* 169–182.

Cusick, P. (1973). *Inside high school: The student's world.* New York: New York: Holt, Rinehart, & Winston.

Custer, G. (1994). Psychologists ease school transition. *American Psychological Association Monitor, 25* (11), 44.

Damon, W. (1981). Exploring children's social cognition on two fronts. In J. Flavell & L. Ross (Eds.), *Social cognitive development: Frontiers and possible futures* (pp. 154–175). Cambridge: Cambridge University Press.

De Parle, J. (1991, September 27). Number of people in poverty shows sharp rise in U.S.: Americans' incomes slip—data touch off debate on toll of recession. *New York Times,* p. A1.

Dodge, K., Asher, S., & Parkhurst, J. (1989). Social life as a goal-coordination task. In C. Ames & R. Ames (Eds.), *Research on motivation in education: Vol. 3. Goals and cognition* (pp. 107–135). New York: Academic Press.

Duck, S. (1988). Socially competent communication and relationship development. In B. Schneider, G. Attili, J. Nadel, & R. Weissberg (Eds)., *Social competence in developmental perspective* (pp. 91–106). Dordrecht, The Netherlands: Kluwer.

Dweck, C. (1986). Motivational processes affecting learning. *American Psychologist, 41,* 1040–1048.

Eccles, J., Midgley, C., Wigfield, A., Buchanan, C., Reuman, D., Flanagan, C., & MacIver, D. (1993). Development during adolescence: The impact of stage-environment fit on young adolescents' experiences in schools and in families. *American Psychologist, 48,* 90–101.

Eder, D. (1985). The cycle of popularity: Interpersonal relations among female adolescents. *Sociology of Education, 58,* 154–165.

Eisenberg, N. (1982). *The development of prosocial behavior.* New York: Academic Press.

Elkind, D. (1982). *The hurried child: Growing up too fast too soon.* Reading, MA: Addison-Wesley.

Erikson, E. (1968). *Identity: Youth and crisis.* New York: Norton.

Faltis, C. (1993). Critical issues in the use of sheltered content teaching in high school bilingual programs. *Peabody Journal of Education, 69,* 136–151.

Fetterman, N. (1990). *The meaning of success and failure: A look at the social instructional environments of four elementary school classrooms.* Unpublished doctoral dissertation, Bryn Mawr College, Bryn Mawr, PA.

Flavell, J. (1985). *Cognitive development* (2nd ed.). Englewood Cliffs, NJ: Prentice-Hall.

Flavell, J., & Ross, L. (1981). Social cognitive development: Frontiers and possible futures. New York: Cambridge University Press.

454,000 U.S. teens binging on alcohol. (1991, June 7). *St. Louis Post-Dispatch.*

Freud, S. (1953–1974). In J. Strachey (Ed. and Trans.), *The standard edition of the complete psychological works.* London: Holgarth Press.

Furth, H. G. (1980). *The world of grown-ups: Children's conceptions of society.* New York: Elsebier North Holland, Inc.

Garbarino, J., Dubrow, N., Kostelny, K., & Pardo, C. (1992). *Children in danger: Coping with the consequences of community violence.* San Francisco: Jossey-Bass.

Gilligan, C. (1982). *In a different voice.* Cambridge: Harvard University Press.

Good, T., & Brophy, J. (1994). Looking in classrooms (6th ed.). New York: Harper & Row.

Hacker, A. (1992). *Two nations: Black and white, separate, hostile, unequal.* New York: Scribners.

Haycock, K. (1990, June). *Closing remarks.* Presentation at the AAHE/College Board Conference on Mainstreaming University/School Partnerships, Chicago.

Heckhausen, H. (1991). *Motivation and action.* (P. Leppmann, Trans.). Berlin Heidelberg, Germany: Springer-Verlag.

Herrnstein, R., & Murray, C. (1994). *The bell curve: Intelligence and class structure in American life.* New York: Free Press.

Jackson, P. (1968). *Life in classrooms.* New York: Holt, Rinehart, & Winston.

Kohlberg, L. (1969). Stage and sequence: The cognitive-developmental approach to socialization. In D. Goslin (Ed.), *Handbook of socialization theory and research.* Chicago: Rand McNally.

Kounin, J. (1970). *Discipline and group management in classrooms.* New York: Holt, Rinehart, & Winston.

Krampen, G. (1987). Differential effects of teacher comments. *Journal of Educational Psychology, 79* (2), 137–146.

Marcia, J. (1980). Identity in adolescence. In J. Adelson (Ed.), *Handbook of adolescent psychology.* New York: Wiley-Interscience.

McCall, R. (1994). Academic underachievers. *Current Directions in Psychological Science, 3* (1), 15–19.

McCaslin, M. (in progress). *Adaptive learning: A co-regulation perspective.*

McCaslin, M., & Good, T. (1992). Compliant cognition: The misalliance of management and instructional goals in current school reform. *Educational Researcher, 21,* 4–17.

McCaslin, M., & Good, T. (1993). Classroom management and motivated student learning. In T. M. Tomlinson (Ed.), *Motivating students to learn: Overcoming barriers to high achievement* (pp. 245–261). Berkeley, CA: McCutchan.

McCaslin, M., & Good, T. (1996). The informal curriculum. In D. Berliner & R. Calfee (Eds.), *The handbook of educational psychology.* New York: MacMillan.

McCaslin, M., & Murdock, T. (1991). The emergent interaction of home and school in the development of students' adaptive learning. In M. Maehr and P. Pintrich (Eds.), *Advances in motivation and achievement* (Vol. 7, pp. 213–259). Greenwich, CT: JAI Press.

McCaslin Rohrkemper, M. (1989). Self-regulated learning and academic achievement: A Vygotskian view. In B. Zimmerman & D. Schunk (Eds.), *Self-regulated learning and academic achievement* (pp. 143–168). New York: Springer-Verlag.

Mergendoller, J. (Guest Ed.). (1993). Middle grades research and reform [Special Issue]. *Elementary School Journal, 93,* 443–658.

Minicucci, C., & Olsen, L. (1992). *Programs for secondary limited English proficient students: A California study.* Washington, DC: National Clearing House for Bilingual Education.

Natriello, G., McDill, E., & Pallas, A. (1990). *Schooling disadvantaged children: Racing against catastrophe.* New York: Teachers College Press.

Noddings, N. (1992). *The challenge to care in schools.* New York: Teachers College Press.

Nolen, S. (1988). Reasons for studying: Motivational orientations and study strategies. *Cognition and Instruction, 5,* 269–287.

Ogbu, J. G. (1992). Understanding cultural diversity and learning. *Educational Researcher, 21,* 4–14.

Parker, J., & Asher, S. (1993). Friendship and friendship quality in middle childhood: Links with peer group acceptance and feelings of loneliness and social dissatisfaction. *Developmental Psychology, 29* (4), 611–621.

Piaget, J. (1983). Piaget's theory. In P. Mussen (Ed.), *Handbook of child psychology: Vol. 1. W. Kessen (Ed.), History, theory, and methods* (pp. 103–128). New York: John Wiley & Sons, Inc.

Powell, A., Farrar, E., & Cohen, D. (1985). *The shopping mall high school: Winners and losers in the educational marketplace.* Boston: Hougton Mifflin.

Rest, J. (1986). *Moral development: Advances in theory and research.* New York: Praeger.

Reston, J. (1991). *Deadline: A memoir.* New York: Random House.

Rohrkemper, M. (1984). The influence of teacher socialization style on students' social cognition and reported interpersonal classroom behavior. *Elementary School Journal, 85,* 245–275.

Rohrkemper, M. (1985). Individual differences in students' perceptions of routine classroom events. *Journal of Educational Psychology, 77,* 29–44.

Rohrkemper, M., & Bershon, B. L. (1984). The quality of student task engagement: Elementary school students' reports of the causes and effects of problem difficulty. *Elementary School Journal, 85,* 127–147.

Rohrkemper, M., & Brophy, J. (1983). Teachers' thinking about problem students. In J. Levine & M. C. Wang (Eds.), *Teacher and student perceptions: Implications for learning* (pp.75-104). Hillsdale, NJ: Erlbaum.

Rohrkemper, M., & Corno, L. (1988). Success and failure on classroom tasks: Adaptive learning and classroom teaching. *Elementary School Journal, 88,* 299-312.

Rose, M. (1989). *Lives on the boundary: The struggles and achievements of America's underprepared.* New York: Free Press.

Rosenhotlz, S. & Simpson C. (1984). The formation of ability conceptions: Developmental trend or social construction. *Review of Educational Research, 54,* 31-63.

Rotter, J. (1966). Generalized expectancies for internal versus external control of reinforcement. *Psychology Monographs, 80,* 1–28.

Sadker, M., Sadker, D., & Klein, S. (1991). The issue of gender in elementary and secondary education. In G. Grant (Ed.), *Review of research in education* (Vol. 17, pp. 169–234). Washington, DC: American Educational Research Association.

Schunk, D. (1989). Social cognitive learning. In B. Zimmerman & D. Schunk (Eds.), *Self-regulated learning and academic achievement: Theory, research and practice* (pp. 83–110). New York: Springer-Verlag.

Sears, S., & Milburn, J. (1990). School-age stress. In L. E. Arnold (Ed.), *Childhood Stress* (pp. 223–246). New York: Wiley-Interscience.

Selman, R. (1980). *The growth of interpersonal understanding.* New York: Academic Press.

Simon, H. (1969). *The sciences of the artificial.* Cambridge, MA: MIT Press.

Simmons, R., & Blyth, D. (1987). *Moving into adolescence: The impact of pubertal change and school context.* Hawthorne, NY: Aldine de Gruyter.

Skinner, B. (1953). *Science and human behavior.* New York: Macmillan.

Spencer-Hall, D. (1981). Looking behind the teacher's back. *Elementary School Journal, 81,* 281–290

Steele, C. (1992). Race and the schooling of Black Americans. *The Atlantic, 269* (4), 68, 70, 72, 74–78.

Stipek, D. (1986). Children's motivation to learn. In T. Tomlinson & H. Walberg (Eds.), *Academic work and educational excellence* (pp. 197–221). Berkeley, CA: McCutchan.

Sullivan, H. (1953). *The interpersonal theory of psychiatry.* New York: Norton.

Tomlinson, T. (1993). Educational reform: The ups and downs of good in good intentions. In T. Tomlinson (Ed.), *Motivating students to learn: Overcoming barriers to high achievement* (pp. 3–20). Berkeley, CA: McCutchan.

Vygotsky, L. (1962). *Thought and language.* Cambridge, MA: MIT Press.

Vygotsky, L. (1978). *Mind and society: The development of higher psychological processes.* Cambridge, MA: Harvard University Press.

Weiner, B. (1986). *An attributional theory of motivation and emotion.* New York: Springer-Verlag.

Weiner, B. (1992). *Human motivation: Metaphors, theories, and research.* Newbury Park, CA: Sage.

Weinstein, R. (1993). Children's knowledge of differential treatment in school: Implications for motivation. In T. M. Tomlinson (Ed.), *Motivating students to learn: Overcoming barriers to high achievement* (pp. 197–224). Berkeley, CA: McCutchan.

Weinstein, R., Marshall, H., Brattesani, K., & Middlestadt, S. (1982). Student perceptions of differential teacher treatment in open and traditional classrooms. *Journal of Educational Psychology, 74,* 678–692.

Wertsch, J. (1985). *Vygotsky and the social formation of mind.* Cambridge, MA: Harvard University Press.

Wertsch, J., & Stone, C. (1985). The concept of internalization in Vygotsky's account of the genesis of higher mental functions. In J. Wertsch (Ed.), *Culture, communication, and cognition: Vygotskian perspectives* (pp. 162–182). New York: Cambridge University Press.

When I grow up. (1990). *New York Times.*

INTERVIEWING STUDENTS

❖ INTRODUCTION

◆ DEFINING THE INTERVIEW

Social scientists have been debating the strengths and limitations of interviewing for a long time (e.g., Bingham & Moore, 1931, 1959; Ericsson & Simon, 1980; Jones, 1990; Meichenbaum, Burland, Gruson, & Cameron, 1985; Nisbett & Wilson, 1977), and interviews have been defined in various ways, including clinical interventions, supportive "active" listening, and public opinion polls. Bingham and Moore (1959) define an interview as a "conversation directed to a definite purpose other than satisfaction in the conversation itself" (p. 3). Following Bingham and Moore, we define the classroom interview as a purposeful conversation between the teacher and individual students about teacher and student perceptions of classroom events—what has happened and what could happen. In our view, conversations can exist on two levels. First, the conversation is about a specific content of interest, and second, the conversation provides a structural scaffold that co-regulates student mediation of events (see Figures 1.1–1.4). Teacher-student conversations can emphasize one or both levels and range from the give and take of casual repartee, to information getting and giving, to co-regulated problem solving. Our emphasis in this chapter is on intentional conversations rather than more casual encounters.

◆ MULTIPLE REASONS AND MULTIPLE CONTEXTS

Interviews can be conducted for varied reasons, including securing information and opinions, giving information and interpretations, and trying to influence attitudes or behavior. The uses of interviews are equally varied. For example, information obtained through interviews is used in employment decisions, employer-employee supervision, vocational counseling, public policy, judicial procedures, law enforcement, and print and television journalism. The reasons for and uses of interviewing are considerable; however, the research *on* interviewing is relatively scarce.

Even so, there is a rich literature on techniques of interviewing; and, although the research base is not large, it is useful (e.g., Brenner, Brown, & Canter, 1985; Meichenbaum et al., 1985; and Schuman & Presser, 1981). Further, professionals have accumulated a wealth of practical knowledge about strategies for interviewing. In this chapter, we will discuss some general concepts that provide a useful framework for thinking about how to conduct interviews. Although most of this advice is derived from clinical settings and/or other professional experiences (e.g., vocational counseling), we think it provides a satisfactory set of recommendations that will be useful to teachers who want to interview students.

◆ CLASSROOM INTERVIEW RESEARCH

Researchers' attempts to interview students systematically about their perceptions and knowledge of classroom settings are fairly new (Rohrkemper, 1981, 1982; Weinstein et al., 1982). Hence, there is comparatively little research evidence available on how researchers should interview students. For example, how might interview structures and strategies differ with hyperactive students? those who are shy? aggressive? Even less is known about the role of the *teacher* in interviewing students. For example, how can the teacher demarcate "teacher," who evaluates and judges the correctness of student answers, from "interviewer," who is nonjudgmental about student verbal reports? How might the teacher help students make the transition in and out of the interviewee role? help a student to understand his/her role as an interviewee and know what to do when the interview is over?

We begin this chapter with a set of suggestions for interviewing, based upon research and practice, that seem of value to classroom teachers. Second, we discuss some of the special constraints that apply to teachers as interviewers because of their special relationship with students. As we shall see, the teacher's role as an interviewer in some ways is easier than an outside professional's because of teacher knowledge of and familiarity with students (e.g., teacher can more effectively challenge or probe student report). However, in other ways, teacher role (e.g., a continuing daily relationship) makes the interview a more difficult task than it would be for a researcher.

This chapter discusses considerations associated with general interview formats as well as strategies for conducting "problem interviews." Other chapters have provided content and structure for specific interviews (e.g., student mediation of classroom assignments in Chapter 1, student goal coordination in Chapter 2). Here we address: 1) how to prepare for and design an interview, 2) general considerations relevant to conducting an interview, and 3) specific considerations that directly address classroom interviewing.

❖ PREPARING FOR THE INTERVIEW

◆ GOALS

Bingham and Moore (1931, 1959) stress the importance of preparing for the interview. The interviewer should have a firm understanding of what s/he wants to accomplish. Even if the interviewer has had experience in conducting interviews, it is advantageous to write down goals, list possible problems and issues that may arise, and select possible "back-up" strategies to address them. Indeed, many experienced interviewers begin just this way. For example, a sixth-grade teacher who decides to interview students briefly as part of an orientation to the class at the beginning of the year should clarify whether his/her goal is: 1) to get information from the student that might be useful in planning instruction (e.g., exploring student enactive strategies), and/or 2) to make the student comfortable in the new setting. Clearly, the questions and issues discussed (and elaborated upon) would be quite different, depending upon these two goals. Simply put, if the interview is to be successful, the teacher must begin with deliberate consideration of her/his goals.

◆ INTERVIEWER BIAS

We have known for some time now that it is possible for interviewers unintentionally to influence the outcomes of their inquiry. For example, Rice (1929) found interviewer bias in a study of the physical and social characteristics of 2,000 destitute men. Interviewer-obtained explanations for destitution varied by the interviewers' backgrounds and attitudes (more than their *subjects'* backgrounds and attitudes). For example, one interviewer, who was a strong prohibitionist, indicated that while only 7 percent of destitute cases could be attributed to economic conditions, 62 percent were primarily due to the abuse of liquor. In contrast, an interviewer who was a socialist reported that only 22 percent of the cases were due to liquor and 39 percent of the cases could be linked primarily to economic conditions (e.g., layoffs, etc.).

What is perhaps even more fascinating is that Rice presented data suggesting that the background of the interviewer also influenced subjects' actual responses. The interviewer with a prohibitionist background was told by 34 percent of the applicants that liquor was the primary cause of their difficulty, whereas 42.5 percent indicated environmental reasons. In contrast, the socialist was told by 11 percent of the men he interviewed that liquor was the primary problem, whereas 60 percent said their demise could be linked to environmental or industrial conditions. These data underscore that an interview is a discrete example, a microcosm, of co-regulation of mediational processes;

both interviewer (teacher) and interviewee (student) influence the interview process and each other.

In recent times, there has been considerable effort focused on identifying interviewer bias or expectancy biases. In particular, there has been considerable experimental research in social psychology to illustrate that fictitious information can be given to experimenters in ways that impact on how they interact with subjects (and the data they actually obtain). Jones (1990) presents considerable experimental evidence to illustrate that expectations of interviewers—and how they then communicate with interviewees—can be significantly affected by information given to them about test performance, group placement, classroom behavior, physical appearance, race, gender, ethnicity, etc. The communication of expectancies is sometimes so subtle that they are hard to detect even when conversations are audio- or videotaped. However, there is also evidence to illustrate that teachers can guard against developing and communicating expectation effects if they are sensitive to the process (Good & Brophy, 1994).

Thus, interviewers need to work deliberately and systematically to be sure that they do not bias respondents when they are asking questions. And equally important, interviewers have to listen carefully to what individuals say so that they do not bias their interpretation of what has been said. This is especially important in our culturally diverse society, in which teachers are often of a cultural or ethnic group different from many of their students. For example, a teacher who is working with a student s/he believes to be a frequent discipline problem in the classroom may have to work especially hard to be sure that s/he does not look for information that *confirms* the perception that the student has been involved in difficulty once again. "Confirmation bias" (Kahneman & Tversky, 1973) is one of the more common errors in judgment we make as humans and as researchers—even though one goal of research is to control systematically for confirmation bias. Teachers, because of the complexity and ambiguity of classroom events—and the concurrent, chronic demands for immediate response—are apt to be especially vulnerable to confirmation bias errors.

Along these lines, Spencer-Hall (1981) conducted an interesting classroom research study relating teachers' perceptions about student misbehavior to observed sanctioning behaviors of teachers. She described how some students are much better at impression management than others because they have developed the ability to misbehave in ways that escape their teacher's (but not their peers') attention. Hence, teachers could begin an interview with a student who they believe is a model student (or a discipline problem) with questions that confirm, and worse yet, promote that belief, when in fact the student may be rather typical in her/his behavior.

◆ INTERVIEWEE POINT OF VIEW

Another proactive step that Bingham and Moore recommend in planning for the interview is to put oneself in the place of the person who will be interviewed. That is, try to anticipate what the individual will think of you, the issues, and try to understand what might be useful or important to know from the other person's perspective. One term frequently used to describe this disposition is *empathy*. In order to listen to and understand another's perspective, it is important to attempt to see the problem as the other person sees it and to try to understand how s/he conceptualizes the problem or situation, how s/he feels about it, and how s/he feels about discussing it with you.

◆ PARTICIPANT'S STORY

Bingham and Moore stress that the participant should be able to tell her/his own story, using her/his own concepts and "story grammar." They suggest that although a "free narrative" may be less complete, it is more likely to accurately convey the participant's perception than is a rigid set of questions. They note that after the interviewee has had the opportunity to tell her/his story (unconstrained by interrupting questions), it is then possible to ask questions that help to fill in some of the details. They note that obtaining insight into a person's unique perspective takes time and skill to develop. Later in the chapter we will build upon the work of Rohrkemper (1982) and explore question structures and strategies for encouraging students to share their stories. At a minimum, if a teacher is to convey empathy, s/he must be genuinely interested in what the student has to say and *how* s/he says it.

◆ DECODING AND UNDERSTANDING

Just as sensitive interviewers know that their biases and attitudes may influence what someone tells them, it is also the case that even relatively neutral statements can be interpreted in strikingly different ways. One of the enriching yet troublesome characteristics of most languages is the ambiguous nature of many phrases and the multiple ways in which they can be interpreted. For example, the statement, "I am unhappy today," may be stated in oppositional terms, suggesting an unstable event. That is, the speaker is typically happy, but today is unusual and the speaker is unhappy. "I am unhappy today" may suggest instead continuity or stable events and that this is simply another day in the speaker's unhappy life. Alternately, "I am unhappy today" could mean that the listener is the one who is usually in this state, but today it is the speaker who is in such a funk. And so on. For some time, those writing on the interview process have stressed that the same words will not mean the same things to different individuals (Bingham & Moore, 1959; Heath, 1982). Simple statements like, "Today is very hot," may be interpreted in markedly different ways by someone living in Alaska, Arkansas, or Arizona.

◆ THE WORDING OF QUESTIONS

For some time, we have known that the specific wording of a question has major impact upon the answers that are provided. Questions that appear somewhat similar will often elicit different answers. For example, Bingham and Moore relate the experience of Elmo Roper, who was preparing a poll for *Fortune* magazine. In the pilot sample, he used two questions: "Should the United States do all in its power to promote world peace?" (97 percent of respondents answered yes), and "Should the United States become involved in plans to promote world peace?" (only 60 percent of the respondents said yes). Even slight changes in wording can have a major influence on how individuals respond to a particular question. Not only individual words, but the *ways* in which language is *used* affects individual interpretation and response (e.g., Heath & McLaughlin, 1993). This is a particularly important point when we consider the ever-increasing language and cultural diversity among school-aged children (Moll, 1992; Romero, Mercado, & Vàzquéz-Faría, 1987).

Finally, questions can change our very memories of events. In the past two decades, much research has followed a 1975 study by Loftus (Loftus, 1975). She found that eyewitness's memories of an accident changed with time and question. Initial reports were accurate, but one week later an intervening question about a stop sign at the accident site became incorporated into reports about the observed accident. These subsequent reports were inaccurate. Apparently, we can confuse an actual observed event with questions about it. These data have serious implications for designing interviews about student problems—for example, suspected abuse. We will return to this issue in considerable detail in Chapter 5.

❖ CONDUCTING THE INTERVIEW

◆ RELATIONSHIP

Bingham and Moore (1931; 1959) describe the relationship within the interview as critically important. They discuss the important influence that Carl Rogers had on the field, noting that he, perhaps more than anyone, "worked to dispel the notion that technique and strategy were the major concerns of the interviewer. His thesis is that the relationship is all important, that unless the interviewer really accepts and respects the interviewee, little can be accomplished" (p. 15). Teachers, or anyone who chooses to interview, must not only feel empathy, but must also communicate "it"—what Kottler and Kottler (1993) call a "helping attitude"—to the interviewee. We add that the interviewee must be *receptive* (versus resistant) to this overture. Thus, the teacher's and student's shared history sets the relational context for the specific interview.

◆ LISTEN MORE, TALK LESS

Seidman (1991) notes that researchers use interviews because they are interested in other individuals' stories. Personal stories provide a way of knowing—a window of insight into another's perspective. Interviewing is a basic mode of inquiry, and, as Seidman contends, recounting narratives of experience has been a primary way that humans have attempted to make sense of that experience. For Seidman, interviewing is an attempt to understand other people's experience and how they interpret that experience.

Seidman (1991) presents various useful techniques and strategies for researchers to develop in order to become effective interviewers. We think that much of Seidman's advice is relevant for teachers in classroom situations as well.

Seidman explains that listening is the fundamental skill of interviewing and that if one is to interview well, one must concentrate on the interviewee and actively try to understand what s/he is saying. Seidman suggests that one good way to estimate listening skills is to listen to an interview tape and compare the length of the interviewee's paragraphs with those of the interviewer's. If the interviewer is listening well, typically her/his paragraphs will be relatively short and relatively infrequent compared to those of the interviewee. The teacher who is to be an effective interviewer must be willing to listen intently and try to understand what the student is saying. This skill, often referred to as *active listening* (Gordon, 1970), involves a constellation of attending, listening, and interpersonal sensitivity (Kottler & Kottler, 1993). We add that it also involves being comfortable with an interviewee's silence, pauses, false starts, and attempts to regroup.

◆ STARTING AND MAINTAINING THE FLOW OF THE INTERVIEW

Get a Response It makes sense to begin an interview with questions that the participant can and wants to answer. Bingham and Moore note that, in part, cooperation may be attained by establishing *the attitude of answering*. If students begin to answer and feel comfortable, the entire process becomes easier. Similarly, Yarrow (1960) advocates beginning the interview with a question that assures the respondent that s/he can successfully fulfill the interviewee role.

Model Mistakes and Recovery We think it especially important to model what to do if there is a slip. McCaslin trains research interviewers to explicitly, credibly do just that. Approximately 5 minutes into the interview, after the student has successfully engaged the process, interviewers are instructed to get a bit tongue-tied, stop, model how to recover, and continue: "Oops. That's not what I meant to say. Wait a minute. (Pause and look away.) Let me try that again!" It is important that students know their discussion need not be "polished," real conversation is full of false starts. Students also need to learn how to cope with making mistakes, being embarassed, and changing their minds (perhaps *learning* their minds) when thinking and talking things through. McCaslin cautions interviewers to keep the mistakes in the "middle range" so that perception of their general competence and credibility is not threatened. The usefulness of modeling coping with frustration and mistakes is apparent in the subsequent student interview.

Ask a Single Question Clearly   Participants, no matter how sophisticated, can be confused when they are presented with two or three different questions at once. Even if the person can respond to the questions, it may be difficult for the interviewer to separate which answer goes with which question. It has already been noted that different questions with slightly different wording may be interpreted differently; it is equally the case that awkwardly worded questions will be difficult to interpret. Questions should be asked in such a way that they can be understood easily—one clear question at a time.

Easily understood questions, however, are not necessarily "easy" questions. Rohrkemper and Bershon (1984) found that moderately difficult questions—those that require thoughtful consideration by students—are more powerful in exploring how students' perceptions differ from those of their peers. Too "easy" (i.e., too readily answered) questions and those that are too difficult (i.e., personally threatening or simply beyond student knowledge) do not differentiate students' reports. Rather, students' response to very easy and very difficult questions sound alike, as if there were a "single" student perception. Individual differences among students are blurred in these report opportunities. We will return to this issue.

Avoid Reinforcing Responses   Interviewers may unintentionally influence the nature of participants' responses by falling into the habit of making some short affirmative response to participants' statements (I see; that's okay; it makes sense to me; yes; mmmm; oh really?) and, we add, nonverbal responses (leaning forward, looking down, quickly changing topics). Seidman notes that interviewers are often quite unaware that they engage in such transitional behaviors. If they are aware of these behaviors, they are apt to point out *defensively* that these actions show that the interviewer is listening and being attentive or is ready to move on.

We believe that in many instances interviewees interpret these transitional statements as affirming or sanctioning statements and behavior—especially if they follow some statements and not others. For example, a student may infer from the teacher's "I see" that the teacher believes him or thinks that a particular response is "really good." Thus, the student may continue to elaborate on the point, far beyond his own personal opinion or belief. Similarly, a student may believe she has been "cut off" and shouldn't "feel that way" if a teacher appears disinterested in her personal account (i.e., does not affirm with "uh huh"). Whenever possible, it is important in the interview situation to eliminate such differences in transitional statements and markers and, if necessary, to simply ask follow-up questions or questions of clarification in a matter-of-fact tone.

We focus on eliminating *differences* in interviewer statements of acceptance rather than eliminating acceptance statements per se, for two reasons. First, as interviewers, we find it extremely difficult, if not impossible, to eliminate such common conversational markers from our speech. Second, some specialists (e.g., Segal-Andrews, 1994) maintain that interviewer verbal affirmation is essential for establishing and maintaining rapport in the interview.

Thus, we think it is more realistic and helpful for the interviewer to focus on eliminating *differential* acceptance of interviewee report rather than strive to maintain "silent" acceptance.

Finally, "probes," or follow-up questions, should be used sparingly, as they also can suggest a reinforcement or special interest, or lead the interviewee to try to "figure out" what the interviewer wants to hear (Ericcson & Simon, 1980).

Follow Up on What the Participant Says In order to convey listening skills, one must be able to communicate that the participant has been heard. Clearly, the teacher is interviewing a student for a basic purpose. However, it is important to listen actively to students, and when possible, to ask the next question in a way that shows that the teacher has been listening to the students. A word of caution: parroting back student responses (Teacher: "You are upset.") even though intended to convey empathy and "active listening" often does not (Student: "That's what I just *said!*"). Teacher questions and comments need to structure *elaborations* of student report, not mere repetitions.

Kottler and Kottler (1993) provide an instructive example of an appropriate level of elaboration:

> Child: "Mikey keeps hitting me. He won't leave me alone and teases me all of the time."
> Teacher: "Mikey won't get off your back no matter what you do." (p. 44)

◆ ASK PARTICIPANTS TO RECONSTRUCT

Seidman recommends that interviewers should avoid asking interviewees to "use their memories." That is, he suggests (following Tagg, 1985) that when participants are asked to remember, they often become overly self-conscious, as in a school evaluation task where there are right and wrong answers ("What happened in 1588?"). He suggests that a question like "What was your elementary school experience like?" would be a better question than "Do you *remember* what your elementary school experience was like?" Seidman makes this argument, in part, because of the tendency for some people to "freeze" when asked to provide an accurate memory (i.e., to tell the "truth," to be "correct"), but also because reconstruction of past events is only partially based on memory.

In a very real sense, recollection—reconstruction—is based on what the participant feels and believes is important about the past event; and, as we have already noted, it can be influenced by other factors (e.g., questions) in between (Loftus, 1975, 1994). Thus, "recall" and "remember" are more aptly termed "reconstruction" (Neisser, 1982; Piaget, 1983; Vygotsky, 1962, 1978). For example, the actual wording of a rude comment that Sally directed toward Alicia (two days earlier) is perhaps not as important as is how Alicia *now feels* about the event and its perceived effects (e.g., is Sally asking to work with Alicia in a small group?).

McCaslin, Tuck, Wiard, Brown, LaPage, and Pyle (1994) demonstrate the powerful effects of students' *reconstructions* of classroom events and the significance of the *timing* of questions about those experiences. In a study of student experience in small-group learning, they expected students' delayed reconstructions of their experience to differ from their immediate "constructions" of that experience in two ways. In comparison with their immediate reports, students' delayed reconstructions would: 1) overrepresent positive aspects of their small-group behavior, and 2) underrepresent the interfering aspects of their personal behavior in small groups. Comparisons between student responses immediately after (six) small-group lessons with their responses following a 10-day delay, McCaslin et al. (1994) found clear evidence that students reconstruct their memories of small-group experiences in ways that increase their enjoyment, engagement of the task, and active participation in the lesson, and decrease their negative experience, anxiety, and withdrawal.

Thus, it is important to recognize that the ways in which students reconstruct events might not be isomorphic with the observed "actual" event (e.g., if we had a videotape of what actually occurred in the small group; or if we had three students who witnessed the exchange on the way home, etc.). This occurs not only for reasons of self-protection ("I don't want to get in trouble") or self-enhancement ("I'm not the sort of student who would do something like that"), but also because other events do occur that mediate and influence memory in important ways, just like the initial experience. As we have noted, one of these mediational events can be as seemingly inconsequential as a question. Within our model of co-regulated learning, questions can be considered as opportunities. Like other opportunities, they function as scaffolds. Thus, questions (especially if asked by a valued other) structure processes even as they examine them.

Other information also can change our perceptual "filter." For example, perhaps Alicia subsequently learns that Sally had received a failing grade on her Spanish translation and was still angry when she left school. Hearing this, Alicia infers that Sally was having difficulty in handling her own anger, and thus, took it out on her. Or perhaps, the next day Roberto told Alicia that Sally told him—the day before as she was leaving school—that she hates Alicia because she is a teacher's pet who always gets good grades only because the teacher likes her. These two scenarios likely would have important consequences for how Alicia differently reconstructs Sally's remark (and her interpretation of Sally's subsequent invitation to join her small group). For any individual, it is very difficult—if not impossible—to separate the memory of an event from experiences that preceded it and those that follow it. Even though the actual words might be *remembered*, the relived intensity with which the statement was delivered is undoubtedly influenced by many factors that envelop the particular event.

We provide extended comment on this point because this situation is in sharp contrast to a "retrospective" research study, in which an interviewee tells an interviewer about prior experiences and the interviewer does not know the respondent and is unlikely to have any direct experience of his/her own (although they may be interviewing other people from that time period). Teachers (unlike research interviewers) often will be in a situation in which they have their own memory about a particular event and access to other students who participated in the episode. On occasion, they may even have tape recordings of particular events (e.g., the teacher may be taping student conversations during small-group work for instructional purposes). Also, teacher-student interviews become part of the teacher-student relationship.

We think teachers are in a unique position. They should not overreify "the truth" and must understand that student perceptions can not only differ but *change*. When students talk about past events, they are likely to enhance the positive features for themselves and to decrease the negative connotations—especially if they need to cope with similar settings or persons again ("Oh, she really knew that I was kidding." "I'll do better next time if I try harder."). Reconstructions that allow coping with future stressful situations can be adaptive. Thus, one reason for teachers to interview students is to try to understand how students reconstruct events, and equally importantly, how they feel about the event now and what consequences it has for the future.

❖ CONDUCTING INTERVIEWS IN CLASSROOMS

◆ ISSUES OF STATUS

As various educators have noticed, role and status differences between interview participants can prevent the effective sharing of information (e.g., Seidman, 1991). However, as other authors have noted (e.g., Sincoff & Goyer, 1984), it is possible to use interview techniques to obtain useful information between persons with uneven status if the participants are aware of each other's needs and if the individual conducting the interview can do so with general skill and competence. Bingham and Moore (1959) discuss management and employee relationships as examples of an area where cooperation might be difficult to obtain. They note that even in this context:

> In most situations, as for example in industrial disputes, people speak freely and frankly when they feel that they will not be misunderstood and that no unfair advantage will be taken of what they have said. The principle, as it applies to the interview, is that the interviewee is as frank as he can be . . . when he feels that his point of view is appreciated and respected, that the interviewer has some right to the information, and that the questions are relevant and not impertinent. (p. 14)

Teachers, in creating a climate appropriate for an authentic interview, have to be aware of status differences and take steps to reduce this barrier. The best way to begin to build an appropriate climate is to be sure that students 1) understand why they are being interviewed, 2) believe that teachers have a right to such information, and 3) trust that the interview can lead to helpful changes and support, not recrimination.

◆ STUDENTS' UNDERSTANDING OF THE INTERVIEW

When interviewing students, teachers should always identify the situation and the rationale clearly, so that students understand that the teacher is trying to obtain information and further understanding—not attempting to punish. In addition to helping the student to understand the situation (and perhaps how it differs from conversations in front of the entire class), it is important for teachers to create and to communicate a credible tone of interest and concern—but not one of evaluation or emotional intensity (Rohrkemper, 1982). Students need to understand their teacher's expectations (including why they are engaging in the conversation) and be able to trust them with their honest perceptions and information. Students who develop the impression that conversations with the teacher will come back to haunt them understandably will engage in resistance and/or face-saving or ingratiation strategies (Rohrkemper, 1982). Under these circumstances, interviewing students will do little to improve teacher-student relations or to further the teacher's understanding of classroom events.

◆ AVOID TEACHING; AVOID PREACHING

At first glance, this banner may seem totally out of synch with our repeated stance on teachers and co-regulation of student mediation and learning. Let's look at the interviewing guidelines, however, distinguishing teaching and preaching from modeling and scaffolding.

Bingham and Moore (1959) strongly advise all types of interviewers to avoid the role of teacher:

> Most persons do not appreciate having an outsider, often a novice in their special field, tell them how to do their work or run their business. Let the interviewee be the teacher. Do not yourself attempt to harangue or moralize for his benefit, but let him criticize or moralize all he wants to. The only occasion for differing with him is to get him to state his opinions or release his feelings. (p. 73).

Kottler and Kottler (1993), in describing the counseling role in teaching, are a bit more succint:

> Advice Giving. Don't do it. Period. Resist your natural inclination to tell people what to do with their lives. (p. 47).

Following this advice might be especially difficult for teachers, who certainly are *not* "outsiders" or "novices" but who *are* co-regulators and socializing agents of students and who try to foster the development of certain moral perspectives in them. Clearly, the teacher is the classroom authority, but when teachers interview a student, they do so on one or both of two possible levels. First, they may seek to obtain information and to assess perceptions about that which they have limited, incomplete, or wrong information. Second, they ask questions to help structure ways to find, define, and confront conflict and ambiguity in ways that inform goal setting, enactive strategies, and evaluation of progress. Hence, in most interview situations, the student should be treated as the expert from whom the teacher learns, even as the teacher actively scaffolds and models through specific questions and problem-focused, nonjudgmental dispositions. When interviewing students, teachers should think of themselves as learners *and* teachers. We maintain that the role of learner is not inconsistent with the socialization role of teachers. Rather, we believe that teachers model empathy and authentic valuing of another, even where there is disagreement. Interviewing conveys a commitment to *understanding*, a virtue of both teaching and learning.

◆ KNOW YOUR OWN PERSONALITY

All of us have preconceptions and are committed at one level or another to certain beliefs or opinions (recall the earlier discussion on bias). As we prepare for an interview, it is useful to recognize and to think about the biases or commitments that we have that might interfere with obtaining new information or being open to new perceptions. Thus, a teacher who is getting ready to discuss dishonesty may well think about how her/his own opinions (e.g., indignation) may interfere with having a reasonable discussion about the issues. Similarly, if a teacher is inquiring about a discipline problem, s/he need not let the student's past behavior (and the futility of previous discipline strategies) be an overriding concern in obtaining information about the present situation. Background information may be useful to help examine the current event (e.g., the other students think you are going to be mean to them, so they beat you to it), but a student "need not be the victim of her/his biography," to quote Kelly (1966/1970, in Weiner, 1992, p. 225).

◆ SOCIAL PROCESSES

Rohrkemper (1982) stresses that the interview is a *social* process. The relationship between the interviewer (whether teacher or parent) and interviewee (whether parent or student) has considerable potential both in assisting or limiting the success of the interview. When students are having private conversations with teachers, students (especially older students) will enter the conversation with a great deal of information about this teacher and "teachers" in general.

For example, students are well aware of how teachers conduct classroom discussions. The extent to which their teacher is seen as fair and understanding in public contexts will likely transfer to private settings. Similarly, how frequently teachers talk with students privately informs the degree to which teacher-student conversations are seen as an acceptable aspect of classroom behavior. Teachers who frequently talk with students are in a much better position to obtain helpful information about incidents that occur in the classroom than are teachers who seldom engage in such conversations. Indeed, if teachers rarely talk with students, the fact that they are initiating a conversation may have unintended consequences (others' and self-perception that the student is *really doing poorly* . . . or the misbehavior that the teacher is trying to investigate must be *really important*).

To the extent that a teacher can develop conversations with individual students in the classroom as a normal part of classroom practice, we believe that s/he will improve considerably the ability to interact with students as a concerned and interested adult. Teachers should begin the process early in the year so that students become used to brief conversations with their teacher. An early start will help the teacher to become familiar and to build rapport with the students prior to the occurrence of (and may even prevent) any major problems. If you have a history of talking informally with students, it will make subsequent, potentially "difficult" conversations easier.

◆ VALIDITY

To the extent that students are willing to share their perceptions and their beliefs, interviews can take an important role in improving both teachers' and students' understanding of classroom events. Thus, validity (the students' *willingness and ability* to provide the perspective they believe) and invalidity (the degree to which the information the students provide does not reflect "true" facts or feelings) is a significant issue in conducting classroom interviews.

As an important starting point, Rohrkemper (1982) argues that teachers need to examine their biases and expectations and be aware of distortions in student reports that may be elicited by the type of question the teacher asks ("Why did you do that?" versus "Tell me what happened," or "Something happened."). Thus, the teacher's manner affects validity (e.g., perceived blame, support, or neutrality) and is conveyed indirectly through tone and directly through the structure of the "same" questions. The presence of consequences the student may wish to obtain (teacher support), or avoid ("You'll lose gym privileges for a week if what Joan said is true. Now, did you. . . . ?") also affect the validity of student report.

Clearly, not all presentations can be anticipated or controlled. Sometimes teachers will be overly controlling or angry and rushed when they start the interview process, and they may need to reestablish rapport with the student. For example, the teacher may need to say something like, "Jan, I was in such a hurry to find out who took the laboratory chemicals that I probably started this conversation too abruptly. Let me make it clear that I am not blaming you; I am simply trying to be sure that dangerous chemicals are returned to the proper laboratory shelf and that everyone respects proper safety procedures." This teacher not only regains control of the interview, she also models identifying and coping with one's own emotions and learning from mistakes.

At times, when teachers do not feel that they can disassociate themselves enough to obtain valid student information, it may be appropriate to ask a colleague (and occasionally a classmate) to interview the student. Obtaining the professional involvement and advice of a peer teacher (e.g., asking him/her to interview a student) is a good strategy, as is asking peers to observe one's teaching. Collegial exchange can stimulate professional conversations that often are helpful in providing relevant information and useful perspectives (Rosenholtz, 1989; Smylie, 1992). If student behavior seems to form a pattern that calls for additional psychological expertise (e.g., suicidal tendencies, an eating disorder), the school counselor or psychologist should be alerted.

◆ RELIABILITY

Another fundamental issue is the reliability of student information. The typical approach to reliability of interview has been in the test-retest tradition. Would the student provide the same information on Friday afternoon as on Monday morning? The expectation of stability or consistency of student opinion, of course, is an assumption that one cannot take for granted. Some aspects of students' lives are relatively stable, but others are highly unstable; and hence, the report of different opinions is not always an issue of contradiction. Recall (reconstruct!) our previous discussion of memory reconstruction. Thus, we think a better approach to interview reliability is to consider whether the student would report similarly to another trusted adult at that time.

As Rohrkemper (1982) notes, student perceptions are not static and reflection takes time—especially in emotionally charged situations. She argues that one useful strategy for increasing the probability that information accurately reflects students' thoughts and identified emotions is to interview students *after* they have calmed down. Once students are removed from the immediate situation, they are more likely to have an opportunity to reflect on their experience, have more valid insights, and be better prepared to understand, and thus, to report on and learn from their perceptions. Therefore, unless an issue demands immediate intervention, it may be better to wait before holding student interviews. Generally, students' reports are much more likely to be representive after they have had an opportunity to emotionally distance themselves from the original event. However, time for reflection does not always serve validity (Rohrkemper, 1982): a teacher who is concerned with how the student feels *in* a situation, clearly should talk to the student at that point rather than delaying.

◆ IS INFORMATION ACCESSIBLE?

The optimal distance between the time of an event and the time it is discussed will vary and depend upon involved students (for example, the student's age or whether s/he was directly involved in the event or simply an observer) and the goal of the interview. An important constraint on the utility of interviewing is the accessibility of information (Ericsson & Simon, 1980; Meichenbaum et al., 1985; Nisbett & Wilson, 1977). Often, students may not have the relevant information. For example, if some time has passed since the event, the student may have forgotten the details—in which case a simple reminder would help to move the interview along. And students may *no longer* have the information to report. That is, they may no longer be aware of their thoughts and perceptions because they have become automatic, "thoughtless," and are no longer accessible to them. The "story" that the student then tells may not represent the *actual* processes, but it may carry forward and play an important role in future self-fulfilling-prophecy effects (Meichenbaum et al, 1985, p. 7). Again, the role of the question opportunity in student mediation emerges as a key issue in interviewing.

In other cases, students may have suppressed or repressed details or distorted an event to avoid stress and anxiety (e.g., abuse cases). More simply, the student may not have the desired information; s/he never knew it in the first place because it was outside the student's experience or level of awareness (this factor is especially relevant when working with younger children). It takes a sensitive interviewer to distinguish the cause of a child's responding, "I can't remember" or "I don't know," and to be able to follow up appropriately. We think one useful heuristic is to accept the student's self-assessment, provide a clue to trigger recall; and, if not helpful, recognize the student's effort, provide your assessment of the event, and move on.

◆ ISSUES OF SOCIAL DESIRABILITY

Social desirability is like a first date: the attempt to put one's best foot forward can be a problem—especially if the interviewee senses that s/he is being evaluated or that there is a "good" right answer. Classroom research has suggested that some students will exhibit a tendency to over- or underreport certain interaction patterns they share with the teacher for social desirability reasons, both to enhance themselves and their teacher. For example, Gustafsson (1977) found some students to be reluctant to report that their teacher provided different amounts of help to different students (which was the case). Instead, these students commented, "Miss X does as good as she can. She comes to all of us." The bulk of research evidence, however, illustrates that students can and will give accurate information under appropriate conditions (Cooper & Good, 1983). McCaslin et al. (1994) remind us that "recall conditions" and reconstruction of experience go hand in hand.

When interviewing students, teachers must recognize that some students will be anxious in that situation—particularly the first time or two that they confer with the teacher. One strategy for reducing student anxiety is to suggest that others have felt the same way the student does. The teacher can mention various feelings or actions that some people experience without stating preferences or making value judgments (Rohrkemper, 1982). For example, a teacher might state, "Everybody gets bored sometimes. In our class, I notice that some students get bored when the work's too hard and others when it's too easy. Other students get bored in some classes but not in others. Some students only get bored during seat work, and other students only get bored when the teacher is lecturing." After making these observations, the teacher could ask, "What about you? When do you get bored? Why do you think that is?" By letting students know that the teacher understands that everyone gets bored—and that's okay—the teacher can reduce student anxiety about discussing an issue that potentially could be "threatening" to the teacher. By suggesting a range of possible situations that could be boring, the teacher is more likely to put the student at ease and to obtain information about how the student really feels.

By using such techniques, the teacher can help students to deal with a variety of issues. For example, if the teacher is aware that a student is being teased frequently in a small-group setting, the teacher might want to understand better how the student feels about it before attempting any intervention. The teacher could ask something like, "Some students like small-group work better than others—how about you?" Subsequently, the teacher might want to ask a question like, "Some students report that they often feel uncomfortable during small group because sometimes the students they work with are not supportive and sometimes they are even mean to them. How about you? Have you ever felt that way?"

When interviewing students, it is important to attend to the sequence of questions and avoid the temptation to rush and do too much too soon. Earlier, we noted one interview strategy that is often recommended is to be sure that the individual can successfully answer the opening question (Rohrkemper, 1982; Yarrow, 1960). Given status differences and the fact that the teacher often evaluates the student, this strategy seems especially important in the classroom. Assuring that the student can answer the first question successfully enables the teacher and student to set a positive climate and involves the student more directly with the content (rather than defending or trying to avoid embarrassment, etc.).

Thus, it is a good strategy to save the more difficult and sensitive questions for later in the interview, after rapport has been established and after students have become more competent in the interviewee role. We also suggest that the interview close with "success" questions—especially if sensitive topics have been discussed. The "shape" of such an interview is an hourglass. Like an hourglass, the section of heightened sensitivity and vulnerability is kept small and sandwiched between progressively larger areas of relatively smooth and nonintrusive discussion that highlights student competence and promotes confidence.

In some situations, it may be desirable for a teacher to use a "funnel" strategy, in which the interview conversation proceeds from relatively broad to specific questions, in the shape of a funnel. Using such a technique, the teacher may open a discussion with a series of questions that become increasingly specific: "What do you think about learning in small groups? What do you think about learning mathematics in small groups? How is it different from what you expected? If you had to name three good things about small groups, what would they be? If you had to name three things you would like to change about small groups, what would they be?"

One advantage of the funnel technique is that by asking broad questions the teacher prevents the student from responding with a simple yes or no answer. However, the possibilities of "I don't know" and shrugs remain. Another advantage is that the student is less likely to feel "tricked" by similar questions that seem designed to see if s/he is telling the "truth" (as actually is often the case in questionnaire studies *and* teacher tests). Reliability is often defined as "truth"—or at least consistency: we expect certain recurring responses to similar (and opposite) questions for the report to be considered reliable. A third advantage is that funnel interviews directly involve students early on in the process of thinking and responding. As the interview continues, the teacher could restrict the scope of later questions to his/her specific concern, or invite the student to suggest topics (Rohrkemper, 1982).

◆ STRUCTURE AND TYPE OF QUESTION

Yarrow (1960) identifies several dimensions that are useful in constructing and conducting interviews. Considerations he advances include the degree of standardization of the question (teacher preparation of specific questions versus general topics), the degree of structure and directiveness in the teacher's behavior (the teacher maintaining close control of what is discussed versus spontaneously following student contributions), and the degree of structure in the questions and in the type of responses that are desired (e.g., "Do you understand why I want no more than three students out of the room at one time?" versus "How can we be careful not to have accidents?" or "What about the Golden Rule?"). This latter dimension concerns the openness of questions. Several researchers (e.g., Meichenbaum, et al., 1985) advocate open-ended questions ("What do you want to do?") rather than closed questions ("Do you want me to tell your mom?"). Open-ended questions allow student constructs to emerge and, at the very least, do not afford minimalist yes/no responses. Notice that this is a bit more differentiated than the suggestions by Bingham and Moore (1931; 1959), who considered all preset questions rigid. Open-ended questions can be predetermined but not necessarily "rigid" in that students respond in their own terms to the standard questions.

Teachers can present questions to students in a direct, indirect, or projective fashion. Yarrow notes that direct questions can elicit factual information but contends that indirect questions are better when one desires more information about complex student attitudes, feelings, and expectations. As a case in point, Rohrkemper (1982) argues that if a teacher is concerned about a particular student's lack of interest in social studies, the teacher may want to ask the student an indirect question based on observation of student behavior and an analysis of what is involved in the social studies lesson.

For example, the teacher might inquire: "Of reading, math, and social studies, which do you like best (dislike least)?" Similarly, the teacher might ask, "If you could choose to read quietly, have a class discussion, or listen to a lecture, which would you choose first? what next?" and so on, to narrow down what it is about social studies that interferes with the student's classroom work. Rohrkemper (1982) notes that in such a sequence, the student was not asked what he *didn't* like. Rather, information concerning his least-preferred choice was obtained without the student having to feel that he was complaining or being critical. It is also instructive that the example includes a "back-up" question that is prepared in advance, in case the initial question is not understood or is not relevant to the student's frame of reference. In general, back-up questions, like the initial question, should be prepared in advance and should be nonemotional and nonjudgmental.

Finally, much research and interview criticism (e.g., Nisbett & Wilson, 1977) indicates that questions phrased as *how* or *why* invite response problems. Often *how* is not known (or as we explained earlier, no longer known), especially by younger students; but the desire to respond prevails. The result can be irrelevant and, worse yet, misleading information. *Why* questions can be seen as threatening and even hostile. This is particularly the case because teachers typically ask *why* questions more in discipline situations ("Why can't you keep your hands to yourself?") and when students have made mistakes ("Why did you set up the equation like that?") than in opportunities for students to display their talents ("Why did you choose to play soccer?").

Why questions are likely to trigger self-justifications and defensive reactions. If used, *how* and *why* questions need to be posed carefully to convey an interest in *process* not a disappointment in the *outcome* of that process. For example, consider how your tone when asking *why* can convey a genuine concern for the way in which a student is conceptualizing a situation ("*Why* did you do that?"). Compare this with your tone when exasperated over the effects of that conception: "Why did you do *that*?"

Making Questions Concrete It is often useful to make questions very concrete in order to facilitate student understanding. The benefits of this technique are especially relevant when interviewing younger students, students who are less verbal, and students who may be generally anxious. Making questions more concrete is especially advantageous when asking students about specific people. For example, rather than require a student to say that she does not want to work with a certain classmate, the teacher could ask: "Pretend that Ted, Jan, and Mark all live on your street. Who do you think you'd like best? If Mark's sick (the student's first choice) and can't play, whose house would you go to next?" Alternatively, the teacher might ask, "If you could choose Tom, Mark, Chris, or Danielle to be your partner in reading, who would you like to work with most? If Tom's sick today, who would you choose to work with next?"

Hypothetical Questions and Situations Projective questions can also be useful when interviewing and listening to students. Rohrkemper (1982) puts the case this way: "When the teacher feels the student has repressed memory of an event, has severely distorted his recollections, or is simply leery of being directly critical of the teacher, the teacher can ask projective questions that concern hypothetical situations. For instance, a teacher who is concerned that a low-ability student is becoming detached and withdrawn might relate a situation about a fictional student from another class with the same behavior and ask the student, 'How do you think he felt in school? How do you feel about it? What about other kids? What do they think?' " (p. 91). By using hypothetical situations, the teacher allows the student to discuss his/her own concerns with less anxiety (see also Segal-Andrews, 1994).

Use of Stories Stories can also be useful in understanding how students perceive the teacher's behavior toward, attitudes about, and expectations for students—and toward classroom rules. For example, teachers could use the following stories (after Rohrkemper, 1981, 1984, 1985). "Tonya could do good work in school, if she tried. Tonya hardly ever does her assignments even when she promises her teacher she will. Today during work time everyone is busy except for Tonya. She is writing in her diary."

"Dan is not very smart in school. Even though Dan often tries hard, he has trouble learning new things, and lots of time he answers wrong and tries to act like he doesn't care. Today the class began a new topic in math. Everyone was working except Dan. The teacher asked Dan if something was the matter. He said that he tried but he couldn't do his work; it was too dumb and too confusing."

"Julia is upset. Today her small group was supposed to be working on a social studies project, but they had so many disagreements they got hardly anything done. Julia wants to ask the teacher a question, but the class rule is that students can't ask the teacher unless they have already asked the students in their small group: 'First ask three, then me.' Julia is so angry at her group members that she doesn't want to *talk* to them let alone ask for help."

After presenting such stories, teachers could ask, "Pretend I was Tonya's (Dan's or Julia's) teacher. What would I say if that happened? What would I do?"—followed with, "Why do you think I would do those things? What would I expect Tonya to do? What would I think about Tonya? If you were Julia, what would you do? If Julia did that, what do you think the teacher would do? How come?"

Using stories in this way could facilitate teachers' explorations of how students perceive teacher motives, behavior, and expectations for students, as well as certain classroom routines (e.g., requiring students to talk to other group members before the teacher). Teachers could use this information to help correct inaccuracies in students' perceptions or to change their own classroom presentations to make their behavior consistent with their intentions.

❖ PROBLEM-SOLVING INTERVIEWS

We begin with generic procedures for interviewing students about specific problem incidents that involve them. Most educators stress that the teacher stay calm and methodically gather information from all participants. It is crucial that each student has a turn to tell her/his story without interruption and to perceive that others are listening. The teacher can facilitate problem-oriented interviews by structuring the initial ground rules and facilitating the presentation of each student's perspective. Teachers, with the students, can then proceed to discuss discrepancies in testimony and to search for acceptable ways of handling such incidents in the future.

The key to implementing this approach is a nonpejorative problem-solving stance. Students are encouraged to discuss and consider their own feelings and perspectives while also having the opportunity—the requirement—to listen and reflect upon others' perceptions. Teachers report that this method is especially useful when dealing with problems among students that begin innocuously but escalate (fights, arguments, etc.). In conducting such interviews, teachers have the opportunity to (and should) state their own feelings about unacceptable student behavior, as well as communicate their expectations for appropriate student behavior and teach strategies to meet them. Thus, while scaffolding how to deal with a short-term problem (the content level of the problem-solving interview), the teacher can also help students to think proactively about classroom conditions and behavior that are important for everyone to consider (the structural level of mediational scaffolding).

When appropriately used, a problem-focused interview can help to provide teachers with information that will help them better understand and thus, more appropriately co-regulate, student behavior. Often, teachers will become sensitive to motivations and attitudes that they never would have predicted from simply observing student behavior. Increased teacher understanding may help teachers not only to resolve present anomalies and conflicts but also to "read" their students more accurately in the future, thereby facilitating teacher ability to monitor and stimulate—co-regulate—student growth in the classroom. We now describe one specific approach to the problem interview, termed a *life space* interview, that has been found effective with hostile, aggressive students.

◆ LIFE SPACE INTERVIEWS

Morse (1971) proposed a life space interview based on work by Redl (Redl & Wineman, 1951; Redl, 1966) that is intended to improve the life conditions of hostile, aggressive students (and their peers) in a classroom setting. Following some serious misbehavior, the teacher talks to the student privately in order to obtain his/her perceptions of the incident, the events that preceded it, and issues and feelings that followed. The goals are to allow the student to experience a degree of catharsis and to vent anger, and to provide the teacher an opportunity to model his/her interest in listening and helping the student.

It is important that teachers understand generally what took place and how students *react* to the event. For example, two students who were involved in the same episode (a fight on the playground) may be angered by different aspects of the incident. For example, two days after the event, one student may still be angry because s/he was picked on by a peer; whereas the other student may not be angry about the fight (these things happen), but about the way the playground supervisor intervened in it (the student feels that she was unduly held responsible for the event). Reconstructing the event and assessing how the student feels about it now, the teacher can communicate acceptance of particular feelings that a student expresses—although the teacher does not necessarily (indeed, often does not) accept the student's actions.

Once the reconstruction is explored, the interview/discussion can begin to focus on what can be done at this point. The *experience* of emotion is distinguished from its *expression*. The teacher works together with the student to find ways to reduce the problem—how can the problem be prevented in the future, and what are the consequences if the problem happens again? As Good and Brophy (1995) note, it is important for the teacher to avoid needless threats or inappropriate moralizing (see also Gordon, 1970). Instead, it is more helpful to focus on how the student might identify and cope more appropriately with her/his emotions because current behavior is self-defeating.

◆ SOME PROBLEM-SOLVING INTERVIEW GUIDELINES

The guidelines for conducting problem-solving interviews with students that are presented in the following example stem from our integration and extensions of work by Bingham and Moore (1931, 1959) on the counselor interview; Redl's (1966) original problem-focused interview and Morse's (1971) elaboration of it in the life space interview; and recommendations by Good and Brophy (1995), Gordon (1970), Meichenbaum (1977), and Rohrkemper (1982). We believe that teachers should provide these types of support and supportive structures that envelop a life space interview, following the model of *co-regulated* learning we described in Chapter 1.

Co-Regulated Problem-Solving Interview Guidelines

1. Make the interview a cooperative undertaking. The student should be assured that nothing is being concealed, no predetermined action is going to be forced upon her/him, and there is no hidden agenda.

2. Maintain a professional demeanor at all times. Thus, the teacher should generally be sympathetic and engaged but should not appear surprised or shocked at students' disclosures. Unpleasant issues and content should be examined in terms of their implications for remediation of the problem.

3. Help the student release emotion (e.g., anger, anxiety) by expressing sympathy and understanding for the *emotion*—not necessarily the *behavior*. Deal with emotions that the student may now feel (embarrassment and/or guilt which sometimes follow an emotional outburst).

4. Work with the student to understand her/his perceptions, attributions, and expectations for his/her own behavior, needs, wishes, desires.

5. Help the student identify her/his *goal* in the present event. Help the student identify multiple goals and their relationships, and consider strategies to coordinate among them (see Chapter 2 for extended discussion). Encourage critical goal review.

6. Encourage the student to consider the perceptions of others. Clarify values and note how particular student behaviors might interfere with others' rights, goals, and needs.

7. Encourage the student to accept "reality" (e.g., "You were fighting") and to abandon defensive distortions (e.g., "I was trying to get away").

8. Help the student identify which aspects of his/her perceptions, inner speech, and behavior are inappropriate and self-defeating, and not helping meet her/his own goals.

9. Work with the student to identify strategies that would better help her/him meet goals and deal with emotions and problems more appropriately. Teach and practice these strategies with the student or refer her/him to support personnel who can work in this way (e.g., perhaps the school counselor or psychologist for extra support with highly anxious or aggressive students, the reading specialist for students with learning disabilities).

10. Help the student formulate her/his own plan of action that incorporates goals, strategies to meet them, and actions (including cognitions) to substitute for previous inappropriate behavior.

11. Encourage the student to accept responsibility for his/her plan, its enactment, and evaluation of progress.

12. Be prepared to have multiple conversations with and extended monitoring and support of the student as he/she follows through on her/his plan. Behavior is hard to change, and volition is not easily learned; respect and support the size of the task the student has engaged.

13. Note some progress that has occurred in relatively specific ways, even though there are issues that remain. Teach and encourage student realistic self-evaluation of progress (after Zuckerman, 1994). Reinforce *realistic* appraisals—no matter what their "objective" level.

14. Maintain open communication and offer to talk with the student on subsequent occasions to see how the student is progressing and where additional support might help.

15. Talk about *other things*. Remember: the student is more than her/his "problem."

In brief, points 1 and 2 deal with establishing the tone and reaffirming the teacher-student relationship. Points 3 through 5 prioritize student *motivation*—what we previously termed reality contact, to stress the importance of identifying emotion and setting and coordinating reasonable goals given current capabilities and the realities of the situation.

Points 6 through 10 emphasize student *enactment* strategies, the arena of reality testing we previously defined as recognizing and exerting control over oneself and control over the persons (e.g., teachers, peers) and physical resources of the classroom. Enactment strategies can be evaluated in terms of their service to goal attainment, the focus of points 11 through 14. In this section, concern is with *evaluation* of student progress toward and acceptance of goal attainment by both the teacher and student. Earlier, we identified evaluation as the arena of reality feedback. We argued that realistic student self-evaluation, defined by congruence between teacher and student self-assessment—independent of the level of progress—is a key task for the promotion of student learning and mental health. Finally, point 15 brings the interview suggestions full circle and reasserts the teacher-student relationship and its functional role in the co-regulation of student mediational processes.

The 15 points presented here are heuristic guidelines that are based on, even as they deepen, co-regulation and the teacher-student relationship. Obviously, the points are not meant to be a rigid set of steps to be followed, in order, from beginning to end—although we consider the opening and closing points important no matter what occurs between them. Rather, teachers likely will prioritize specific mediational areas of concern (i.e., motivation, enactment, evaluation) at a given time.

Our discussion of realistic goal setting is important for teachers to bear in mind as well. We recommend that teachers decide the most important arena to target first. We can imagine situations—for example student aggression—where teachers may want to prioritize enactment strategies over motivation. Student safety has precedence over self-insight. Once behavior is predictably under appropriate (self-) control, then motivational and self-evaluation concerns can be targeted. In comparison, interviews with students who are highly anxious and engage in self-defeating inner speech may first target motivational dynamics to prepare the student for the more difficult task of realistic self-evaluation.

As these examples illustrate, some aspects of a co-regulated problem-solving interview are more difficult than others, with difficulty defined by the complexity of the "objective" task, the student problem presentation, and teacher strategies and dispositions. Thus, we present the 15-point guidelines to help teachers reflect on their own goal(s) with a student, cue strategies that might realize those goals, and stress the need to evaluate progress—both the student's and the teacher's. This example is a mediational scaffold, not a blueprint.

❖ SUMMARY

In this chapter we have defined the classroom interview as a conversation between the teacher and individual students about teacher and student perceptions of classroom events—what has happened, what could happen. We have noted that interviews are used productively in various contexts and that professionals have accumulated over time a wealth of information about how to conduct interviews—although relatively little research on classroom interviews is available. In this chapter we have discussed ways of thinking about preparing for the interview, conducting interviews generally, and classroom interviews specifically. Among other considerations we have stressed that interviews are a social process and that teachers need to establish rapport and express empathy and genuine interest in the student and his/her perspective. We have commented upon the unique features of the teacher-student interview situation and discussed strategies for effective communication to overcome potential difficulties. Finally, we have provided some general interview strategies for discussing student behaviors and set specific guidelines for interviewing students who cause serious or special concern. These interview guidelines themselves scaffold a model of co-regulated learning of mediational processes. Throughout, we have presented communication strategies, within the context of the teacher's role responsibilities.

❖ QUESTIONS AND SUGGESTED ACTIVITIES FOR CHAPTER 3

1. Do you think that teachers would tend to underestimate or overestimate the learning potential of the following types of students: passive minorities; loud, aggressive females; students who are neat and follow directions; students who complain that schoolwork is not interesting? Why do you believe that teachers might over- or underestimate the abilities of these student types? If teachers were interviewing students about whom they held these beliefs, how might beliefs interfere with teacher planning and conducting of the interview?

2. Are teachers already inherently biased when they think in terms of "minorities" rather than about particular types of students?

3. How might your expectations about the person you are interviewing influence: a) the type of questions that you ask, b) the order in which questions are asked, c) the extent to which you probe or ask for clarification, and d) the extent to which you ask open versus directive questions? In what ways might you reduce your potential bias so that you can hear the interviewee as objectively as possible?

4. How might a teacher's emphasis on accepting student responses during an interview interfere with valid student reporting? Give examples of how this process might work. What can be done to eliminate or reduce this problem?

5. What is the role of a backup question? How might an interview structure inadvertently influence student responding? Why?

6. In this chapter, the authors stress the use of open-ended questions rather than direct questions. However, it would seem logical that there are some circumstances and times when direct questions would be better than open-ended questions. Identify three or four such situations and compare your responses with other students' responses.

7. Pretend that you are going to interview Rick, a student who has a speech impediment and who has been teased frequently by his peers during small-group lessons. You know that the students are teasing him and that

Rick's frustration and anger frequently end in him pushing other students or grabbing their materials. Write out four or five questions that you would want to raise during an interview with Rick. What are the critical issues that you want to deal with? How would you start the interview, and, in particular, what strategies would you use for building rapport and assuring Rick that you are interested in his perspective?

8. Alternatively, assume you are going to interview Martha, one of the students who has been teasing Rick. What are the critical questions you would ask? How would you attempt to develop rapport with Martha and communicate interest in her perspective? What difficulties might you have?

9. Define a problem-solving strategy conference that you would conduct with a student. Indicate the problem (e.g., student has been accused of defacing property) that you want to address. Briefly prepare a list of essential questions and issues that you would want to deal with in the problem-solving interview.

10. Assume that a student's parents request to be present for an interview after school. How might this influence how you would start and conduct the interview? What is your rationale for any possible differences (e.g., parents present or not, knowledge of family dynamics)?

11. In general, what types of interview skills and dispositions are the most difficult for you to handle (e.g., be objective, retain focus, etc.)? Why?

12. Assume that a student tells you: a) that she is pregnant, b) that she has been having difficulties in other classes, and c) that she is being mistreated at home. How would you interview the student? In which cases would you keep the information confidential between you and the student? How do you go about making such decisions?

13. In the chapter, it was mentioned that one way to prepare for an interview is to put yourself in the place of the interviewee. Think about questions that you might be asked in an interview in the near future (applying for a job, applying for a graduate assistantship, etc.). How does your role differ from that of the interviewer? To stimulate your thinking further, you may want to read various sources that discuss how to prepare for the interview (see, for example, Richard Beatty's *The Five-Minute Interview*).

14. Often when we read material, it stimulates more questions than answers. Consider what you have read about the interview method in this chapter and a) list three or four questions that address issues about which you would like to have more information, or b) list concepts and strategies with which you disagree or have concern. Discuss your ideas and reactions with other classmates.

❖ REFERENCES

Bingham, W., & Moore, D. (1931). *How to interview*. New York: Harper and Brothers.

Bingham, W., & Moore, D. (1959). *How to interview* (4th ed.). New York: Harper and Brothers.

Brenner, M., Brown, J., & Canter, D. (Eds.). (1985). *The research interview: Uses and approaches.* London: Academic Press.

Cooper, H., & Good, T. (1983). *Pygmalion grows up: Studies in the expectation communication process.* White Plains, NY: Longman.

Ericsson, K., & Simon, H. (1980). Verbal reports as data. *Psychological Review, 87,* 215–251.

Good, T., & Brophy, J. (1994). *Looking in Classrooms* (6th ed.). New York: HarperCollins.

Good, T., & Brophy, J. (1995). *Contemporary Educational Psychology.* White Plains, NY: Longman.

Gordon, T. (1970). *Parent effectiveness training.* New York: Wyden.

Gustafsson, C. (1977). *Classroom interaction: A study of pedagogical roles in the teaching process.* Stockholm: Gruppen.

Heath, S. (1982). Questioning at home and school: A comparative study. In G. Spindler (Ed.), *Doing the ethnography of schooling* (pp. 102–131). New York: Holt, Rinehart, & Winston.

Heath, S., & McLaughlin, M. (Eds.). (1993). *Identity and inner-city youth: Beyond ethnicity and gender.* New York: Teachers College Press.

Jones, E. (1990). *Interpersonal perception.* New York: W. H. Freeman.

Kahneman, D., & Tversky, A. (1973). On the psychology of prediction. *Psychological Review, 80,* 237–251.

Kottler, J., & Kottler, E. (1993). *Teacher as counselor: Developing the skills you need.* Newbury Park, CA: Corwin.

Loftus, E. (1975). Leading questions and the eyewitness report. *Cognitive Psychology, 7,* 560–672.

Loftus, E. (1994). The repressed memory controversy. *American Psychologist, 49* (5), 443–445.

McCaslin, M., Tuck, D., Wiard, A., Brown, B., LaPage, J., & Pyle, J. (1994). Gender composition and small-group learning in fourth-grade mathematics. *Elementary School Journal, 94,* 467–482.

Meichenbaum, D. (1977). *Cognitive-behavior modification: An integrative approach.* New York: Plenum.

Meichenbaum, D., Burland, S., Gruson, L., & Cameron, R. (1985). Metacognitive assessment. In S. Yussen (Ed.), *The growth of reflection in children* (pp. 3–30). Orlando, FL: Academic Press.

Moll, L. (1992). Bilingual classroom studies and community analysis. *Educational Researcher, 21,* 20–24.

Morse, W. (1971). Worksheet on life space interviewing for teachers. In N. Long, W. Morse, & R. Newman (Eds.), *Conflict in the classroom: The education of children with problems* (2nd ed.). Belmont, CA: Wadsworth.

Neisser, U. (1982). *Memory observed: Remembering in natural contexts.* San Francisco: W. H. Freeman.

Nisbett, R., & Wilson, T. (1977). Telling more than we can know: Verbal reports on mental processes. *Psychological Review, 84,* 231–259.

Piaget, J. (1983). Piaget's theory. In P. Mussen (Ed.), *Handbook of child psychology: Vol. 1. W. Kessen (Ed.), History, theory, and methods* (pp. 103–128). New York: John Wiley & Sons.

Redl, L. (1966). *When we deal with children.* New York: Free Press.

Redl, L., & Wineman, D. (1951). *Children who hate.* New York: Free Press.

Rice, S. (1929). Contagious bias in the interview: A methological note. *American Journal of Sociology, 35,* 420–423.

Rohrkemper, M. (1981). *Classroom perspectives study: An investigation of differential perceptions of classroom events.* Unpublished doctoral dissertation, Michigan State University.

Rohrkemper, M. (1982). Teachers' self-assessment. In D. Duke (Ed.), *Helping teachers manage classrooms* (pp. 77–96). Alexandria, VA: Association for Supervision and Curriculum Development.

Rohrkemper, M. (1984). The influence of teacher socialization style on students' social cognition and reported interpersonal classroom behavior. *Elementary School Journal, 85,* 245–275.

Rohrkemper, M. (1985). Individual differences in students' perceptions of routine classroom events. *Journal of Educational Psychology, 77,* 29–44.

Rohrkemper, M., & Bershon, B. (1984). The quality of student task engagement: Elementary school students' reports of the causes and effects of problem difficulty. *Elementary School Journal, 85,* 127–147.

Romero, M., Mercado, C., & Vàzquéz-Faría, J. (1987). Students of limited English proficiency. In V. Richardson-Koehler (Ed.), *Educators' handbook: A research perspective* (pp. 348–369). White Plains, NY: Longman.

Rosenholtz, S. (1989). *Teachers' workplace: The social organization of schools.* White Plains, NY: Longman.

Schuman, H., & Presser, S. (1981). *Questions and answers in attitude surveys: Experiments on question form, wording, and content.* New York: Academic Press.

Segal-Andrews, A. (1994). Understanding student behavior in one fifth-grade classroom as contextually defined. *Elementary School Journal, 95,* 183–197.

Seidman, I. (1991). *Interviewing as qualitative research: A guide for researchers in education and the social sciences.* New York: Teachers College Press.

Sincoff, M., & Goyer, R. (1984). *Interviewing.* New York: MacMillan.

Smylie, M. (1992). Teachers' reports of their interactions with teacher leaders concerning classroom instruction. *Elementary School Journal, 93,* 85–98.

Spencer-Hall, D. (1981). Looking behind the teacher's back. *Elementary School Journal, 81,* 281–290.

Tagg, S. (1985). Life story interviews and their interpretations. In M. Brenner, J. Brown, & D. Canter (Eds.), *The research interview: Uses and approaches.* London: Academic Press.

Vygotsky, L. (1962). *Thought and language.* Cambridge, MA: MIT Press. (Original work published, 1934.)

Vygotsky, L. (1978). *Mind and society: The development of higher psychological processes.* Cambridge, MA: Harvard University Press.

Weiner, B. (1992). *Human motivation: Metaphors, theory, and research.* Newbury Park, CA: Sage.

Weinstein, R., Marshall, H., Brattesani, K., & Middlestadt, S. (1982). Student perceptions of differential teacher treatment in open and traditional classrooms. *Journal of Educational Psychology, 74,* 678–692.

Yarrow, L. (1960). Interviewing children. In P. Mussen (Ed.), *Handbook of research methods in child development* (pp. 561–602). New York: John Wiley & Sons.

Zuckerman, G. (1994). A pilot study of a ten-day course in cooperative learning for beginning Russian first graders. *Elementary School Journal, 94,* 405–420.

STUDENTS IN GROUPS

In this chapter, we focus on one interview goal: understanding students in small groups. Much current school reform and curriculum intervention encourages the use of small student work groups in the classroom. Various professional bodies are urging teachers to spend less time working with the class as a whole and more time allowing students to engage in small-group activities (where they can explore, manipulate, "dialogue," argue, etc.). We, too, believe that classroom teachers could profitably invest more classroom time in designing and implementing small-group lessons.

For example, work on project science at the University of Michigan has illustrated that students' active participation in small-group work can enhance learning and involvement (Blumenfeld, Krajcik, Marx, Soloway, 1994; Krajcik, Blumenfeld, Marx, & Soloway, 1994). Further, in our collaborative work on mathematics curricula with teachers in Missouri, we have found that in some contexts well-designed lessons can have useful impact on students' involvement and learning (Good, McCaslin, & Reys, 1992; McCaslin, Tuck, Wiard, Brown, LaPage, & Pyle, 1994).

We do not see small-group instruction as a panacea. Many small-group learning tasks are poorly designed and inadequately implemented (Blumenfeld, 1992; McCaslin & Good, 1992; Mulryan, 1992). In addition, much effective teaching can and does occur in large-group settings (Fenemma, Carpenter, & Peterson, 1989; Good, Grouws, & Ebmeier, 1983; Mason & Good, 1993).

In our opinion, external sources (e.g., National Council of Teachers of English; National Council of Teachers of Mathematics) will continue to encourage teachers to use small-group lessons, and we want teachers to understand the issues inherent in this model. There are numerous articles available that discuss the *advantages* of small-group learning and numerous sources that provide detailed information about constructing and maintaining cooperative groups. Interested readers are referred to Bennett and Dunne (1992); Cohen (1986); Good and Brophy (1994); Slavin (1990); and Slavin, Sharan, Kagan, Lazarowitz, Webb, and Schmuck (1985). Our goal is to contribute to this literature by directing much of our attention to illustrating several difficulties and potential costs that have to be recognized if the model is to work well. We also suggest ways that teachers might frame these difficulties to better afford their solution. One of the fundamental structural issues associated with small-group learning is that most students will be working independently away from the teacher (i.e., the teacher can be with only one small group at a time). This is a feature of small-group learning that has important consequences for student mediation. Although this can be an advantage, it can also be a disadvantage (e.g., when one or two other groups perform poorly, it is difficult to understand their problem). Thus, it seems to us that increased use of small-group models makes interviews and conversations with students even more necessary and valuable for understanding the dynamics associated with student subject matter learning in a small peer-group context. In this chapter, we will illustrate some of these practical issues associated with implementing small-group models and conducting teacher-student interviews.

❖ RESEARCH ON COOPERATIVE LEARNING

◆ LIMITED RESEARCH FOCUS

There has been much research on cooperative learning methods (Johnson, Johnson, & Maruyama, 1983; Slavin, 1990). The results are generally positive, but outcomes used to measure learning are at a relatively low level. That is, achievement comparisons in small-group learning have been made in reference to computational skills, simple concepts, and simple application problems (Davidson, 1985). Many other possible learning outcomes that one might be interested in (e.g., problem finding, problem solving, extrapolation, etc.) have not been explored. We agree with Davidson that a relatively narrow range of achievement outcomes has been studied and that much more information is needed about how higher-order skills are influenced by small-group learning. This seems especially important given that educators are increasingly advocating instruction that emphasizes *understanding* rather than the recall of isolated facts or display of discrete skills (Cohen, McLaughlin, & Talbert, 1993; Good & Brophy, 1995; Newmann, 1992).

◆ THEORETICAL CONCERNS

Cooperative learning methods also have been questioned on their theoretical premises about group motivation and group goals. For example, research by Stipek (1986) indicates that teachers need to pay careful attention to what happens to student motivation when cooperative behavior is maintained by the use of external incentives (e.g., concrete rewards, public recognition) over an extended period. This seems especially important when within- (intra-) group cooperation is instilled and maintained by between- (inter-) group competition (as in, for example, Teams-Games-Tournaments designed by Slavin (1990). Hence, there are some questions about the impact of small-group learning that is maintained by extrinsic rewards on students' intrinsic motivation to learn (Pepitone, 1985).

Some theorists, such as Pepitone (1985), further argue that if a group is to work cooperatively, it must work on goals that are important to group members, not just *assigned* curriculum goals and tasks. Yet, the concept of group goals has largely been ignored in cooperative-learning research, although distinctions between task goals and group goals have long been central to the literature (e.g., Deutsch, 1949). Simply put, some would argue that cooperation is not a true definition of *group* process unless the group is pursuing its *own* goals. In our observations, it appears that the pursuit of others' goals in small groups can change the meaning of *cooperation* from *cooperate* to *obey* or *comply* as in, "I expect you students to cooperate with me today." Conversations with individual students or small groups of students (three to five) can help to determine the extent to which students feel ownership of group goals and how that ownership might facilitate their learning and cooperation.

◆ LIMITED PROCESS DATA

One important limitation of research on cooperative learning is that there are few observational data that describe how students *actually interact* during groups and how these process dimensions are associated with student achievement and affective experience. A lack of process information for describing students' social abilities, perception, and affect is an especially important concern for teachers and researchers who are interested in student personal development as well as the quality of achievement outcomes. Theorists such as Noddings (1989) advocate that small groups might be potentially interesting and useful because they can help students to develop prosocial skills, increase their capacity for generating alternative approaches to problem solving, and generally grow in their ability to work with others. Our research suggests as well that small-group experiences teach students how to recognize and cope with social frustration and conflict and how to develop a certain "hardiness" that facilitates being one's own person as well as a peer. Consider the give and take of peer accountability and face saving illustrated in this exchange among third-grade students. This group consists of all boys:

S: You went over there and copied off of 'em.
S: No, I didn't.
S: Yes you did.
S: (Overlapping) Yes you did.
S: I just went to get tell Miss Smith something.
S: Wrong.
S: It it . . .
S: You looked on the paper.
S: Man, I didn't look on the paper!

S: Yes you did.
S: If he's gonna tell us what to do . . .
S: Did not.
S: Did too.
S: Did not. Did not do it. Did not. Did not.
S: Did too.
S: Did not.
S: Did too.
S: Did not.
S: Did too.
S: You did too look at the paper.
S: I know.
(Group returns to fraction problem.)

For some time, researchers have been encouraging more study of group processes in order to determine the extent to which the putative goals of small-group instruction are being obtained (Bossert, 1988–1989; Good & Biddle, 1988; Good, Mulryan, & McCaslin, 1992). Bossert (1988–1989) noted that research results are difficult to interpret because researchers have often failed to verify whether students have even engaged in cooperative interactions. When researchers have observed instructional processes, their results have not always supported theories of cooperative learning (e.g., in some instances, students in control groups cooperated as much as students in the experimental group). Thus, too often teachers are given overly optimistic accounts of the positive effects of small-group instruction and do not receive information about difficult and problematic effects of implementing and using this model.

◆ ADVANTAGES AND DISADVANTAGES

We suspect that the effects of small-group instruction vary according to the purpose for using the method and how well it is implemented. Simply increasing the amount of small-group instruction is unlikely to make the discussion *or* learning of a subject more meaningful. Good and Biddle (1988) and Battistich, Solomon, and Delucchi (1993) argue that small-group instruction is not a panacea but an attractive instructional format that, when properly implemented (e.g., careful organization, appropriate curriculum task), can enable students to achieve certain goals. These goals might include meaningful learning of subject matter of appropriate difficulty and interest, learning prosocial skills, developing alternative approaches to problem solving, exploring, conjecturing, generalizing, verbalizing mathematical ideas, and growing in social intelligence (Noddings, 1989).

As Good, McCaslin, and Reys (1992) and McCaslin and Good (1996) note, there are many reasons why cooperative groups *may enhance* students' achievement and social relations. The many desirable potential features of small-group learning include: 1) subject-matter knowledge is increased; 2) students value shared academic work; 3) students can regulate their own resources; 4) students learn to manage other resources; 5) students develop appropriate dispositions toward challenging work on shared tasks; 6) school tasks are similar to those outside school; 7) group members serve as models for one another; and 8) students develop an expanded understanding of self and others.

However, Good, McCaslin, and Reys (1992) also note that there are *possible negative outcomes* associated with small-group instruction, depending upon the quality of implementation and the type of curricular material selected. Some of the potential disadvantages are: 1) students' misconceptions are reinforced when they work with other students; 2) students shift dependency from teacher to peer; 3) students value the product more than the process; 4) students value group process more than the academic product; 5) students receive differential attention and status; 6) some students believe they are not able to contribute; 7) some students may learn that they do not need to contribute; and 8) group accountability may mediate failure-avoiding and success-enhancing behavior.

◆ STUDENT INVOLVEMENT

The problematic nature of small-group instruction as articulated by Good, McCaslin, and Reys (1992) has been illustrated by other researchers who find that some students do not flourish in small-group settings. For example, Mulryan (1989, 1992) studied students' behavior during small-group mathematics instruction. She found that students did exchange information when working in small groups, but the frequency of question asking was relatively low. Low achievers asked more questions and high achievers gave more information. Mulryan argued that helping roles that emerged in many small groups did not appear adaptive. Often the same students consistently played each "giving and receiving" role: I give, you receive (with gratitude). These dynamics appear to create a caste system that discourages the active involvement of at least some students. In addition to observational data, Mulryan noted that during interviews some students indicated that they perceived low achievers as a burden to the other members of the cooperative group.

Extending Good's (1981) passivity model, Mulryan identified six types of passive students: The unrecognized student; the discouraged student; the unmotivated student; the despondent student; the bored student; and the intellectual snob. (For more information about student types, see Mulryan [1992]). Mulryan's work illustrates that there are different *types* of student passivity that are not apparent by only observing student behavior. These distinctions in student motivation emerged from interviewing students in addition to observing them. Further, it may be that certain types of passivity are adaptive in certain contexts (e.g., it is someone else's turn to take the lead), whereas other types of passivity are dysfunctional (e.g., fears that one's contributions will be ridiculed). These types of motivational differences in seemingly apparent student behavior are especially important considerations for teachers who use small-group learning formats.

Other researchers also have observed problems in small-group interaction. King (1993) reported that small-group discussion and task initiation were dominated by high-achieving students. In general, only high-achieving students played leadership roles. King's case study indicated that even though low achievers were passive during group work, they reportedly enjoyed working in small groups (especially the social aspects) and looked forward to more opportunities for small-group work. In short, small-group learning experiences are not straightforward!

Good, McCaslin, and Reys (1992) have noted that students' affective reports of satisfaction with group work on questionnaires (or in delayed, retrospective interviews) may mask important problems in group functioning; and McCaslin et al. (1994) have demonstrated this point empirically. Thus, teachers who use small-group work as a method for engaging students in "problem-solving and higher-order thinking" or any other learning outcome, must monitor and inquire about group processes (the sooner, the better) if they are to assess the quality and utility of student interactions during group.

Teachers need to develop strategies for *monitoring* group processes (e.g., occasionally tape-recording a group, sitting in on a group) in order to assess the quality of group discussions that take place. Our data indicate that students often "perform" quite well for teacher observation, but that performance does not represent typical group interaction or accurately reflect group members' level of understanding. Indeed, tape transcribers of student "table talk" during small groups in our research (McCaslin, Sisk, & Thompson, in progress) can often predict a teacher comment; abrupt changes in student behavior from off-task or reactive interaction to on-task concern with learning and procedures, cue teacher proximity. Teacher monitoring is especially difficult in small groups, and teacher comments meant to keep students on task often not only miss their mark but also create confusion. Teacher "with-it-ness" (Kounin, 1970) is very difficult because teachers are literally "out-of-it"—out of the group process. Consider, for example, the inappropriateness and likely effect of what this teacher meant to be a supportive prompt on the students' (here, all girls) attempt to make—or at least believe—the task meaningful:

S: Bang.
S: I'm gonna, s,s,s, first, second, first . . .
S: You have to put first, second, first.
T: Uh huh, just circle them.
S: Thanks ma'am.
S: K–M . . .
    (Inaudible comment.)
    (High-pitched humming.)
S: We got it right (?)
    (Pause.)
S: Oh, I messed up somewhere.

(Clucking noises made with tongue.)

S: Jesus!
(Giggling.)
(Pause.)

S: You know why he want to tape players that sound like pots and pans whenever, it's on my tape player, it sounds like pots and pans. If you ever do that on a tape player. That's, that's on every tape player. You just make pots and pans.

S: Shhhh.

S: Yeah, what if we broke . . .

S: Shhhh.

S: . . . pots and pans.

S: . . . so we'll be grounded. What if you broke a pot and two pans and you broke them on accident?
Loud sigh.

S: . . . What would you have?

S: One whole thing . . .

S: (Overlapping) No you'd have two . . .

S: . . . No you'd have a weapon. No, you'd have a weapon.
(Giggling.)
(Pause.)
(Whispered comment.)

S: What!? You know where I'm comin' from.

S: You broke up a pot and pan. You would have, don't you have a whole one? And then you break it in two. And then you remember two.
You guys (Pause.)

S: What do we have to do to get a whole, whooolle . . .

S: (Overlapping) Have you guys done it yet?

S: . . . Whoolle piece.

S: I had a whole four of them.

S: (Simultaneously) Yes.

S: (Simultaneously) You guys.
Banging.

S: I hope we had whole four. (Smacking noises) We broke it in four pieces.

S: I wonder what that means.

S: I don't get this.

T: (At this point, teacher approaches group) Now you're, you're ready for page 2.

S: Ohhhh.
(Group moves to page 2.)

As this exchange illustrates, teachers may want to interview students about the preconceptions they bring to their small group—preconceptions about the concepts to be studied and how work will be evaluated. In-process interviews would help the teacher better intervene in student thinking and learning during small group. Further, if teachers are to understand student perceptions and motivation, they need to be willing to interview or hold conversations with students and to discuss interpretations of what is happening in small groups and why.

◆ EFFECTIVENESS VARIES WITH TASK

There are data to suggest that some tasks seem to be more useful for cooperative or small-group learning than are other tasks. Phelps and Damon (1989) present data to show that fourth-graders (of equal abilities) working in pairs could make more progress in understanding basic mathematics and spatial-reasoning concepts than students working alone. They studied 152 students over 2 years who were divided into four groups: two control groups (individuals) and two treatment groups (pairs learning mathematics and spatial reasoning). In assigning tasks, the investigators had students work in pairs solving problems or completing tasks that neither could do previously (hence, the tasks were reasonably difficult).

The results clearly indicated that the effectiveness of peer collaboration varied with the task. For example, the peer sessions had little impact on performance dealing with missing addends and multiplication sets. However, when working on tasks like ratio and proportion, the collaboration resulted in improved student performance. Very similar results were obtained in the spatial domain. For example, model-copying performance was not improved by peer collaboration, whereas collaboration improved performance on spatial-perspective problems.

Phelps and Damon conclude that peer collaboration is a good method for promoting conceptual development and for thinking about mathematics, but not for enhancing rote learning. They note in this research that tasks least effective for peer collaboration tended to involve formulas, procedures, and basic skills that can be presented and learned directly. In contrast, collaboration appears to facilitate learning of concepts that apparently are not as amenable to direct instruction (e.g., proportionality). Given that the *match* between student collaboration and type of task assigned is so important, it seems that teachers will need to gather process data in order to understand how to design (and redesign) new tasks. Conversations with students—where students have an extended opportunity to explain and demonstrate their thinking—would appear to be one promising way to enhance instructional decision making. This is especially important because most of the early research in small-group learning and most of the materials that have been developed for use in small groups have focused on basic facts and skills.

◆ NATURALISTIC STUDY OF WORK GROUPS

Observations of small groups in classrooms also illustrate the problematic nature of the effects of small-group instruction and reinforce what many educators have long contended: frequency and type of instructional method is notably less important than *quality* of method (Good, 1983).

Good, Reys, Grouws, and Mulryan (1989–1990) administered a survey to over 400 teachers that examined how often they reportedly used small, cooperative work groups. These investigators were interested in exploring what teachers and students actually did during work-group instruction. Through survey data, they identified teachers who reported using work groups more than once a week and for at least half of the mathematics period. An observational study was conducted with these teachers in the intermediate grades (3–5). The investigators noted considerable variation among teachers, in the sense that work groups appeared more effective in some classes than in others. For example, in many classrooms, students were more active learners and had more opportunities to: 1) interact with peers, 2) explore more interesting mathematics, and 3) become involved in more mathematical thinking. However, the study also indicated that the work-group lessons had some apparent disadvantages.

Inadequate Curriculum   The paucity of curriculum materials that were designed explicitly and appropriately for small-group instruction was perhaps the largest hinderance to the effective use of work groups that the investigators found. The lack of materials forced teachers to use or adapt textbooks or to develop their own lessons, as most problems in mathematics textbooks are designed for students who work alone. Although some teachers were adept at constructing appropriate materials, many used inappropriate materials. When that occurred, student learning was not very successful. For example, in these lessons, some students learned that other students were faster and smarter, and that their contributions were not really needed. (We will return to this topic later.)

Student Role Assignments   Although some in-service programs strongly recommend that students be assigned roles to fulfill in small groups, these researchers' observations indicated that this is a highly questionable practice. Designation of students as leaders, recorders, or material managers seemed artificial and futile in many cases (i.e., students fought over roles or ignored role assignments). Although this strategy might be useful for very young children or for students who are first learning how to function in cooperative groups, the functional value of role assignment seems to dissipate quickly with student experience.

Student Passivity   The positive climate that led to active learning and more peer interactions for some students did not improve the active learning of a notable subset of students. These students were content *not* to contribute to small-group work. If teachers did not address this problem (e.g., by calling on passive students to summarize group work for the entire class or by emphasizing diversity rather than speed of responding), some passive students were content to allow other students to do the work or simply could not fit in, even if they tried. Other students seized their opportunities without giving their more passive peers proper time and attention.

Lesson Structure and Accountability   Unfortunately, in many cases, Good et al. observed groups that were not held accountable for completing tasks. Nor did students have the opportunity to discuss what they learned with the teacher or students in other groups. Too many lessons ended abruptly without adequate time for students to summarize what they had learned. Not surprisingly, some students developed the attitude that what they were doing during small-group work was not important: they did not discuss it with others and they were not graded on it.

❖ COOPERATIVE-LEARNING GROUPS AS SOCIAL/INSTRUCTIONAL ENVIRONMENTS

Teachers design small groups and the tasks students are to engage in, but because of the inherent monitoring difficulties in this format, students play a large part in determining what the small-group experience will be for its members. Thus, when we think of small groups as social/instructional environments as described in Chapter 2, we need to think of the increased role that students have in the co-regulation of their own and peer learning. In Chapter 2 we described social/instructional environments and the functions of context. We explained that classrooms are "also places in which intentional and incidental instruction and learning about things that matter is pervasive. Students learn, for example, about tolerance for ambiguity, recognition and negotiation of conflict, personal and class pride and responsibility. Contexts, then, ever so subtly, continuously teach and socialize". Here we add that sometimes "teaching and socializing" is not the least bit subtle in small groups. The give and take of working with peers away from the continuous supervision of the teacher can get a little rough—rough enough to convince us that the skills important to small-group learning include knowing how to tease and how to not ask the "wrong" question. Consider, for example, how this student gets involved in his own set-up in a small group of boys:

S: Give it to me man, I want to write.
S: Fine.
S: Let Greg do it if he wants to do it.
S: (Overlapping) I'm not ashamed to be in his group.
      (Long pause.)
S: Come on Greg, get busy.
S: Duh. Go.
S: Shut up.
S: Get busy.
S: Busy. Shut up. I ain't the one saying shut up, so get busy.
S: Shut up.
S: I ain't the one who's saying shut up so get busy.
S: Shut up, man!

S: You want to know why you should never say shut up?

S: Why?

S: 'Cause that stands for you.
    (Pause.)

S: You're just making that up.

S: Okay, whatever, just hurry up. Go, go, go, go! Come on and join us. Come on Greg, go!

S: Yeah Greg.

S: Come on, go.

S: I've got to do it with you.
    (At this point the teacher approaches and intervenes. Her actions indicate she thinks the problem is that the students are not sitting close enough so that all can see materials.)

In short, learning in small groups is not for the faint-hearted. Students *learn* how to profit from them; teachers *learn* how to design them. If small-group learning formats are to function as educative opportunities and supportive social/instructional environments, they will require thoughtful design and deliberate mediation. It is easy to underestimate the social demands inherent in small-group settings, and students who experience little if any anxiety in large groups may experience extreme social anxiety in small-group learning situations. As educators became more interested in small groups and as they use more *performance* measures, teachers may have to become better at recognizing and responding to issues of social anxiety. (For an extended discussion of social anxiety, see Marshal, 1994.)

◆ DESIGNING APPROPRIATE CURRICULUM

Affording small-group social/instructional environments include mindful consideration of the objects (curriculum tasks and procedures), the persons (group members, other groups, and teacher), and their interrelationships. We begin with the objects of small-group instruction—the curriculum materials and goals to be shared by group members.

Curriculum Tasks   Based upon several studies examining small-group interaction (Good, Grouws, Mason, Slavings, & Cramer, 1990; Good, Reys, Grouws, & Mulryan, 1989–1990; and Mason & Good, 1993), we are convinced that one of the major problems in using small-group models successfully is inadequate curriculum materials. As we have noted, the paucity of curriculum materials designed explicitly for small groups is perhaps the greatest hinderance to their effective use. Most problems in mathematics textbooks are designed for students to work alone. When such work is presented as a group task, students usually want to work individually. Rather than consider students "uncooperative" in this situation, it seems more reasonable to examine students' prior learning habits and recognition of task requirements. At best, cooperation on tasks designed for individuals means "divide the assignment up"; typically it means "let the one who does it best do it"; at worst, it is "everyone for him/herself." Such materials actually encourage solitary work because students need only ask for assistance when they have a problem. Students have to learn to cooperate; tasks have to allow that learning (Rohrkemper, 1985).

Thus, teachers who implement small-group lessons with some degree of frequency will have to develop appropriate materials, or at least adapt existing materials that were designed for whole-class teaching or for individual learners. Teachers who build their own curriculum materials have long recognized the value of learning from students by talking to them about the materials and procedures (what was confusing?; how did your group first try to solve the problem?; how did you know what to do next?).

Criteria for Active Learning   Curriculum materials and tasks that promote problem-solving are one concern for a curriculum of active learning. A second concern is the design of small-group lessons that foster social mediation of problem solving. A third is the design of interviews with students that might scaffold their mediation of task and peers and inform the efficacy of teacher efforts. Here we present a few suggestions based upon our work (Good, McCaslin, & Reys, 1992; McCaslin, Sisk, & Thompson, in progress).

First, the problem-solving task should engage all group members. By *group engagement*, we do not mean learning mathematics or biology quickly or efficiently. Rather, we mean students' valuing mathematical, scientific, or writing *processes* (e.g., reasoning involved in solving a problem, the type of persuasion needed for a particular written communication) more than *products* (correct answers). Students' reasoning and responses should be coherent (e.g., internally consistent arguments, models that characterize the problem, etc.), but not necessarily optimal (the best or most efficient response). The purpose of small work groups for problem solving is to encourage thoughtful inquiry, understanding, and appropriate dispositions (e.g., willingness to work cooperatively with others) rather than efficiency in thought or expediency in personal exchange.

Small groups for the purpose of problem solving involve two levels of engagement. First, each student thinks about the problem in a meaningful way (tries to understand). Second, each student participates in *other* students' problem-solving thinking. That is, students listen to other students' ideas and attempt to understand them and to respond to them. Thus, a second dimension of a good work-group problem-solving task is that it should be sufficiently challenging to engage meaningfully collective group interaction on possible solution strategies.

We feel that teachers need to be clear about what they want to occur in small groups. If teachers can conceptualize their goals, then teachers can provide educative opportunities, intentionally model dispositions and strategies, and actively teach them within a supportive classroom SIE that both promotes and requires students to value those strategies and dispositions (Bandura, 1977, 1982; Good & Brophy, 1991).

Assessing Progress   Although teachers may use work groups for review and drill purposes (and most extant curriculum materials have been designed with this intent), we do not feel it is a particularly good use of the small-group format. If the goal is to tutor slower students, then dyadic pairs would appear better than groups of three to five students. Research by Webb (1982, 1989) suggests that one side effect of this use of small groups is the withdrawal of moderate-ability peers who have no role in this context; they are neither tutors or tutees. However, some would disagree and use small-group settings for review or tutorial work. No matter why you choose to use small groups—novelty, practice, tutorials, exploration of new ideas—it is important to be theoretically explicit about your rationale for using them. We (not surprisingly!) add that teachers would also benefit from interviewing students to assess the extent to which teacher goals have been realized. Teachers who are clear on their own goals for small groups (e.g., practice skills and work on turn taking) can better structure opportunities to coordinate and realize those goals. For example, our research (e.g., McCaslin et al., 1994) and work by Bennett and Dunn (1992) would suggest that restricting ability differences within two adjacent levels (e.g., relatively highs with moderates; moderates with lows) will better promote the realization and coordination of nontutorial and nonhierarchical status goals.

In addition, teachers might benefit from a script or picture of what good normative practice would look like (how students should handle conflict, confusion, dead ends, etc.). Too many teachers try to use small-group models without a clear sense of purpose or an articulate, theoretical view of the normative practice they want to influence. Although we have presented some of our thinking about the role of small-group learning that emphasizes group process, we have done so to encourage readers to become explicit about their intended purposes. Some educators would argue a more product-oriented approach than we have suggested here, and some would argue a context of work and accountability rather than one of learning and co-regulation.

◆ PERSONAL RELATIONSHIPS

We have argued that teachers' theory of small-group use informs the design of tasks and how students are to relate to them. Teachers' theory of small groups also informs the assignment of students and how they are to relate with one another, *independent* of the task and *in relation* to the task. For example, teachers must decide which students to place together and how long they should stay together (we will return later to each of these decisions). Our focus here is on the type of cooperation teachers want to affect. To repeat, students learn to cooperate. We have noted that tasks themselves can promote or inhibit that learning. So, too, can the type of cooperation (and level of trust) required.

As Good, McCaslin, and Reys (1992) note, there are multiple ways to conceptualize cooperative learning. Further, different models of cooperative learning may have notably different effects on students' language, form of participation, and type of cognitive engagement. Here we describe three cooperative (interpersonal) task structures based on the work of Bennett and Dunne (1992). Consider what it might be like to participate in each of the structures as you read. What type of cooperation, for example, requires the most trust among peers? Which cooperation structure seems the easiest to learn? The most difficult? Why? Which seems to expose students to the curriculum task the most? least? at what cost?

Independent Students in a Group Students work individually on identical tasks. Each student has his or her own materials and works on his or her own task. *Cooperation* means to seek and give help as needed.

Interdependent Students in a Group Students work individually on different tasks that, when completed, form one shared group outcome (this is often called the *jigsaw* method, after Aronson, Blaney, Stephan, Sikes, & Snapp, 1978). Each student works with material that is informative in its own right and that also informs the larger group project. *Cooperation* means to do one's best on one's part so that it meaningfully contributes to the whole.

Students as a Group Students work together on the same task for a shared outcome. Students share materials and help each other to produce a single product. *Cooperation* means to engage one's own and others' thinking, skills, and dispositions. (See Bennett & Dunne [1992] for more extensive discussion.)

Just as teachers must make decisions about how much structure they provide students, what content to emphasize, and how to proceed through the curriculum, teachers must also make decisions about the form and degree of complexity of cooperation that are required to engage the curriculum tasks. Such decisions require that teachers be aware of how students perform during small-group work and how they mediate their experience. We have seen that this is no easy task.

◆ RESEARCH TO BE DONE; QUESTIONS TO BE ASKED

Elsewhere (e.g., Good, McCaslin, & Reys, 1992) we have discussed several aspects of small-group learning that need more research attention if researchers are to be more effective in designing instructional tasks and assessing small-group learning. It is beyond the purpose of this chapter to explore in depth areas of needed research. However, it is productive to highlight three areas to illustrate some of the exciting issues that teachers may want to think more deeply about and involve their students in exploring. The three areas that we have chosen to discuss affect student mediation of small group learning experiences in terms of what the individual student "brings" to the (shared) setting: group composition, stability of group membership, and student perceptions. We consider each feature important to explore because, just as teachers co-regulate student mediation, students can co-regulate their peers' mediation—especially in small-group settings. We have noted that peer co-regulation in small group often occurs independent of the teacher. We begin with the two features of small-group SIE that teachers deliberately design and that directly scaffold student experience in critical ways.

Group Composition   The dynamics of a particular group (e.g., the degree to which the group works productively and cooperatively, conflicts are recognized and resolved) is determined, in part, by the mix of students within the group. We know from Webb's (1989) work, mentioned previously, that moderate achievers do less well when placed with high and low achievers in groups with a tutorial goal. It seems important to see if these difficulties are specific to that instructional goal or group composition. Do teachers need to be concerned about moderate achievers when tasks are more complex or students are engaged in different cooperative structures? Which kinds of cooperative group work does group composition especially affect? How can group composition best be determined? Will students with poor social skills benefit more in groups with some empathic and supportive students than in groups with more aggressive, task-oriented, and competitive peers? Is it useful to consider group composition in terms of compensatory relationships (e.g., types of motivation, relative ability) rather than simple range of abilities or other characteristics? What about student friendships? Clearly, these considerations are important if teachers are to understand the social/instructional environments in which they place students. We suggest that, in addition to observing (or tape-recording) students in these different interpersonal learning contexts, teachers interview students about their experiences. The following interview excerpt illustrates the kinds of questions teachers might want to ask students whom they worry are passive or not treated fairly in small groups (McCaslin, 1991).

Introduction:
It seems to me that two things happen in small groups: we learn about math and we learn about working and being with others. Sometimes more learning gets done in small groups, sometimes less. And sometimes students get along better than other times. You know? I want to ask you about getting along in small groups.

1. I've been wondering how you *like* working in small groups. I've noticed that students differ in how much they like to work with their classmates: some like it a lot, some would rather be by themselves, and some don't much care either way. How is it for you—which do you like better? (working alone or in a group?)

    How come? Why do you suppose that is?

    (Say more? Anything else? Hmm.)

Could you give me an example? (Is that unusual or the way it usually is?)

2. What was it like in your small group today? How did your *group* get along?

   Were there any put-downs? (If yes: can you give me an example?)

   Were people nice to each other? (If yes: can you give me an example?)

   Did some people seem to be more "into it" than others? (If yes: can you give me an example?) Why do you think that is?

3. How was it for *you* today in your small group?

   What did you like most about being with the others in your group?

   What did you not like very much?

   Anything else?

4. Think about a student you *like* to be with in small group (no names). What is it about them that you like?

   What do they *do*? Can you give me an example?

   Have you ever done this? (Example)

5. Think about students you'd rather *not* be with in your group (no names). What about them do you *not* like?

   What do they do? Can you give me an example?

   Have you ever done this? (Example)

6. How would you describe yourself in your group?

   What do you do?

   What kinds of things do you think to yourself, say to yourself, when you're in small groups?

   How do you feel?

   Do you think the others feel this way, too? If yes: How come? If no: Why not?

7. Do you sometimes worry about what other group members might think about what you say?

   If yes: Tell me about it.

   If no: Do you think others in your group ever feel that way?

8. What about mistakes? First, how do you feel when you make one?

   Is it different if it happens when the whole class is listening? How do the other students react?

   How about in your small group? How do the people in your small group react if someone makes a mistake?

9. Does it matter what kind of *work* we're doing in small group?

   If no: How come?

   If yes: What kind of work seems to be better in small groups? Why?

What kind doesn't seem to be good?

Why do you think that is?

How was it for today's lesson?

Wrap-up: Well, that's it for my questions. Is there anything we haven't talked about that you would like to talk about?

You've been a special help. I think I have a better sense of what it's like for students like you to work in small groups. Thanks. When you go back to your seat, I want you to start work on. . . .

Stability of Group Membership Another important decision that teachers make when using small groups concerns how long to keep a particular group together. Should it work together for one period? a week? a month? Is the decision better made on content coverage? a lesson? a unit? Surprisingly little research has been directed at the issue of stability, or duration, of group membership.

For various reasons, teachers might change group membership frequently. For example, if two students are truly difficult to interact with, a teacher may want to rotate these students in and out of various groups to minimize their interference in peer learning and quality of small-group experience and to keep all groups functioning more smoothly. As these remarks indicate, teachers may well decide that small groups are not for everyone. Some teachers we have worked with consider small-group participation a privilege, not a right. Students can lose the privilege; whether and how students regain the privilege varies.

Teachers may also want to change student groups frequently for reasons of variety and novelty—the chance to work with different students. This seems especially useful at the beginning of the year. However, teachers may want students to stay together because that is the way they learn how to engage one another as resources appropriately and attempt to really deal with other students as individuals—warts and all.

As with most challenging teaching decisions, there are advantages and disadvantages to having students work together in the same group for a relatively long time (seven or eight lessons, two weeks, in a row). Group stability allows students to become familiar with the work styles, competencies, and personal characteristics of other group members, and allows group norms for student behavior to develop. Group stability per se does not guarantee that students (or their parents) will value that learning, however, students who work in relatively permanent groups might be more likely to resolve differences than students in groups whose membership changes frequently and who can afford to ignore or succumb to conflict.

In contrast, changing group membership after one or two periods may occasionally benefit individual students by allowing them to meet and work with a wider range of students and also to avoid the negative consequences of personal conflicts and disagreements that could characterize more stable groups. Changing group memberships might also keep students from "unidi-mensionalizing" one another ("She can't spell." "He's not smart." "She is mean.")

Student Perceptions Student perceptions—including their estimates of their own qualities (e.g., ability, fairness, kindness) and those of peers—would seem to have a fundamental influence on their behavior during small-group instruction (consider the previous interview with passive students). Student perceptions are also influenced fundamentally by the configuration of group membership and the stability of that membership (e.g., McCaslin et al., 1994; Rohrkemper & Bershon, 1984). We have surprisingly few data to inform such questions as: "What expectations do students have for themselves and others?"; "Do some lower-achieving students expect to be less involved and less able to make a useful contribution to group activity than other students whom they perceive as more able?"; and "Do other, more altruistic students agree?"

We know even less about students' beliefs about and perceptions of "be-longingness" and its relation to conflict. "How do students perceive the cohesiveness of the group in which they work and the degree to which the group values them as coworkers?" Research by Mulryan (1989) indicated that low achievers, especially those attending remedial instruction outside regular classrooms, are frequently excluded from on-going group activity by the "in-group" members. The extent to which students are aware of their rejection and the value they place on it differently mediates their small-group experience and learning.

To repeat, small learning groups are designed by teachers and directly structure the social/instructional environments students will navigate—typically independent of teacher supervision. Small groups provide the opportunity for peers to co-regulate one another's mediation of experience. Small groups need to be mindfully constructed and deliberately assessed. Interviewing is one useful strategy for exploring student perceptions so that teachers can make better decisions and achieve their goals for small-group learning. One starting point might be to ask students what they believe *cooperation* means and what it looks like in their group. These questions, excerpted from a series of interviews designed to assess students' changing beliefs about cooperation with increased experience (some in stable groups, others in changing membership groups), might provide a useful model (McCaslin, 1990). The first interview excerpt targets student-generated beliefs; the second and third, student actual experiences.

Introduction: As I mentioned, I am interested in how students think about math and learning together in small groups. There are no right or wrong answers, I just want to know what *you* think.

1. What kinds of things do students do who are "good" cooperators?
2. How about you? What do you do when you cooperate?

Can you think of a time that you did *not* cooperate so well? What kinds of things did you do then? Why do you suppose that is?

Can you think of a time that you cooperated *really well*? What things did you do? Why do you think that happened?

Instructions: It's good to have time to talk again. This time, I would like you to think about the math activities that we have been doing in small work groups this last week. Can you remember working in small groups? Good, I want to ask you some questions about what it was like.

1. First of all, do you remember who was in your group(s)? (If yes: Who? If no: Why do you suppose that is?)

   If you could choose who was in your group, who would you choose? How come?

   If you could choose how long you stayed in your group—like, say, everyday for a whole week, a month, or just one day—what would be best *for you*?

2. Were there things about working in your small group that you liked? (If no: How come? If yes: What were they? [After each: Why did you like that? Do you think the other students in your group liked that, too?])

3. Were there things about working in the small group that you did *not* like? (If yes: What were they? [After each: Why didn't you like that? Do you think the others in your group didn't like that either?])

4. What kinds of things happened in your group(s) that were the *most* cooperative? Why do you think that happened? Do you think that will happen again?

5. What was the *least* cooperative thing to happen in your group(s)? Why do you think that happened? Do you think that will happen again?

Instructions: It's good to have time to talk again. This time, I would like you to think about the math activities that we have been doing in small work groups this week. Can you remember working in small groups? Good, I want to ask you some questions about what it was like.

1. First of all, do you remember who was in your group(s)? (If yes: Who? If no: Why do you suppose that is?)

2. Did anything happen in your group that helped you learn math better than if you were working all by yourself? (If yes: What? If no: Why do you suppose that is?)

3. Did anything happen in your group that made it harder to learn math than if you were working all by yourself? (If yes: What happened? If no: Has that ever happened?)

4. Do you remember saying anything to yourself while you were working in your small group? What were you thinking? Did that help?

5. Some students seem to work longer on their math if they work in a small group. Other students seem to stay with it longer if they are by themselves. What about you? What helps you work longer?

Not only are students' emotions, experiences, and perceptions of interpersonal relationships important, so are their perceptions about the subject matter. For example, how will students who perceive mathematics as primarily involving speed, drill, and practice react to work-group experiences that involve exploration and experimentation—false starts, restarts, and dead ends?

We hope that these three examples illustrate that questions about how to design constructive small-group experiences is an exciting area of inquiry. Teachers and researchers have much to learn. We suspect that students will play critical "informant" roles in this learning. Actually *using* small groups, and to what purpose, involves deliberate teacher decision making regarding goals (motivation), design strategies (enactment), and assessment of progress (evaluation). Teachers mediate classrooms just as students mediate them. Together, teacher and students co-regulate classroom social/instructional environments. We now provide extended examples of what this co-regulation can look like. First, we attend to small-group learning in project-based science from a curriculum goal perspective. Second, we illustrate small-group learning from the interpersonal process perspective.

❖ ACTIVE SMALL–GROUP LEARNING IN SCIENCE

As noted earlier, various professional groups are describing a new, normative image of teaching that emphasizes, among many factors, the need for students to work on cooperative problem-solving tasks and to have more opportunities to become involved in discourse about the subject matter they learn. Thus, learning how to use small groups appropriately is a fundamental task that many teachers face. How to create student groups, design new curriculum materials, and evaluate student learning in groups are just some of the questions that teachers must address if they are to help students become actively involved in group and project learning.

Investigators (Blumenfeld, et al., 1994; Krajcik, et al., 1994) working with teachers on project-based science, attempted to create "driving questions" as tasks (rather than specific projects or specific questions). The driving question helps to organize concepts and principles and, thus, drives activities in a general way. Their goal was to provide students the opportunity to pursue specific investigations and become involved in doing science in a realistic, reflective way. As students explore solutions to a particular question or issue, they have the opportunity to develop meaningful understanding of key scientific concepts. Krajcik et al. (1994) argue, as an example, that:

A question such as, What is the Ph of rain water in our city? allows students to explore concepts such as acids and bases, Ph, and concentration. The question also organizes activities around planning and carrying out investigations to measure the acidity of rain water and the effects acid rain has on living and nonliving things. A question such as, How do you light a structure? allows students to explore principles such as parallel and series circuits, voltage resistance, current, and power. Activities would be organized around students designing and building structures that they could light. Good questions or problems are: (a) *feasible* (students can design and perform investigations to answer the questions/problem), (b) *worthwhile* (contain rich science content, relate to what scientists really do, and can be broken down into smaller questions), (c) *contextualized* (related to the real world, important), and (d) *meaningful* (interesting and exciting to learners). (pp. 486–487, emphasis added)

The project-based science project allows students the opportunity to pursue solutions to real questions and, as they search and collect information (debating ideas, making predictions, gathering information), they reformulate the questions and develop new pathways for exploring the problem.

The products that students create are real artifacts that allow for examination and feedback (e.g., a written report, a videotape, a computer program, etc.). However, as we have noted, it is difficult to deal with the process unless the teacher develops some mechanism to understand how students are attempting to construct the artifacts, how they handle debates and conflict (when they are criticized or teased), etc. Thus, new models for engaging in scientific inquiry and dialogue, just like new models of cooperative problem solving in mathematics and social studies, provide a learning mechanism in which students will often be working on their own and with each other away from the teacher. Teachers who can develop interview and conversational strategies with students to explore their thinking will be in a better position to understand the social and cognitive learning that is occurring during project work.

It is clear that the design of driving questions and problem-solving lessons is an important first step in stimulating thoughtful student engagement (Blumenfeld, 1992). However, much can and does go wrong during group work. Researchers and teachers need to explore and better understand group processes.

❖ ACTIVE SMALL-GROUP LEARNING: INTERPERSONAL DYNAMICS

The literature is replete with specific examples to illustrate that students often become involved in side issues, plot against students who are not in the group, or are cruel to group members. However, many groups also *recover* from these forays. Our intent in these next examples is to shift the emphasis from how students get off task and on each other to how students get back on task and off each other.

Of course students can, on occasion, be unkind; some students more so than others. However, if students are to recover from and learn to resolve conflict, they need to experience conflict in the first place. Students learn to be hardy; negotiation of conflict is part of that learning. As you read the remainder of the chapter, valuable questions to ask might include When does group conflict lead to resolution versus escalation? What role might the task play? teacher? How might students learn better to anticipate patterns of social exchange?

◆ SECONDARY-SCHOOL EXAMPLES

We have provided numerous examples of elementary- and middle-school students in small groups. We now briefly turn to the high-school student. Much of research on cooperative-learning dynamics has occurred with younger students; however, difficulties high-school students have with this instructional format have been represented in the field for some time (e.g., DeVries, Muse, & Wells, 1971). The following hypothetical secondary examples will serve to illustrate the type of dialogue and issues that can occur in junior high and secondary school settings. As you read these examples, think about *if* you would respond, and if you would respond, *how* and *when* would you. We will return to these three brief cases at the end of the chapter.

Physics Class   Linda, Kathy, Paula, and María are members of a small, cooperative group who are working together on an assigned computer project in an advanced physics course. The students attend high school in an affluent suburb near Chicago. They are working with a peer team in Brooklyn at a science magnet high school, sharing data via a computer network.

Kathy (complaining loudly so that students in an adjoining group can overhear): I'm tired of working with this cheap computer. The computer I have at home is at least three times as good as this computer in terms of its speed and access capabilities.

Linda: I'm not sure that the speed of the computer will detract us from this assignment (laughing but annoyed). I'm sure that those *7 seconds* that we lose are going to cost us dearly!

Kathy (with contempt): Why are you always so negative and criticize everything that I say and do? You know that the real problem is that we don't have a good graphics package to make our project look good so we can get a good grade.

María (trying to smooth the friction and move the group forward): Our team in Brooklyn can handle that problem. They've got a great graphics package.

Linda, Paula, and María (in unison): Let's get busy on this project. It's really an interesting assignment. Our team in Brooklyn is counting on us.

Economics Class   Matt, Ricardo, June, and Leroy are 12th-grade students enrolled in an advanced-placement economics course. The four students have worked together on a group project dealing with homelessness in America from an economic perspective. They have met in a group for the past seven classes and are now putting the final touches on their report.

Matt (clearly emotional): I had no idea that so many of the homeless were little kids. This is horrible. I feel so guilty.

June (with finality): Matt, it's not you, it's society—the rich get richer.

Leroy (with considerable enthusiasm): Remember those figures we placed in Table 4 a week ago—our society now leads the world in income inequality. The top one percent of Americans have most of the money and lots of people have none.

Ricardo (pointedly notes): The demographic data we looked at several days ago showed all this, Matt. We *know* that more and more kids are living in poverty.

Matt (fighting back tears): This isn't just an assignment to me. I care about what's happening. I want to add a new section to our report. To hell with the economic consequences to society—I want to talk about what we can do for homeless children.

June (with some empathy, but clearly patronizing): Matt, that's not the assignment we agreed to do. We're finished.

Government Class   Julie Dorn, the ninth-grade government teacher, had her students brainstorm possible topics for cooperative projects. She emphasized that for their project, students should select a *topic* that was of interest to them, not a *classmate*. Ms. Dorn's appeal worked in this case because Juan, Gloria, Amos, and Helen chose the topic, "The Death Penalty," for their project, even though they barely knew one another. During these past 6 weeks, Ms. Dorn has used the first part of the class to lecture and the second part for each group to work on their project.

"The Death Penalty" group is behind. One week remains before final projects are due, and they still do not have a working copy of their paper. By this time, they had expected to be doing final edits, and, as Juan had said, "writing those special 'integrative' sentences that teachers like." Instead, they are bringing each of their sections together for the first time.

Gloria (glancing at Amos' one-paragraph report. In a rage, she rips it in half): You let us down. If I had known you were such a jerk, I would never have agreed to work on a group project with you.

Amos (red faced): You didn't even read my report. It's only a paragraph, but it's very good. It cites two recent Supreme Court cases.

Gloria (ignores him, loudly): You let us down.

She stares at Amos and accuses: Juan has done a great job describing the emotional and economic toil on the victim's family, Helen has provided some really interesting information on the extraordinary cost of taxpayers' monies in fighting endless appeals, and if I do say so myself, I've done a good job of documenting the cruelty of forced death.

Amos (looking out the window) responds: Well, I'm not sure I'm really against the death penalty.

(All three students glare.)

Juan (with exasperation): Now you tell us.

Amos (getting mad): The purpose of this report was to find out what we really believe. I've thought about this a lot, and I think that in some cases, the death penalty makes sense.

(The other three group members groan in unison).

Amos (with clear disdain in his voice): The idea is to develop and support your beliefs—not just to appear to be politically correct.

Juan (half standing): You don't get it, do you? Amos abruptly leaves the table.

Spanish Class   Tomás, Hank, Ted, and Marcello are four members of a cooperative group who have been assigned to write a new ending for a short story they have just finished reading in Spanish. The idea of the assignment is to come up with an ending that is different and creative but still plausible, given the general context of the story. It is to be written in Spanish.

(The group is beginning its deliberations.)

Marcello (to Hank): Where did you get those high-top black tennis shoes? They look like the Boston Celtics in the 1950s.

Hank (angrily): I worked hard to earn money to buy these shoes. Some of us don't have everything handed to us on a silver platter. I work at McDonald's for my money, and I don't have the money to pay three times the price of these shoes to get a shoe that you think looks better!

Marcello (extremely defensively): Hey, I wasn't trying to start a war.

Hank (defiantly): Back off, rich kid, or you'll be the first casualty—whether you want war or not!

◆ GROUP PROCESS DIMENSIONS

As we have noted earlier, when teachers consider what takes place in small groups, it is useful to have a frame of reference to think about—to scaffold—the meaning and value of group work for students' and teacher goals.

Students as Their Group   One frame of reference might be to describe how the group functions *as a group*. In Chapter 1, we discussed at length individual student mediation—motivation, enactment, and evaluation. It seems that the co-regulation framework is also a useful scaffold for understanding students as a group. For example, how does the group coordinate the goals of getting along, getting the work done, and meeting a standard of excellence? It seems that some opportunities and group compositions might allow their coordination more readily than others.

Pepitone (1985) reminds us that goal ownership might also facilitate coordination of group goals. Is the task goal one that the group itself set or negotiated with the teacher and/or one another? Or did the teacher impose the goal, allowing students only to decide how (or how fast) to pursue it? What *degree of commitment* do students have to the established goal? Are they genuinely interested in solving or completing the task, or are they simply engaged in "time on task"? Yet another lens that could be used in reflecting upon group functioning would be to consider the *group focus*. Is group attention proportionately greater on the academic task? on personal issues (e.g., what might self-handicapping, face-saving strategies look like in small groups)? on social issues (e.g., flirting, off-task discussion, etc.)?

There are many other ways to think about how the group functions. For example, it is possible to consider the *affective climate* of the group—to what extent is group talk enhancing (e.g., supportive compliments), hostile or demeaning (frequent criticism, oneupsmanship, etc.)? Are interpersonal relationships compatible (e.g., cooperative), independent, antagonistic (e.g., competitive)?

We have previously mentioned *division of labor*—how the group distributes the work load. Is the group generally egalitarian and collegial such that work tasks are shared equally, or at least proportionately (e.g., each according to her/his ability) or fairly (e.g., everyone gets to touch the stuff)? Or is the group marked by elitism and/or passivity where only some members do the work? Do some students dominate, whereas others lead? Is it the case that some "passive" students listen intently and actively try to construct the meaning of group process, whereas other passive students silently disengage and withdraw from the academic task?

In sum, describing a group *as a group* is important because it is a social/instructional environment in its own right, and because we hope students eventually can learn how to share resources—when it makes sense to do so—and to function effectively in a group setting. There are many good reasons and contexts in which we want an effective committee, group, or team. Thus, one way to think about a small group is how the group *qua group* functions: is there a shared goal? Is there cohesive and proactive exchange? Is there a reasonable division of labor? Does the group raise critical issues and function productively? Teachers, in some contexts, may be as concerned about group-level functioning as with the performance of individual students.

Individuals in Groups   Yet another lens for viewing group behavior is the performance of *individuals* in groups. This is the most typical way to view students—as individuals. However, as we have stressed throughout, we consider any distinction between group and individual in a complex social setting a relative one. Boundaries and tensions between an individual and a group context and among individuals within the group are not possible to draw with finality—that's what co-regulation and social/instructional environments are all about. For example, the experience of a generous student in a group marked by hostility and conflict likely differs from that of a generous student in a supportive, cohesive group. The specific contributions to that experience, however, are not easily identified. We know that in some groups students talk too much and too little, talk at appropriate and inappropriate times about appropriate and inappropriate things. We could go on, but our main points are these: 1) individual students in small groups are likely even more vulnerable (or receptive) to peer co-regulation than students in whole-class settings, and 2) student mediation is not apparent. Teachers will need to interview students if they are actively to scaffold student mediation of their experience even as they learn more about it. For example, some students may have difficulty coordinating goals in small group (a motivational difficulty) and following through on learning priorities (an enactment difficulty) (e.g., a group member's teasing is making it difficult to concentrate—face saving just preempted fractions). Students also may have may have difficulty engaging self-evaluation in such close proximity of peers (e.g., a student notes her individual progress but can't help also noticing that she is the first one who "gets it"—as do the other group members).

❖ SMALL GROUP LESSON: SOME EXAMPLES WITH COMMENTS

In our collaborative work with teachers (Good, McCaslin, & Reys, 1992) on the design and implementation of small-group mathematics lessons, we encouraged teachers to tape record lessons (their presentations and students' work in groups) to learn more about small-group processes. The brief descriptions of small-group interactions that follow are summaries from actual transcripts (we acknowledge the assistance of M. B. Llorens). In one study, students in 24 different classrooms during a 2-week period participated in three small-group cooperative lessons dealing with fractions.

The type of cooperation required of students varied so that, in one lesson, students used the independent students in a group model; in another lesson, they used the interdependent students in a group model; and in the third lesson, they used the students as a group model (the models, based on Bennett & Dunne [1992] were described earlier in the chapter). Students knew that the tapes of their small-group work would be heard by their teacher, as well as by university researchers who wanted to learn about what happens during small-group work. The students were told to act as natural as possible, and a tape recorder was placed in the middle of their work group. We term the type-scripts of their work group "table talk."

As you can imagine, some of the discussions that occurred in particular groups were very surprising (teachers did not predict the conflict or social concerns of students or groups), and some discussions were edifying and rewarding to teachers. As you read the examples that follow, think about your goals and expectations for small-group work. Think about what you think students should be doing in small groups and see how these examples fulfill your definition of student conversations during work-group assignments.

> *General description:* This mixed-gender group of four stays on task and works well together. Though Elisa is initially confused and uncomprehending, José helps to clarify Elisa's part of the task and leads Elisa to discover her own answers. Elisa is the first to contribute a response (which is correct) to the group task and continues to contribute heavily for the remainder of the lesson. José and Tom act to regulate the group by setting the pace of the task progress. At one point, the teacher interrupts and confuses the students by asking them to add the fractions for an unknown reason. They recover

from this and go on to complete the lesson—an accomplishment they relish.

Comment: A teacher listening to this tape recording of small-group dynamics would know that students are facilitating one another's needs, and that students are beginning to provide their own structure. Listening to the dynamics that preceded his/her visit to the small group might also help a teacher understand how the intended intervention was confusing to students, given where they were in the discussion. Under some circumstances, the teacher might want to return to the students the next day to get and give feedback. Even if it is too late to intervene with this particular group, this understanding may serve as a useful reminder to the teacher to be sure s/he understands where the students are (ask students to provide information and to elaborate on their understanding *and* their difficulty) before intervening in future situations.

General description: This group of three has a lone male, because the second boy is absent. The group stays fairly task focused, although they are distracted by discussion of their favorite pizzas and by designing them (which is part of the fraction lesson). June asserts that she would like to be the recorder, and even though Hank at first opposes this, she prevails. Lisa has a sore throat but actively plays the vocal role of "group monitor" throughout. Lisa thinks Hank is "the smart one" of the group. Hank agrees, but his stature is not obvious from his task contributions. The group is having some difficulty with their work. At one point, Hank calls on the teacher for help. Throughout, a class "helper" interacts with the group frequently but offers little—unless it is helpful to point out that June is doing some work on her own when the entire group is "supposed to be collaborating." Hank finally insists that the group is finished. Lisa protests that they are not; she prolongs the task briefly to "win."

Comment: In our experience, teachers implementing small-group instructional strategies often report that students spend a great deal of time arguing about who will play what role within the group. Frequent argument (or prolonged discussions about roles) indicates the need to discuss general principles with the class again if role assignments are to be: 1) used and 2) realized. Also, it is our experience that food and other concrete examples sometimes lead to disagreements and fights over the "correct image" (e.g., "Does the pizza have pepperoni? I hate pepperoni."). Clearly these distractors should be dealt with if the intended learning task is to be engaged! Another salient issue in this example is clarification of the "helper" role. This helper is playing an evaluative role, attending to group process, not group learning.

General description: This mixed-gender group of four is engaged primarily in interpersonal concerns, mostly relating to cross-gender attraction. They begin by arguing over whose supplies to use and which responsibility each will assume. They finally start working on the assignment after the teacher intervenes. Their primary focus is on decorating their pizzas, however, despite teacher reminders to move on. Bill adds an off-color comment to the off-task talk by speculating on other group members' sexual desires and liaisons. Kate joins in this somewhat; Tom and Sonya *seem* mostly to ignore it. However, Sonya then tells Kate to put her leg down because she is wearing a miniskirt. Later, all but Bill participate in putting down a group member's older brother. During what little lesson-focused discussion there is, the students regenerate the same wrong algorithm for adding fractions, but no one notices.

Comment: Cross-gender attraction imposes both positive and negative possibilities in the classroom. Teachers will have to think through their expectations and guidelines for dealing with such behavior. (See Chapter 5 for an example of helping a student discuss sexual harassment.) Clearly, these cross-gender issues differ by grade. (See Chapter 2 for general developmental considerations.) In addition to interpersonal issues that may have to be dealt with, the tape also reveals considerable off-task behavior and apparently little academic progress even though students are "decorating" their pizzas—part of the assigned task. We would not be surprised if group member perceptions were that "they did not get done" (i.e., ran out of time), rather than "they did not do it."

General description: This group of four with a lone girl is conflictual, although mostly task focused. Sam is aggressive and often rude to other group members. He congratulates himself and puts others down. Kevin also is aggressive; he challenges Sam, especially when he is sure of "being right." Tanya seems the most diligent group member and acts as the group monitor. She doesn't back down from the boys' dominance, although she frequently opts not to respond to them. Eric is mostly quiet throughout until near the end when he accuses Sam of "looking off of" his paper. No one backs Eric.

Comment: This vignette is difficult to react to without knowing more about what has happened in the group in previous encounters, or without knowing more about the students. Perhaps Sam is simply having a bad day and a general "Golden-Rule" reminder to the entire class is sufficient. If Sam consistently plays off and intimidates his peers, however, a more specific problem-solving interview and intervention may be warranted—either with Sam alone or with Kevin, too (see Chapter 3).

General description: This group of four with a lone girl is very task-focused and productive. Group members consider Iris the most knowledgeable, but everyone demonstrates a solid understanding of the concepts, particularly Ken. The lesson begins with Iris stating that she will, for once, do nothing and allow the others to do everything. This is *not* what happens. Indeed, Iris later states that she would be glad to do everything. The group proudly acknowledges their ability to work well together. They are polite and compliment each other. At one point, for example, Iris tells Chris that he writes beautifully. They are careful to take turns and include everyone in the task recording and question answering process. This proves to be somewhat frustrating to Matt. He thinks it's "boring" because "it takes a lot longer."

Comment: In general, this data would seem to suggest that the group is functioning quite well. However, if the teacher identifies a number of students like Matt in the classroom, it might be useful to make a few general comments in class. Recalling that it is a common error for students to equate "speed" with "smartness" and "learning," it might be useful to make a few general comments in class. Teachers may want to discuss (again) reasons why we talk about process, why alternate answers are important, and why during most group tasks we are not concerned about speed. Students *learn* the difference between timeliness and speed.

General description: This group of four has a lone girl. Sam and Kevin dominate the group interaction. The group is easily distracted from the assigned task. Eric tries to act as group monitor, to get the others back on task. His methods are fairly subtle, and he is generally quiet throughout. When Eric offers answers to assigned questions, they are generally wrong. The other group members accept them as correct except once, when Kevin questions an answer. Much of the group talk is off task and often involves sexual innuendo. The teacher interrupts the entire class several times as she tries to spur this group on.

Comment: We now have the opportunity to observe a previously described group a couple of days later. Given the continuing difficulty, the teacher might want to consider spending most of his/her time with this group during the next class period. That is, rather than interrupting the class several times to deal with this group, it might be more constructive simply to participate as a group member for an entire period. As a group member, the teacher could actively demonstrate and model adaptive group skills for the students to emulate *and practice*. At a minimum, the teacher needs to consider the difference between "spurring on," and "reigning in," and their juxtaposition.

General description: This is a model group of four with a lone female, who seems to be the highest ability member of the group. Group members work well together and stay on task. They do begin, however, with an extensive debate over who will write the name of the group members on the task sheet. Group members are not particularly concerned with speed; they want to understand the fraction concepts being explored. Joe makes the fewest task contributions and comments the least overall, but he remains invested in the group's progress and is attentive. He simply seems less competent in this area. At one point, when the teacher hurries the class, Veda objects, "Really, you're rushing us." When they do finish—which is before the other groups—they begin to work on extensions, at the teacher's suggestion. Veda summarizes her understanding of the nature of fractions. The teacher compliments the group on their collaboration, cooperation, and good learning.

Comment: Hearing this tape, a teacher might conclude that teaching is a very rewarding profession! When a small-group lesson "clicks," there is nothing quite like it. Some effective, productive, and authentic things happen.

General description: This group of four with a lone girl is unable collectively to engage the task. Tanya continually tries but fails to focus peer attention on the task questions. Eventually she pursues the worksheet on her own, with only occasional questions asked of the group. Tanya doesn't demonstrate any intense frustration: she seems to accept the group dynamics as normal, even though not what the teacher wants. Tanya expresses her concern that the teacher will hear group conversation on the tape. The teacher intervenes regularly to push and direct the group. At one point, the teacher gives them explicit, step-by-step instructions on how to proceed. As soon as she leaves, however, the group reverts to disruptive behavior. One student comments that the lesson is not graded.

Comment: The student comment that the lesson is not graded may suggest an underlying sense that is shared by other students in the class. That is, if students are not occasionally held accountable—either tested as a group or group products figured into individual grades, many students are likely to conclude that small-group work is simply "filler" time and that it is not important. Again, this is a group situation that suggests that the teacher's presence for an entire lesson or two would be useful in helping the students to develop proactive group skills and appropriate performance expectations.

General description: This group of three has a lone boy. The group members seem to work fairly well together and stay task focused. Most of their talk is about fractions. The teacher intervenes initially to correct their understanding of the assignment but does not interfere again, even when Bobby calls for her assistance. The group expresses a sense of completion at the end of the transcript.

Comment: Here, again, we see a situation in which a teacher might take considerable pride in his/her decision making. It is very difficult to judge when to intervene with a group, when it is not necessary, and when it may be counterproductive. Teachers need to support the development of *students'* capacity for identifying and solving their own problems. Here we see that the teacher's decision not to go back and help the group was a good one. They were able to rise to the occasion—learn from the lesson required by the opportunity.

General description: This group of three with a lone boy is task focused, some members are talkative and fairly productive. Joan is incessantly questioning Mary Beth about her answers. Mary Beth always responds that she does not know. Joan repeatedly asks the group whether they are done; no one responds. Mary Beth and Felipe suggest possible question answers. Felipe refers to the "dumb" chart the teacher had given them previously. At one point, the teacher states to another group that "this is an individual activity." The teacher seems to misunderstand the work-group structure. The group expresses a sense of completion.

Comment: Teachers who use multiple group formats (and we think they should) may, in the short run, confuse students unless they are very clear about the task structure under which students are expected to function. It might even be useful, after explaining the lesson activity, to once again remind students about which cooperative task structure they will be participating in before they begin group work. It may be necessary to review what *cooperation* means in this structure, why different models are important, and how each occurs in authentic adult work. At least, teachers need to be very clear about the task structure and about their assumptions of students' ability to engage in a particular task. Sometimes teachers can move too quickly, asking students to engage in more mature types of cooperation before they are able.

❖ PRACTICE EXAMPLES FOR ANALYSIS

As you read the following 10 descriptions, make notes about the kinds of interaction that appear to be represented in them. Identify why you believe as you do. We did not analyze these descriptions, because we want you to form your own impressions and complete your own analyses. As you read them, in addition to noting possible themes, also try to identify what types and sources of other information you might want about the group (e.g., the frequency of the particular pattern of behavior). In at least two of the cases, identify situations where you would want to interview one or more students in order to: 1) clarify student perceptions and 2) identify ways in which students might be more proactive and successful during small-group instruction. The co-regulation model of student mediation—motivation, enactment, and evaluation—may provide a useful heuristic to guide your questions. Consider how questions about group or "socially situated" work might differ from questions about individual work.

1. *General description:* This mixed-gender group of four is somewhat argumentative but generally good-natured. Members are intense and exasperated throughout. They spend a long time designing and arguing about their pizzas. Cindy says less than the other group members and tries to keep the group moving along. At one point, however, she loses her patience with John and decides to "do it" herself. Jennifer twice attempts to ask the teacher how to proceed. The second time she is stopped by John, who insists that group members are supposed to rely on one another and not on the teacher. John's reaction contrasts with his previous deference toward Jennifer. This group seems highly aware of the taping process and concerned that their teacher will hear their interactions. The teacher intervenes periodically throughout.

2. *General description:* This group of four with a lone boy is mostly task focused but not proficient with the fractional concepts being studied. Jim begins by contributing equally to the group interaction, although his statements are mostly critical or demanding of other group members. The teacher comments that Sue is not trying to contribute to the group work. However, Sue makes comments regularly to the group, even though Jim frequently criticizes her. Jim encourages the group to ask the teacher for help. He also accuses members of the group of cheating because they are copying off one another. By midlesson, Jim has become almost silent. Charlene and Heather talk the most, arguing actively about the problems and competing solutions. Neither has a strong grasp of the material—some of their ideas are completely incorrect—but each is struggling to understand. The group never seems to get a good start on the lesson. As the teacher ultimately points out, they have jumped to the questions without preparing their pizzas and have no concrete reference on which to base their answers.

3. *General description:* This group of three with a lone girl is loosely focused on the task. Andy never seems to take the task or his group members seriously. He mimics the teacher; he belittles Jeff's anxiety and his attempts to learn and seek help. Jeff insists, then begs, Andy to answer his questions; Jeff ignores Elisa, who by her comments seems much more knowledgeable and thoughtful about the assignment. This submission to Andy aggravates Elisa. When Jeff turns to the teacher for help, she redirects him to his group members. This increases Jeff's frustration. Elisa works on questions, showing considerable insight at first but becoming less confident

and thoughtful as the lesson goes on. The teacher intervenes occasionally, and near the end of the lesson, suggests to the class that they design and divide their pizzas *before* attempting their questions. This group points out that the example on the task sheet was not "done for you," as claimed.

4. *General description:* This mixed-gender group of four is task focused but unproductive. The lesson begins with Sarah deferring to Jay's leadership. Jay states, "I'm not the boss of this group, you know." Ginny remains fairly silent throughout the lesson, speaking only occasionally to offer an answer or to direct a fellow group member. Jay dominates the group; the teacher tries to subdue him repeatedly throughout the lesson. The teacher assumes he is taking over for the group; Jay denies it. The group eventually takes turns, presumably to suit the teacher's demands. It is never clear how the group members arrive at their answers despite the teacher's continual prompting to give reasons. The dispute over who is to do what (which involves the teacher) is ongoing.

5. *General description:* This mixed-gender group of five remains fairly task focused but seems to have difficulty understanding the task procedure. Other groups must also be confused, because the teacher stops the class at least twice to reexplain the procedure. She specifies at the beginning that each student must work on his/her unique section of the task *without* help from others within the group. They do this in silence. When they move on to the joint task, their progress is uneven and procedures unclear. Heather begins work asserting that "This is not hard." The teacher prompts the class regularly to explain the reasons for their answers.

6. *General description:* This mixed-gender group of four is task-focused. Shondre is a dynamic and effective group teacher. She explains concepts to group members and systematically controls their progress through the task. Shondre begins by directly engaging Mike in a specific task assignment and patiently explaining how to proceed. Mike seems to be a low-ability student, as indicated by the group's (especially Shondre's) treatment of him and the teacher's request that the group "help Mike." Mike allows himself to be totally dependent on Shondre, but he does occasionally risk a dissenting opinion or answer (although incorrect in one case). Lisa mimics Shondre's behavior—sometimes dominating Mike, reminding him to "pay attention." Hank says very little throughout, except in direct response to Shondre's questions. The lesson ends with the teacher reexplaining the task.

7. *General description:* This group of four with a lone boy spends most of its time negotiating task responsibilities. The discussion is mainly between Bryan, Pauline, and Ayanna, though they discuss Terry's role as well. The group does not make much progress on the task. The teacher refers group members back to their groups for clarification of the task.

8. *General description:* This mixed-gender group of four is task-focused and hostile. The interaction among themselves and with other groups is antagonistic. The background noise from other groups is loud. The teacher in-

tervenes to give the group specific guidance in how to initiate the task. The transcript of the group work is very short and reveals little about the students' individual contributions. Although each participates, no one seems particularly knowledgeable about the concepts being addressed. Lexa seems to take the lead as much as anyone. At one point, Terrance yells at another group to shut up. Burt is challenged by Darren and swears at him.

9. *General description:* This group of four is teacher-dependent and antagonistic. The group includes a lone girl, Tiffany, who is recognized as the most knowledgeable among the group members. She is not especially attentive; however, she didn't realize that each group member had a different task, despite the teacher's two comments to this effect. Tiffany occasionally tries to focus the group on the task and ends up doing most of the work, including the unique tasks of the other group members. Her first approach is wrong, but she corrects her answers once the teacher points out the mistake. (The teacher is heavily involved in their progress.) Michael is especially disruptive, trying to antagonize or amuse others. Sonny and Keith try at different times to prompt the group to work, but they are easily distracted.

10. *General description:* This mixed-gender group of three has difficulty progressing through the task. The teacher helps them begin. At one point India takes over as the leader, telling everyone specifically what to do—even once referring to them as "children." When anyone contradicts her, she tells them to shut up. India makes sure to tell the recorder that she is doing all the work. She does seem to have a clear idea of how to proceed but eventually gives up on the task before it is done. India asks the teacher if they are to be graded; she hopes not, because she feels they "don't understand." Group members are quick to put each other down but seem tolerant of this type of exchange. At times, each of them tries to draw the group to the task, but over all they seem unable to maintain task focus. They recognize that the "aren't doing too good." The teacher interrupts the group several times.

❖ SUMMARY

In this chapter, we have argued that contemporary interest in reforming the curriculum will most likely lead to more emphasis on small-group teaching and project work. Students working in small groups are difficult to monitor. Thus, it would seem that conversations and interviews with students are one important way to enhance students' and teachers' understanding of the learning—about subject matter, personal mediation, and interpersonal dynamics—that occurs in small groups.

Although we are generally positive about new curriculum influences (e.g., project-based science instruction, cooperative group learning in mathematics and other areas), we have noted that the research base supporting these in-structional methods is incomplete. There is considerable research to support cooperative methods and student learning of relatively simple concepts and skills. However, the research support for cooperative methods and higher-order thinking and problem solving is limited.

In this chapter, we have discussed the difficulties of implementing small-group instruction, and we have identified areas that need continued research and attention from the teacher if small-group learning is to meet teacher goals. In addition, we have provided numerous examples that illustrate how interview topics might emerge from the natural on-going processes that take place when students learn in small groups. We remind teachers that peers also co-regulate one another. Small groups are social/instructional environments that, although designed by the teacher, function largely independent of the teacher. Thus, in these contexts, student mediation of one another, the task, and "self in relation to others around the task" are important co-regulation dynamics to understand if students and teachers are to meet their goals.

Thus, although there are many areas of classroom life where interviews and conversations with students would be useful, it seems critical that they occur in connection with small-group work if student learning is to be: 1) real-ized and 2) understood.

❖ QUESTIONS AND SUGGESTED ACTIVITIES FOR CHAPTER 4

1. Select any 2 of the 10 unanalyzed vignettes and write out in detail your per-ceptions of strengths, weaknesses, and important areas where you need more data.

2. Select any 2 of the 10 unanalyzed vignettes and indicate situations where follow-up interviews would be useful. Explain why you believe that and then generate three or four critical questions that you would want to discuss with the students.

3. Reexamine the comments that the authors made following the initial 10 vignettes that were presented in the chapter. Do you disagree with some of the comments? Why?

4. As we have noted before, reading often generates new questions and concerns. Now, after reading this chapter, identify three or four new questions or issues that you would like to explore. How might you interview students to learn how they acquired certain structures within their group or how they ap-proached a problem? Can you identify one or two examples of instances that would call for interviews?

5. Whether a teacher is conducting an interpersonal process or a problem-solving interview, it is possible that under certain circumstances s/he might want to interview all three or four members of a small group at the same time. Would you think that this is generally advisable or generally undesirable?

What are the circumstances that might make individual or group interviews more or less appropriate?

6. As we can see in the physics-class example, Kathy's peers clearly reject her petulant and self-indulgent behavior. In addition to group dynamics, however, the example opens up some extremely important issues involving computers. How might teachers design tasks that involve computer use that keep students focused on the learning goals rather than distracted by relatively less-important qualities like rate and appearance? To what extent do teachers need to monitor students' participation in data banks or collaboration with students elsewhere to be sure that they are truly collaborating on the intended task?

7. Consider the three models of cooperation described in this chapter (independent students in a group, interdependent students in a group, and students as a group). Which model most appeals to you? Why? Is one model better for children of different ages? experience? abilities? Why?

8. We discussed possible advantages and disadvantages of keeping group membership stable. In general, what is your preference? How often would you change group membership? Why? Do you think secondary students would prefer to stay in a group for some time or change daily or weekly? Why do you believe this?

9. Assume you have a student who is very disruptive during small-group lessons but who is characteristically cooperative during large-group lessons. You have switched the student to three different groups, but independent of who the peers are, the student remains disruptive in all small-group situations. Assume you plan to hold a problem-solving discussion with the student. Develop an outline of the questions that you would ask during the interview.

10. Is there any necessary reason that *all* students should participate in all small-group work? Is it reasonable to allow students who dislike small-group work or who interfere with others' learning to often work alone? What are the advantages and disadvantages of such flexibility?

11. One of the students working on the project, "The Economic Consequences of Homelessness in America," becomes emotionally involved to the point of becoming personally upset over what he is learning. To what extent should teachers intervene in the affective experiences of students to help them better understand their own emotions? Does this exceed the teacher/student role? To what extent should teachers avoid assigning materials that may be affectively charged?

12. In the death-penalty group project, three students are pressuring Amos to take their position. What kinds of group projects require consensus? How might teachers structure some group assignments so that students can have their own voice and still participate cooperatively within the project? How might minority opinions (in the sense of the Supreme Court) function in cooperative group projects? More broadly, how can teachers assure that students are able to cooperate freely within small groups without coercion?

❖ REFERENCES

Aronson, E., Blaney, N., Stephan, C., Sikes, J., & Snapp, M. (1978). *The jigsaw classroom*. Beverly Hills, CA: Sage.

Bandura, A. (1977). *Social learning theory*. Englewood Cliffs, NJ: Prentice Hall.

Bandura, A. (1982). Self-efficacy mechanism in human agency. *American Psychologist, 37*, 122–147.

Battistich, V., Solomon, D., & Delucchi, K. (1993). Interaction processes and student outcomes in cooperative learning groups. *Elementary School Journal, 94*, 19–32.

Bennett, N., & Dunne, E. (1992). *Managing small groups*. New York: Simon & Schuster.

Blumenfeld, P. (1992). The task and the teacher: Enhancing student thoughtfulness in science. In J. Brophy (Ed.), *Advances in research on teaching* (vol. 3, pp. 81–114). Greenwich, CT: JAI Press.

Blumenfeld, P., Krajcik, J., Marx, R., & Soloway, E. (1994). Lesson learned: How collaboration helped middle-grade science teachers learn project-based instruction. *Elementary School Journal, 94*, 539–551.

Bossert, S. (1988–1989). Cooperative activities in the classroom. In E. Rothkopf (Ed.), *Review of research in education* (vol. 15, pp. 225–250). Washington, DC: American Educational Research Association.

Cohen, D., McLaughlin, M., & Talbert, J. (Eds.). (1993). *Teaching for understanding: Challenges for policy and practice*. San Francisco: Jossey-Bass.

Cohen, E. (1986). *Designing group work: Strategies for the heterogenous classroom*. New York: Teachers College Press.

Davidson, N. (1985). Small-group learning in teaching of mathematics: A selective review of the literature. In R. Slavin, S. Sharan, S. Kagan, R. Lazarowitz, C. Webb, & R. Schmuck (Eds.), *Learning to cooperate, cooperating to learn* (pp. 211–230). New York: Plenum.

Deutsch, M. (1949). A theory of competition and cooperation. *Human Relations, 2*, 129–151.

DeVries, D., Muse, D., & Wells, E. (1971, December). *The effects on students working in cooperative groups: An exloratory study* (Report No. 120). Baltimore, MD: Johns Hopkins University, Center for Social Organization of Schools.

Fenemma, E., Carpenter, T., & Peterson, P. (1989). Learning mathematics with understanding. In J. Brophy (Ed.), *Advances in research on teaching: Vol. 1. Teaching for meaningful understanding in self-regulated learning*. Greenwich, CT: JAI Press.

Good, T. (1981). Teacher expectations and student perceptions: A decade of research. *Educational Leadership, 38*, 415–423.

Good, T. (1983). Classroom research: A decade of progress. *Educational Psychologist, 18*, 127–144.

Good, T., & Biddle, B. (1988). Research and the improvement of mathematics instruction: The need for observational resources. In D. Grouws & T. Cooney (Eds.), *Perspectives on research on effective mathematics teaching* (pp. 114–142). Hillsdale, NJ: Erlbaum.

Good, T., & Brophy, J. (1991). *Looking in classrooms* (5th ed.). New York: HarperCollins.

Good, T., & Brophy, J. (1994). *Looking in classrooms* (6th ed.). New York: HarperCollins.

Good, T., & Brophy, J. (1995). *Contemporary Educational Psychology*. White Plains, NY: Longman.

Good, T., Grouws, D., & Ebmeier, H. (1983). *Active mathematics teaching*. White Plains, NY: Longman.

Good, T., Grouws, D., Mason, D., Slavin, R., & Cramer, K. (1990). An observational study of small-group mathematics instruction in elementary schools. *American Educational Research Journal, 27*, 755–782.

Good, T., McCaslin, M., & Reys, B. (1992). Investigating work groups to promote problem solving in mathematics. In J. Brophy (Ed.), *Advances in research on teaching* (vol. 3, pp. 115–160). Greenwich, CT: JAI Press.

Good, T., Mulryan, C., & McCaslin, M. (1992). Grouping for instruction in mathematics: A call for programmatic research on small-group process. In D. Grouws (Ed.), *Handbook of research on mathematics teaching and learning* (pp. 165–196). New York: MacMillan.

Good, T., Reys, B., Grouws, D., & Mulryan, C. (1989–1990). Using work groups in mathematics instruction. *Educational Leadership, 47*, 56–62.

Johnson, D., Johnson, R., & Maruyama, G. (1983). Interdependence and interpersonal attraction among heterogeneous and homogeneous individuals: A theoretical formulation and a meta-analysis of the research. *Review of Educational Research, 53*, 5–54.

King, L. (1993). High and low achievers' perceptions and cooperative learning in two small groups. *Elementary School Journal, 93*, 399–416.

Kounin, J. (1970). *Discipline and group management in classrooms*. New York: Holt, Rinehart, & Winston.

Krajcik, J., Blumenfeld, P., Marx, R., & Soloway, E. (1994). A collaborative model for helping middle-grade science teachers learn project-based instruction. *Elementary School Journal, 94*, 483–497.

Marshall, J. (1994). *Social phobia*. New York: Basic Books.

Mason, D., & Good, T. (1993). Effects of two-group and whole-class teaching on regrouped elementary students' mathematics achievement. *American Educational Research Journal, 30*(2), 328–360.

McCaslin, M. (1990). *Understanding math and cooperation interviews*. Unpublished manuscript, University of Missouri at Columbia.

McCaslin, M., (1991). *Passive student interview*. Unpublished manuscript, University of Missouri at Columbia.

McCaslin, M., & Good, T. (1992). Compliant cognition: The misalliance of management and instruction goals in current school reform. *Educational Researcher, 21*, 4–17.

McCaslin, M., & Good, T. (1996). The informal curriculum. In D. Berliner and R. Calfee (Eds.), *The handbook of educational psychology*. New York: MacMillan.

McCaslin, M., Sisk, L., & Thompson, E. (manuscript under review). *Learning with friends, learning to be friends: The dynamics of friendship in small-group learning*.

McCaslin, M., Tuck, D., Wiard, A., Brown, B., LaPage, J., & Pyle, J. (1994). Gender composition and small-group learning in fourth-grade mathematics. *Elementary School Journal, 94*, 467–482.

Mulryan, C. (1989). *A study of intermediate-grade students' involvement and participation in cooperative small groups in mathematics*. Unpublished doctoral dissertation, University of Missouri at Columbia.

Mulyran, C. (1992). Student passivity during cooperative small groups in mathematics. *Journal of Educational Research, 85*, 261–273.

Newmann, F. (Ed.). (1992). *Student engagement and achievement in American secondary schools*. New York: Teachers College Press.

Noddings, N. (1989). Theoretical and practical concerns about small groups in mathematics. *Elementary School Journal, 89*, 607–624.

Pepitone, E. (1985). Children in cooperation and competition: Antecedents and consequences of self-orientation. In R. Slavin, S. Sharan, S. Kagan, R. Lazarowitz, C. Webb, & R. Schmuck (Eds.), *Learning to cooperate, cooperating to learn* (pp. 17–67). New York: Plenum.

Phelps, E., & Damon, W. (1989). Problem solving with equals: Peer collaboration as a context for learning mathematics and spatial concepts. *Journal of Educational Psychology, 81*, 639–646.

Rohrkemper, M. (1985). Individual differences in students' perceptions of routine classroom events. *Journal of Educational Psychology, 77*, 29–44.

Rohrkemper, M., & Bershon, B. (1984). The quality of student task engagement: Elementary school students' reports of the causes and effects of problem difficulty. *Elementary School Journal, 85*, 127–147.

Slavin, R. (1990). *Cooperative learning: Theory, research, and practice*. Englewood Cliffs, NJ: Prentice Hall.

Slavin, R., Sharan, S., Kagan, S., Lazarowitz, R., Webb, C., & Schmuck, R. (Eds). (1985). *Learning to cooperate, cooperating to learn*. New York: Plenum.

Stipek, D. (1986). Children's motivation to learn. In T. Tomlinson & H. Walberg (Eds.), *Academic work and educational excellence* (pp. 197–221). Berkeley, CA: McCutchan.

Webb, N. (1982). Student interaction and learning in small groups. *Review of Educational Research, 52*, 421–445.

Webb, N. (1989). Peer interaction and learning in small groups. *International Journal of Educational Research, 13*, 21–29.

ETHICAL CONSIDERATIONS

As we write this book, it seems that American schools are asked to play an increasingly important role in the lives of children and adolescents. For some time, educators have lamented that American teachers are asked to do too much with too few funds (Good, Biddle, & Brophy, 1975; McCaslin & Good, 1992; Shavelson & Berliner, 1988). Concerns about the competitiveness of the American school (e.g., Is the quality of subject matter learning—test score performance—sufficiently high?) are long standing, but society now also expects the school to address fundamental personal issues (e.g., student personal and social responsibility) that once were the primary responsibility of the community and the family.

For example, we recently read an editorial that appeared in the Chicago *Tribune* (reprinted in the *Arizona Daily Star*, December 27, 1993): "Ending violence in the schools is not a matter of discovering effective methods, 'replicating' them nationally and watching the index of incidence go down. It requires something much more difficult: nurturing our children to civility."

We agree that teachers must address pressing issues that confront American youth—the type of issues that are more pervasive and serious (even deadly) than failure to complete homework. Indeed, this book has advocated actively that teachers must enter the interpersonal world of students. Only by understanding students' social lives in the school can teachers help students to merge their affective and intellectual lives. Increasingly, educational researchers have realized that students mediate instruction and that student mediation of instruction (e.g., perception of teachers' intentions, the value of assigned work, etc.) influences student learning in the classroom (Ames, 1992; Good, 1983; McCaslin & Murdock, 1991; Rohrkemper, 1981; Rohrkemper & Corno, 1988; Schunk & Meece, 1992).

We argue that classroom opportunities need to influence student mediation and learning beyond the classroom as well. If students are to cope in a complex world, they must be able to merge cognitive and affective problem-solving dimensions so that their talents do not develop independent of their values. Throughout this book we have identified the integration of the affective and intellectual in student mediation as interdependent processes of motivation, enactment, and evaluation. We have located student mediation in the context of teacher supportive scaffolding and provision of opportunities in what we term teacher-student "co-regulated learning."

We realize that arguments for increasing teachers' interest in the affective lives of students adds new demands to teachers whose role is already difficult and complex. In time, we hope that citizens and government will fund education more generously (to provide for smaller classes and perhaps more school counselors). However, students are more than simply learners, and they need adult mentors who can help them to integrate their affective and intellectual lives within and beyond the classroom.

❖ DEALING WITH STUDENT CONFIDENTIALITY: GENERAL GUIDELINES

Earlier in the book, we provided our rationale for dealing with the affective and social concerns of students, and we have noted that other educators also call for more interest in the affective and social aspects of students' lives in school (Martin, 1992; Noddings, 1992). Further, we have provided specific arguments about the benefits of entering into conversations for purposes of listening to students, and we have discussed various strategies to both increase communication and actively structure—co-regulate—student mediation.

If teachers actively listen to students and make more systematic efforts to obtain students' perspectives (e.g., by conducting private conversations and discussion groups, tape recording students during small-group lessons, etc.), teachers—whether intended or not—will gain access to the students' private world and personal information. Making distinctions about what information should remain confidential and what information should be communicated to others (something a parent should know or something that by law must be reported to a state agency, as in the case of abuse) is often a difficult decision. The purpose of this chapter is to help the classroom teacher recognize potential ethical considerations inherent in knowing students as more than learners of the curriculum and to develop ways to reflect on and deal with such issues in a thoughtful manner.

As we have noted earlier, from our normative and philosophical view, the teacher's primary responsibility and relationship is with the student. Thus, we focus in this chapter on fulfilling ethical responsibilities to students. Although teachers must be responsible to others, including parents and obviously state and local laws, the frame of reference here is on the responsibilities of the teacher-student relationship.

Other support personnel in schools—for example, school psychologists—define their primary responsibility differently. We have appended excerpts from the National Association of School Psychologists (NASP) ethical guidelines (see Appendix A). These guidelines name the student and the parent(s) as the school psychologist's primary concern; NASP guidelines do *not* refer to the classroom teacher. Teachers need to be aware of the ethical requirements of those from whom they may seek help in supporting a student. The school psychologist becomes the advocate of the student and parent(s)—not the teacher—once a student is referred.

All teachers need to know how to *handle* student information, no matter how oriented they are toward understanding students' affective perspectives. In organizing the information in this chapter, we begin with issues that concern *all* teachers. First, we consider teachers' desired role and the context in which they hold discussions with students. Second, we suggest that ways of dealing with student confidentiality vary from school to school and we stress the need for teachers to understand their school culture. Third, we emphasize that legal issues also serve as a fundamental and major influence on teachers' role responsibilities—at least in certain areas. After presenting general guidelines relevant to all teachers, we turn to topics that are important for those teachers who choose to play a more deliberate and active role in students' school lives. Among the various topics addressed are protecting student privacy, individual differences in students, and ways of increasing schoolwide awareness of ethical issues involving student rights.

◆ ROLE CLARITY

In most circumstances, teachers are employed to further the academic and social development of students in school settings. They are not expected to deal with students' deeply rooted emotional problems or to serve as therapists for family problems. Further, teachers usually do not have extensive training as school counselors, school psychologists, or as clinical interviewers. Accordingly, we believe that teachers' conversations with students should be relatively specific and tied to authentic themes that emerge in the classroom (achievement progress, relationships with peers). The focus of conversation is primarily to help the teacher understand and influence how a student perceives, values, and responds to the academic and social aspects of a classroom. However, the boundary between social relationships in school and out of school is often blurred. Further, as noted at the start of this chapter, society often implicitly (and explicitly at times) asks teachers to play roles in educating youth other than that of instructional leader of "routine" subject matter or "typical" students (e.g., teachers are asked to engage in AIDS instruction, to value and respond to diversity so that mainstreamed children feel comfortable, etc.).

Even when teachers confine themselves to relatively formal communication roles, students will still provide private knowledge that teachers may feel compelled to act upon. Thus, *all* teachers (even teachers who strive to minimize private contact with students) will have unintended exposure to private student feelings and information. Thus, we encourage all teachers to communicate to students early in the semester exactly the type of information that the teacher cannot keep confidential. Such proactive communication will enhance student trust and reduce potential threats to the teacher-student relationship.

The teacher's role is to be a professional who acts in the students' best educational interest and an adult with whom children and adolescents can share sensitive information (e.g., the student's enormous fright in making a public presentation; a student's inability to deal with teasing; a student's concerns about obesity, etc.), with the reasonable expectation that such information will remain private and confidential. We have appended excerpts from the ethical guidelines toward students and teacher bill of rights adopted by the National Educational Association (NEA) to provide another overview of basic teacher role responsibilities and rights with students (see Appendix B).

◆ CLASSROOM FOCUS

As an orienting principle for ethical conduct, we believe that teachers' initial motivation should be to ask students questions that are intended only to understand their affective and academic lives *in* school. However, teachers cannot look the other way; when they possess important information about students' lives *out* of school (e.g., abuse), teachers must respond appropriately. Our point here is that the teacher is not a detective *looking* for threatening or actual misbehavior, but teachers should respond if students *initiate* conversations that involve home, intensive feelings about peers, and/or criminal issues.

The bandwidth of potential teacher responses, however, is large, encompassing a wide range of actions, including:

Engaging in more conversation with the student about the issue.

Indicating that this is a topic the teacher would prefer not to discuss with the student.

Referring the student to a school counselor, psychologist, or other specialist for more specialized discussion/conversation.

Typically, teachers would proactively involve *individual* students in discussing school-related issues: classroom, playground, hallways, bathrooms, school parking lot, school-sponsored activities, etc. A teacher might also proactively involve the *class* in discussing issues that impinge on their lives as a group: drug abuse, gangs, AIDS, etc.—where the intent is to provide prospective and appropriate structures for understanding these issues rather than discussing individual behavior.

◆ SHARED COLLEGIAL EXPECTATIONS

Teachers, at a minimum, must understand how privileged communication is defined and treated in the school, the school district, and the community. For example, if a teacher visits another classroom for the purpose of exchanging ideas, s/he should know whether that information is private or whether the principal can, at some later date, use teacher observation and discussion—independent of either participant's wishes—to support a nontenure or merit-ladder decision. School-home norms are also open to different definitions. If a parent requests that a teacher provide him/her with all essays that his/her child has written in class that year (e.g., the parent may want to see if the child is writing about an acrimonious divorce that the family is undergoing, or perhaps simply to see if the teacher has appropriate standards for grading grammar), what will the principal do or suggest regarding such requests? Will the principal support teacher decision making?

For the most part, legal distinctions have not been made concerning who owns, in a final sense, work done in school. Certainly even less is known about who owns conversations that occur in school (e.g., should a student's apparent or reported unhappiness in school be communicated to parents, guardians, fellow teachers, or school counselors?). Thus, we recommend that teachers explore within their school the informal and formal understandings about privileged information (i.e., the school culture) and be sure that principals are specific about what informational rights teachers, parents, and students have. Since teachers' rights to keep information confidential are not protected by strong professional and specific norms, it is important to identify local norms and make such expectations clear *before* issues of communication/confidentiality occur. Possessing such information, teachers can communicate to students even more clearly their professional and personal role.

◆ LEGAL REPORTING REQUIREMENTS

Teachers must also explore local, state, and federal laws that mandate the reporting of certain information. Laws in some states are quite explicit about information that must be reported. Thus, by law, confidentiality must be broken in certain instances, such as when a teacher becomes aware of or has a strong suspicion of child abuse or neglect (we will return to this issue). Further, schools often have explicit rules about what students cannot bring to school (e.g., weapons, bandannas, skateboards), and teachers' failure to report such violations can result in very strong sanctions (for teachers and students).

Teachers will, on occasion, hear information that they must report. If they are aware of reporting requirements, teachers can enhance their ethical role by proactively informing students that some information cannot be kept confidential. Making students aware of the extent to which information can be held confidential is an important step to take before engaging students in private conversations. Moral and legal judgments are involved in reporting issues, and on occasion, such considerations produce notable tension (e.g., can reporting abuse exacerbate it?).

Teachers who understand local norms and laws concerning the confidentiality of information and who make students aware of the limits of privileged information in the classroom will be in a good position to handle most "informational" issues professionally.

◆ ABUSE OF CHILDREN AND ADOLESCENTS

Parkay and Stanford (1992) estimate that roughly 2 million school-aged students suffer from neglect or abuse each year, and this likely is a conservative estimate. Most states have laws that require teachers to report suspected cases of child abuse to the state's Child Protective Service. What constitutes abuse is sometimes difficult to define or to determine. However, as Weinstein and Mignano (1993) note, "states generally include nonaccidental injury, neglect, sexual abuse, and emotional maltreatment" as indicative of child abuse (p. 263).

According to Arizona law (A.R.S. 13–3620), child *abuse* involves any injury including but not limited to bruising, bleeding, burns, fractures, injuries to any internal organ, failure to thrive, malnutrition, or any physical condition which imperils a child's health or welfare. *Neglect* is an act which constitutes a clear and present danger to the child's health, welfare, and safety. In

Arizona, these broad definitions are operationalized further. For example, *child abuse* is identified in three categories—it includes acts of commission (physical abuse, sexual abuse) and acts of omission (neglect). *Physical abuse* is defined as an act which results in 1) physical injury, or 2) emotional trauma, or 3) places the child in imminent danger. *Sexual abuse* is defined as sexual contact with or exploitation of the child, including fondling and/or intercourse. *Neglect* is defined as failure to provide for the basic physical, medical, and/or emotional needs of the child.

In Arizona, *acts of omission include failure to help an abused child*. Indeed, failure to report a suspicion of child abuse in Arizona is a Class 2 misdemeanor, and the maximum penalty for the first offense is 4 months imprisonment or a $750 fine. Citizens who, in good faith, report possible child abuse to Child Protective Services are protected from civil and criminal liability.

The figures on child abuse are alarming, and as noted above, may vastly underestimate the amount of child abuse and neglect that occurs in the United States. Further, they fail to describe the severity or duration of specific instances. As we work to resolve this shared community problem, it is clear that teachers and other responsible persons who work with children (e.g., doctors, ministers, nurses, psychologists) must be willing to respond to acts of abuse.

As Weinstein and Mignano (1993) advocate, it is essential for teachers to recognize signs of abuse and to report the strong suspicion of abuse when appropriate. They note that in most states absolute proof is not required, and teacher action early in the process may stop the problem before it escalates and causes additional harm. Thus, teachers must be able to recognize some of the signs of abuse; on the next page we outline some of the salient indicators that state agencies have noted.

We caution all teachers to *minimize* direct and close-ended questions with the student (see Chapter 3 to review types of questions). Recall that questions about an event can be confused with the experience of that event. Thus, to maintain the integrity of student memory, a teacher should refer any student with whom he/she has initial discussion of alleged abuse to the designated school authority. The goal is to protect the student, and admissibility of student report in court may be key to that safety. Further, teachers need to be able to maintain their relationship with the student. Students should be assured that their teacher will not be "in trouble" for listening and getting them help; nor will the student be "in trouble" for telling or being the victim of abuse.

❖ GUIDELINES FOR TAKING A MORE ACTIVE ROLE IN LISTENING TO STUDENTS

We have discussed issues that all teachers must address in respecting the rights of students in the broader community. We now turn to a discussion of

PHYSICAL AND BEHAVIORAL INDICATORS OF ABUSE AND NEGLECT

Type of Abuse or Neglect	Physical Indicator	Behavioral Indicators
Sexual abuse	• Somatic complaints, including pain and irritation of the genitals • Sexually transmitted disease • Pregnancy in young adolescents • Frequent unexplained sore throats, yeast or urinary infections	• Excessive masturbation in young children • Sexual knowledge or behavior beyond that expected for the child's development level • Depression, suicidal gestures • Chronic running away • Frequent psychosomatic complaints, such as headaches, backaches, stomach aches	• Drug or alcohol abuse • Avoidance of undressing or wearing extra layers of clothes • Sudden avoidance of certain familiar adults or places • Decline in school performance
Emotional abuse	• Eating disorders • Sleep disturbances, nightmares • Speech disorders, stuttering • Failure to thrive • Developmental lags • Asthma, severe allergies, or ulcers	• Habit disorders such as biting, rocking, head-banging, thumb-sucking in an older child • Poor peer relationships • Behavioral extremes, overly compliant or demanding; withdrawn or aggressive	• Self-destructive behavior, remaining oblivious to hazards and risks • Chronic academic underachievement
Physical abuse	• Unexplained bruises and welts • Unexplained fractures/dislocations • Unexplained burns • Other unexplained injuries may include: lacerations, abrasions, human bite marks, or pinch marks, loss of hair/bald patches, retinal hemorrhage, abdominal injuries	• Requests or feels deserving of punishment • Afraid to go home and/or requests to stay in school, day care, etc. • Overly shy; tends to avoid physical contact with adults, especially parents • Displays behavioral extremes (withdrawal or aggressiveness)	• Suggests that other children should be punished in a harsh manner • Cries excessively and/or sits and stares • Reports injury by parents • Gives unbelievable explanations for injury
Neglect	• Height and weight significantly below age level • Inappropriate clothing for weather • Child abandoned or left with inadequate supervision • Untreated illness or injury • Lack of safe, sanitary shelter • Lack of necessary medical and dental care	• Begging or stealing food • Falling asleep in school, lethargic • Poor school attendance, frequent tardiness • Chronic hunger • Dull, apathetic appearance	• Running away from home • Repeated acts of vandalism • Reports no caretaker in the home • Assumes adult responsibilities

Source: This material is taken from a pamphlet prepared by Child Protective Services (Arizona Department of Economic Security 1991–1992).

factors to be considered by those teachers who choose to be more actively involved with students' concerns and perspectives.

◆ DEALING WITH AMBIGUOUS BEHAVIOR

Teachers will often be confronted with information that is ambiguous—not only in terms of the meaning of the act or the behavior (e.g., *why* does it take place and what does it mean?) but also in terms of whether the teacher should do anything further with the information. Conversations often have unintended consequences.

For example, a chemistry teacher who is asking only about a students' lack of attention may suddenly find herself confronted with an issue of sexual harassment. Consider the following scenario:

> Ms. Segal likes to have lunch with one student a week to discuss general instructional issues in the chemistry class. Today she asks, "Ann, you and Rob Thornton were in a quiet but clearly intense conversation for most of the third period. Was the class that boring?" Ann responds, "Look, Ms. Segal, every day I have to put up with some lewd comment from Rob. Today he told me that I should lean over the table more so he could have a better look at my breasts. I am tired of his harassment, and I spent most of the period basically telling him to keep his mouth shut, his pants zipped, and generally letting him know what a jerk he is."

Unexpected information of this type may lead the teacher to pursue conversations they never intended which are seldom easy and difficult to ignore.

Seemingly innocuous instructional data-collection efforts can reveal private and potentially painful information. For example, an essay on a state assessment exercise may find many students in the state writing directly or indirectly about suicide. Local teachers read such essays and must decide what, if any, action to take ("Is this an expression of intended suicide, part of normal adolescent reality testing, or simply a literary metaphor?"). Teachers, of course, have their own direct experiences as well. "Simple" writing assignments like, "What was most important about your best-remembered event of this last summer?" may promote a variety of stressful responses (e.g., parent divorce, stealing, witnessing a shooting, etc.).

One typical data-collection strategy for assessment of student performance is to examine student work (e.g., workbooks, portfolios, notes). However, collecting student notebooks for the purpose of seeing what materials and ideas students believe are most significant may reveal notes and pictures that are disturbing. For example, a geometry teacher reviewing student notebooks may find a student who frequently sketches a hangman's noose or graphic portraits of violence. A teacher may find that several students in the room consistently place a common symbol in the lower right-hand corner of their papers, as though it were the sign of membership in some sort of club. Another teacher may find that three or four students in the room are consistently defacing the symbols that other students use or crossing out specific letters on their papers, suggesting possible gang involvement. The English literature teacher may find a student frequently asking in her/his notes, "I wonder if the author of this poem used drugs? committed suicide?"

The range of dilemmas that a classroom teacher may face are endless. Some of the concerns that students express will be fairly contained and about other students or family members: "He's too noisy"; "She doesn't care about our group work"; "I hate my sister"; "He has bad breath and I hate to work with him." Other conversations with students will reveal information that has moral consequences: "She steals my pencils"; "He copies my work"; "Ted is always asking me for information during exams"; "Ann threatens to beat me up on the way home from school if I don't give her my money."

Yet other information from students may be designed to "set the teacher up." For example, comments like "Someone stole my copy of *Beowolf* at the slumber party," may stretch the limits of credibility (a topic to which we shall return). Still, other information might deal with issues that occur outside of the school setting and which may or may not have important implications for the school situation: "Tim's parents are out of town and he's going to throw an all-night party at his house"; "Ruth and I plan to elope next week—she's pregnant"; "I know that my manager at work is regularly stealing food." Teachers who choose to become active participants in students' lives will have to be willing to deal with troublesome reports.

In short, the range of information that a teacher may be exposed to is diverse and varies from the trivial to the critical—and it is not always possible to know which is which. We think a solid ground rule to guide teacher decision making on following up student report is the extent to which the information, if true, hinders the student's ability to profit from classroom experience. Whenever events detract from a student's safety, ability to learn, and sense of belonging, teacher attention and possible action are required.

◆ LIMITS ON PROTECTING STUDENTS' CONFIDENCE

As a culture, educators are somewhat accustomed to work with children that involves some amount of deception ("See? You could do that and it was a hard one!"). A considerable amount of research in the behavioral, educational, and social sciences uses deception as a part of the research process in order to draw more focused research conclusions (e.g., the study entraps students to steal so that researchers can more closely analyze conditions or pressures under which students will engage in inappropriate behavior). Consider the following two examples, abridged from Thompson (1992).

> A third-grade boy sits alone with a female researcher whom he has just meet. After a few moments of rapport building, the researcher says, "I want to see how fast you can solve puzzles." The boy performs quickly and successfully, and receives praise from the researcher. Now, the nine-year-old receives several difficult problems which he cannot solve, and the researcher proceeds to ask him several questions about his perceptions of his puzzle-solving behavior and his school achievement abilities. She then tells him not to feel bad, because the puzzles were very difficult. "He then returns to his classroom, where he is in a special

group for slow learners, wondering whether she told him the truth." (Thompson, 1992, p. 32)

And, we add, wondering "Will she tell my teacher that I didn't do very good?"

An eighth-grade girl enters the experimenter's room and is given several academic tasks to complete. She is told not to go into the adjoining room because the experimenter is working on her next task. As she works, she hears considerable sound coming from the adjoining room and eventually she opens the door, only to find the room empty. Subsequently, the researcher asks if she looked into the room, and she tells him that she did not. The researcher "debriefs" the student, telling her that he is working on a study to determine when an adolescent will violate an adult's request. He informs her that he had observed her behavior through a one-way mirror: he saw her look into the adjoining room. Later in the day she wonders, "Am I dishonest?" (Thompson, 1992, p. 18).

Teachers, of course, will have to decide (and get principal support) whether they will allow researchers to conduct deception studies with students in their classrooms. Researchers can sometimes reconcile with the ethics criteria of their professional organization (e.g., American Educational Research Association, American Psychological Association) experiments that involve deception, pain, and self-doubt on the basis of the long-term benefits of the research to society. For example, the short-term distress of a child who is separated from his/her mother may be justified in terms of long-run societal benefits (e.g., our more complete understanding of attachment leads to better design and staffing of child-care and children's hospital facilities). However, we maintain that it is important that *teachers not engage in deception* in working with students. For example, if a child suffers from obesity and brings his concern about his weight to his teacher, the teacher cannot pretend that the problem is trivial or does not exist.

In brief, teachers need to be clear with students about the type of problems that can be kept private and those that cannot. If information cannot be kept privileged, a student should not have the illusion that it can. When teachers are discussing student behavior, performance, progress, and potential with students (or parents), they need to be sure to engage in positive and supportive communication in ways that are also candid and provide a realistic appraisal. In general, it appears that teachers have relatively little power in keeping information confidential. Therefore, they must be very clear about the things that can and cannot be kept confidential so that students have appropriate expectations about the relationship they share with the teacher—and the potential consequences they face when they confide in her/him.

◆ CLEAR PURPOSES AND UNTHREATENING PROCEDURES

Teachers should make very clear when they talk with or interview students why they are doing so. Similarly, teachers need to be clear when opportunities for private conversation begin, how they differ from more typical classroom settings, and how students are to reengage classroom-setting procedures and the student role when the "special time" ends. For example, the teacher who decides to collect randomly and discuss notes from three or four students should be very clear and candid about his/her reasons for doing so. "I want to see how you are relating course materials and concepts. I may find that I have been unclear and need to reconsider some aspects of course content with you." Of course, if you have used such procedures previously, you can make a stronger case. "In the past, students and I have benefited because. . . ."

Although it is not always essential, we believe that teachers should also maintain a relationship with students that allows students *meaningful choice* of whether to participate and provides the opportunity for declining to participate in a nonthreatening way. For example, the teacher might say, "If I choose your notebook for review, I don't care about grammar, how well you write, neatness, etc.; I simply want to see how you have captured course content. I will always request the notebooks on a Wednesday afternoon at the end of the day and return them to you on Thursday. When you leave the class, place your notebooks on my desk. If you would prefer not to share your notebook, that is your right, and I appreciate your decision."

Teachers who implement such a procedure early in the school year will have communicated with students their intent to use student notebooks as a way of learning about students' approach to learning subject matter—before the students have written anything (or very much) in the notebooks. Ethically, teachers have given students a clear and unobtrusive way *not* to share personal notebooks (they can staple certain pages together or choose not to leave the notebooks as they file out of the room). Furthermore, teachers have advised students clearly that certain types of information in the notebook (e.g., gang-related drawings and graffiti) will likely lead to action by the teacher. Thus, if presented to the teacher, such information needs to be followed up on; this may well be the student's intention in submitting it.

Student submission of course notebooks need not be voluntary, however. Student note taking could be conceptualized as part of the normal classroom procedures and assignments, and thereby subject to routine evaluation (to be assessed for completeness, etc.). Our point is that any procedure that is at all *atypical* should involve student cooperation, and rights of participation should be protected.

◆ Classroom Assignments Can Be Intrusive

Relatively straightforward classroom discussions and assignments may inadvertently require students to yield private information that may be painful for them. For example, Ms. Cox, a high-school teacher attempting to make an introductory statistics lesson as relevant as possible may ask students to name their favorite music video. The intention of the teacher is understandable (she wants to use interesting topics around which to organize the teaching of how to make a graph), but revealing such information may embarrass students, especially those who are called upon first (e.g., students might have to divulge that there is no TV in their home, that their family cannot afford cable, or that their parents do not allow them to watch MTV; an insecure student may worry that her/his musical taste will be ridiculed by peers). Further, student "favorite music video" contributions may lead student commentary away from the intended task, graphing, and into unexpected terrain (treatment of females, gangsta rap, etc.).

Thus, again we make the point that teaching often involves response opportunities that may make students feel embarrassed, anxious, validated, or energized—each of which may afford teacher-student discussion and perhaps, on occasion, require it. As we have noted earlier, increasing the number of informal conversations has the potential of increasing teaching dilemmas, but it also increases the possibility that teachers will gain useful insight into student mediation of experience thus improving the classroom climate for meaningful, co-regulated, learning.

◆ BELIEVABILITY

Just as teachers need to be concerned about protecting students in their class from any injustices, so must they be alert to the possibility that students, at times, may attempt to create difficulties for others. Some students may see teachers' concern about student personal behavior and safety as a viable mechanism for creating mischief. For example, two students during a seventh-grade, small-group lesson—knowing that the teacher is tape recording the lesson—may joke about their shoplifting abilities ("We've 'lifted' the top 10 albums every week for the last two months!") simply to get a rise out of the teacher. Students have been known to fabricate stories about abduction, rape, and robbery. For some students, negative attention is better than no attention; occasionally students will start a story (jokingly) but get caught up in it until the story becomes larger than life.

Teachers also need to check on their own stories that result from jumping to large conclusions on too few data. A teacher who happens to find that a student's lunchbox is empty at the start of school need not conclude that s/he has found a case of child neglect; the student may simply be dumping out food on the way to school because s/he hates carrots and peanut butter. Hence, teachers must use common sense, collect appropriate information, and use good judgment before reporting claims that students make or making their own generalized inferences from discrete observation.

Awareness that students may misremember or invent stories is especially important when the consequences are major. Understanding when children can remember and provide accurate detail (e.g., when providing eyewitness testimony), is a complex topic. Even investigators who do primary research on memory currently are calling for more research in order to understand the reliability of children's memory and their capacity to participate in important proceedings, such as court cases (e.g., Doris, 1991; Loftus, 1994). Making judgments here is very difficult and complex, and teachers who become involved in important moral and legal issues may want to examine some of this literature more extensively (e.g., Garbarino et al., 1992; Zaragoza, 1991).

We have already noted that teachers at least should be aware that the way in which they initially frame a discussion or ask a question may have important impact upon how students remember and report events. Research by Loftus and others indicates that questions, especially if repeated by a trusted other, can change student report. As we have repeatedly stated (and we take the risk of redundancy charges), teachers need to design their questions deliberately so that student report, not teacher construction, is best represented (review Chapter 3). Also, teachers need to take care that their questions do not encourage students to underreport or overreport. For example, if an adolescent reports mistreatment and the teacher asks "What kind of clothes were you wearing?", the student likely will view the teacher as unsympathetic and give up reporting the incident. In contrast, a student might be encouraged to overreport if the teacher's initial question after hearing the student report an incident of harassment is something like "How long ago did she start abusing you?"

There are no definitive guidelines that one can use for dealing with student reports. However, it is prudent to keep in mind that students are capable of engaging in deception and that reports may be influenced by the way in which teachers react to the information, the way in which they ask follow-up questions, and how many questions are asked. In most circumstances, the best approach is to allow the student to be as descriptive as possible with an open-ended question ("Tell me what happened"). In situations of abuse or other possible endangerment, rather than have the student "practice" the report in the belief that repetition increases confidence in student truthfulness or helps the student cope, the teacher should seek immediate support from the designated school authorities.

◆ HOME-SCHOOL BOUNDARIES

Just as young people have a right to privacy, so do parents or guardians. For example, in Pennsylvania a school district initiated a screening procedure, including the use of personality inventories, to identify potential drug abusers (following identification, students were to be enrolled in confrontational group therapy). In the case *Merriken v. Cressman* (as described by Melton, 1992), the court ruled in favor of a parent who claimed that the testing violated her constitutional right to privacy because the questionnaire contained private questions about the family (e.g., "Do parents hug me?"; "Why are one or both parents absent?" "What is the family's religion?"; etc.). Thus, teachers should avoid asking students personal questions about private family issues and, we feel, even collecting seemingly innocuous information about the family ("What did your family do for vacation this summer?"; "Where does your father work?"; etc.)

Teachers should also be aware that formal school reporting activities often intrude upon families in unintended ways. There is evidence that reports of abuse often increase after teachers release report cards. Hence, teachers and schools need to work hard to be sure that report cards are not misunderstood or misused by parents or guardians, and that such reports do not lead to abuse of students who bring home low, ambiguous, or family-defined "unsatisfactory" marks. The Baltimore school district, acting upon its concern about reports of student abuse at report-card time, has developed a special communication to parents about how to respond to report cards (see Figure 5.1).

Teachers may want to discuss with students how to handle report cards at home, engage in extensive communication with parents about appropriate strategies for helping, and perhaps hold debriefing meetings with students a week or so after the first report card of the year is distributed.

◆ Do Not Force Compliance

Teachers should be careful in forcing students to provide information about other students for the teacher's own needs or to protect an individual student. For example, the junior-high basketball coach tells the varsity team, "I'm going to play the junior varsity—and none of you will play again until one of you tells me who put that stuff in my locker. I know it had to be one of you, because you are the only ones who had access to my locker." Most adolescents would see this behavior as unfair and would resent the coach for her behavior. Similarly, teachers who choose to hold the class accountable for an individual's behavior are likely to lose students' respect—especially that of older students.

Teachers who play an active listening role will be exposed to situations where their close identification with a student may lead to an overreaction to the student's report. However, if teachers are not sensitive to long-term implications of forcing students to tattle on their peers ("Who said you were pregnant?"), they can create unpleasant, unintended, and unnecessary consequences for the student (a fight after school, friends becoming even more malicious) and for the teacher, loss of respect. Teachers who are used to dealing with students' problems frequently are less likely to overrespond to them than are teachers who are new to the role or who become involved only when confronted with an issue. Although there may be special circumstances that require such procedures (guns, drugs, etc.), typical classroom issues are in the normal, nonlife-threatening range and should not be dealt with by forcing or even encouraging students to reveal others' private behavior.

◆ Developmental Differences in Students

In earlier chapters (especially Chapter 2), we have pointed out various developmental differences in students (loyalty to friends vs. adults; moral orientation; instrumental vs. dependency relationships; etc.) that should influence how teachers think about and respond to problems that students present. In this chapter, we discuss students' developmental differences only in terms of broad implications for ethical behavior. In making decisions about whether to pursue a given issue (e.g, peer teasing vs. "My manager is stealing food."), the teacher has to consider her/his experience and the intended effects of intervention. At a minimum, the teacher must be sure to protect the rights of the

TIPS FOR PARENTS

1 Visit your child's school.
2 Ask to speak to the teacher.
3 Ask the principal if your child can be tutored.
4 Check your child's homework every day.
5 Have your child call for homework help:

AT REPORT - CARD TIME:

● **STOP** *whatever you are doing.*

● **LOOK** *at your child's report card.*

● **LISTEN** *to what your child has to say.*

If you're happy with your child's report card, say so!
If not, use the tips on the other side of this card...

☐ Teachers will help with homework at the
Baltimore Teachers' Union:
DIAL-A-TEACHER **466-1545**
Mon - Thur   4pm - 7pm

☐ Librarians will help at the **Pratt Library**
INFORMATION LINE **396-5430**
Mon, Tues, Wed   10am - 8pm
Thur & Sat   10am - 5pm
Sunday   1pm - 5pm
CHILDREN'S DEPT. **396-5402**
Mon, Tues, Wed   10am - 7pm
Thur & Sat   10am - 5pm
Sunday   1pm - 5pm
NIGHTOWL SERVICE. **396-5557**
Mon, Tues, Wed   9pm - 11:45pm
Thur & Fri   5pm - 11:45pm

☐ Volunteers will help at
KIDSLINE **727-5397**
Mon - Fri   1pm - 6pm

☐ Students will help at
STUDENTS HELPING
STUDENTS HOTLINE **396-8659**
Mon - Thur   5pm - 9pm

*For a list of tutoring programs, call **727-5524**, 1 pm-6 pm*
*For fun activities, call **Dept. of Recreation and Parks: 396-7459***

To learn different ways to deal with your children, call:

PARENTS ANONYMOUS STRESS LINE **243-7337**
24 Hours a Day
FIRST CALL FOR HELP **685-0525**
Information and Referral Service
PACA . . . . **269-7816** or **1-800-422-3055**
National Committee to Prevent Child Abuse

Sponsored By

AN EQUAL OPPORTUNITY CLUB   KURT L. SCHMOKE, MAYOR
BALTIMORE COMMISSION FOR CHILDREN AND YOUTH
THE MAYOR'S OFFICE FOR CHILDREN AND YOUTH
BALTIMORE CITY PUBLIC SCHOOLS

FIGURE 5.1 Report Card Tips for Parents
Reprinted by Permission.

student and *do no harm* to the student or to others. Given that, the teacher needs to self-assess the extent of the knowledge and skills that s/he brings to the situation, the role the teacher desires to play, the developmental level of the student, and the locus of the problem (school, home, community).

Most people believe that students develop and mature in a linear and relatively predictable fashion. Common opinion is that students progressively become more mature as they progress through school and, hence, are less vulnerable to many different types of risks. Indeed, because of these assumptions, research boards that review researchers' ethical processes often scrutinize especially closely research requests for work on young children. This is, of course, because young children have less social power, less ability to reason, etc. Similarly, teacher-education programs focus primarily on children's developing needs and capacity in the preparation of early-childhood and elementary teachers, do much less in the preparation of middle-school teachers (perhaps a course in preadolescent and adolescent development), and may provide nothing at all about the developmental needs of students in the preparation of high-school teachers. This is unfortunate because developmental differences are uneven; issues that may not pose risk for younger children may be quite threatening to older students and be exacerbated by changes in school structures.

Thompson (1992) argues that researchers and those who interview and/or have conversations with young people need to recognize that children and adolescents are a very heterogeneous population. For example seventh-graders, on average, may be more mature than fifth-graders, but many seventh-graders are *less* mature than fifth-graders. Even more important than recognizing the diversity in maturity and competence that exists at a given age, is the realization that risk and age do not always follow a neat, linear pattern. Thompson explains:

> Some risks increase with the child's increasing age; others are likely to decrease. Potential harms to which very young children are especially vulnerable (owing, for example, to their emotional dependence on caregivers) are not significant concerns with older children, whereas older children may be uniquely vulnerable to certain risks (such as threats to the self-concept) that are unlikely to occur with infants or very young children. (p. 4)

Perhaps one of the major differences in degree of vulnerability between children and adolescents falls in the area of privacy (Melton, 1992). Adolescents increasingly want private space—space that no one violates without invitation. Melton argues:

> As children become older, expression of privacy becomes an active choice, with their being less subject to intrusion on their private space, associations, and information. Privacy has a particularly important meaning to adolescents as a marker of independence and self-differentiation. Although being alone is an important element of privacy to adolescents as it is to younger children, adolescents also find maintenance of control over personal information to be particularly critical. (p. 74)

Protecting Privacy   In short, teachers need to be especially sensitive to the privacy needs of adolescents. Although young children may love to share their views (note the popularity of show and tell in the very early grades), older students may not want to share their opinions and beliefs about various performers, who they "hang with," their response to a particular book, or their (changing) career aspirations. Hence, teachers of older students need to consider obtaining information and involving student interests, which makes instruction more meaningful, but doing so in ways that do not violate the students' privacy needs.

Similarly, older students may be less willing to ask questions in class because they understand that questions reveal what they do not know at both the surface (content) and deeper (ability) levels (Moroski, 1986). Thus, question asking can be antithetical to privacy needs. Teachers who recognize the goal conflict older students experience because of their privacy needs (e.g., learn material vs. protect perceptions of my ability) can design question-asking strategies that allow student learning and privacy goals to be compatible rather than antagonistic. For example, the teacher may ask everyone to pass written questions forward and then select questions at random to answer for the class as a whole.

Another example of nonintrusive instruction may help clarify the point. A social studies teacher could distribute a handout asking students to: 1) name what they consider the biggest problem in America today; 2) identify their favorite senator; 3) vote on whether legal immigration should be increased or not; 4) nominate a movie they believe represents an honest portrayal of social injustice or cohesion; and 5) vote on whether the legal drinking age should be returned to 18. Students, after completing the handout, could be assigned by the teacher into one of five work groups, which subsequently would poll the results of the assigned question and lead discussion on it.

In this way, the teacher can allow students to use data involving their personal opinion without requiring any student to reveal private information about his/her personal beliefs in the context of unknown normative peer beliefs (unless the student chooses to do so in the ensuing discussion). Subsequently, the teacher is in a position to use the pooled information to construct graphs, to discuss salient social issues, etc. The point of this illustration is to indicate that students' personal opinions can be collected in ways that do not violate their privacy.

We believe that structured or negotiated choice can be generally good for students; it helps them to reflect upon their interests and to coordinate various goals and enactment strategies that they bring to the "choice" opportunity (see Chapter 1). However, as we described earlier, unstructured choice may only sustain differences among students. Unstructured choice may also conflict with privacy needs.

Participation Vulnerability   Thompson (1992) presents guidelines for thinking about students' vulnerability to research participation that we believe are also useful for teachers who hold private conversations with students. Again, we think it is very useful to understand some of the vulnerabilities of adolescents as well as those of young children, which are more readily recognized (e.g., young children have less ability to cope with stress, need more support, etc.).

Thompson notes that potential threats to a child's self-concept become more stressful with increasing age because students become more committed to an enduring identity (recall Chapter 2). There is considerable research evidence to illustrate that very young children are optimistic following failure; however, middle-school students after a failure may internalize worries about competence which threaten self-esteem. Thompson, writing about vulnerability in research that involves task failure, notes:

> A developmental period of especially heightened vulnerability to these influences may exist in middle childhood when the child's self-referent beliefs are maturing, but during which self-perceptions remain relatively flexible and can be influenced by the short-term performance evaluations that occur. (p. 45)

We note that these experiences are also the daily stuff of schooling.

In our conception, heightened vulnerability is also a period of heightened opportunity for teachers to co-regulate student mediation of competence through supportive scaffolding and provision of opportunities that *promote and require* the development of student enactive strategies and realistic self-evaluation. Thus, in our view, student development is not so much an individual, personal characteristic or description of "the way it is" as it is an *opportunity* for shared, co-regulated, learning between teacher and student.

Thompson continues:

> By adolescence, vulnerability to these risks probably declines because children have developed a more consolidated and coherent system of self-referent beliefs that are less affected by situationally specific evaluative feedback. . . . Adolescents, in other words, are more likely to doubt the feedback they receive than to doubt themselves . . . because their self-understanding is more sophisticated, consolidated, and secure than in middle childhood. (p. 45)

Thompson and others also argue that social comparison information becomes a more significant mode of self-evaluation as age increases. As students become older many of them will be more vulnerable than they were at a younger age to direct or indirect comparisons of their ability with classmates, because with age students acquire a more enduring sense of ability. Adolescents may be especially sensitive to whether their conversations or performance will be shared with peers, other teachers, parents, etc. Sensitivity to social-comparison information apparently increases in direct relation with increases in privacy needs. This is not surprising: as an adolescent is more aware of others and others' performance in relation to his/her, s/he is also aware that others may use his/her personal data in the same way. Both processes co-occur with an increasing capacity to make inferences about others' motives. This suggests that younger students are more apt to take a teacher question at face value, whereas older students may be more skeptical and wonder what the interview is "really" about. Young students are likely to answer a teacher's questions quickly and spontaneously. In contrast, older students are more likely to raise questions about why the teacher wants the information and to have a more complete understanding of the degree of information they are providing and its consequences. Thus, questions about family ("How many people are in your family?"; etc.) may be more threatening to older students than younger ones because they realize that there are judgments associated with different types of families (e.g., single-parent families).

Finally, Thompson also notes that with increasing age, students are likely to become more sensitive to how one's background, ability, etc., is viewed. Hence, teachers—especially teachers of older students—should be sure that the pattern with which they hold conversations or have lunch with students does not reflect any unintended messages (e.g., the teacher only has lunch with low-achieving students; why was a white student first, etc.).

◆ DEVELOPING INCREASED SENSITIVITY TO ETHICAL ISSUES

Protecting Student Time   We close with a few observations about protecting the classroom context that teachers and students create and trust. First, much research is relevant and helpful, some sooner than others, but teachers must judge the value of research in terms of its time, cost, and possible disruption of students leaving and reentering the classroom. Teachers must also consider the possible lingering mediational effects of students' participation on their own personal beliefs and opportunity to learn.

Second, teachers and principals must also evaluate the legitimate interest of business concerns and other organizations that may try to exploit young people (e.g., encouraging them to sell expensive items with only a minuscule return for the student or the school). For example, a major-league baseball team may involve elementary-school children in a large metropolitan area in a contest for which they offer a prize ($50) for the best poster (on safety week, drug-free living, or whatever). Essentially, the team is paying $50 for thousands of student artists to create what amounts to an advertising flier for the team. Similarly, firms like Pizza Hut may sponsor reading programs that indirectly (and directly) encourage students to read short and often unchallenging books in hopes of winning a prize for the largest number of books read in the least time.

As researchers, we think schools should be involved in research that has both short-term and long-term benefits for enhancing students' school experiences. As citizens, we think that what is good for business is not necessarily what is good for students. At a minimum, any intrusion in school life (research, magic show, police or community day, contests run by businesses, career day, etc.) must be evaluated in terms of time lost and personal student cost.

Creating Opportunities for Peer Support and Review   Teachers, in talking with peers and administrators, may find that there has been little focused discussion, and hence, few concrete guidelines for dealing with student confidentiality and other student concerns. Hence, teachers may want to suggest the creation of an ethics review board in the school to meet periodically to discuss and review ethics concerns and to outline appropriate school procedures. Teachers might want to become familiar with literature associated with various professional associations (e.g., see Appendixes A and B) and institutional review boards (university committees that review the ethical procedures used by university researchers [see e.g., Howe & Cutis Dougherty, 1993]) and ombudsman roles in protection of student rights, to learn more about standards of practice associated with privileged information. In-service activities sponsored by the school district might appropriately deal with teacher questions and cases in this area.

There is growing evidence to suggest that teachers benefit from a school culture that encourages the exchange of instructional ideas (Rosenholtz, 1989). Unfortunately and ironically, in too many schools, teacher questions about strategies to manage students or to adjust instruction are seen as signs of teacher weaknesses. We suspect that questions about how to handle confidential information may also be seen in some schools as a sign of weakness or immaturity, or as a threat to the status quo or local myth ("We do not have those problems at Utopia Junior High.").

We encourage beginning teachers to seek out veteran teachers and administrators for counsel and to lobby for institutional structures (e.g., teacher committees, boards that include school personnel and teachers) that allow teachers to discuss ethical issues and ways to respond to various classroom dilemmas involving moral concerns. Most professions *require* peer review and discussion of ethics in dealing with individuals in the professional's care—the professional is not expected to act alone. It should be no different in teaching.

❖ SUMMARY

In this chapter, we have stressed that regardless of whether teachers seek to understand students' social lives, they will at times have access to private information—whether they want to or not. Hence, all teachers must be knowledgeable about laws and/or administrative guidelines that require the reporting of certain types of behavior or information. Further, all teachers need to be knowledgeable about local norms and the school culture as it pertains to the confidentiality rights of students, parents, and guardians. All teachers need to make students cognizant of the type of information that teachers cannot keep privileged. Finally, *all* teachers need to exercise informed judgment, especially when discussing abuse and other life-threatening issues with students so that the teacher does not inadvertently interfere with student safety by contaminating student memory for and report of the abusive or threatening event.

Teachers who want to play a more active role in helping students to integrate their social and intellectual lives need to be aware of issues that go beyond reporting requirements and awareness of local norms. In establishing their role, teachers must be very sure that students understand why they are discussing an issue (e.g., interview a student about her/his experience in a small group) and understand how such information will be used. Teachers need to ensure that students provide such information voluntarily and that there is no risk to the student who does not want to be interviewed or participate. When interviewing students, the teacher must be sensitive to the needs of the individual student, protect home-school boundaries to the extent possible, and be aware that students on occasion may exaggerate or fabricate totally fictitious stories. Further, when teachers work with students they must be sensitive to developmental issues; for example, what constitutes invasion of privacy (physical vs psychological) will vary by age and experience of the student.

Teachers must be prepared to deal with unintended consequences involving private information and be very clear about their role as teachers. Finally, teachers need to protect the classroom social/instructional environment. Their classroom is a context that students trust. Extending student trust to outsiders—be they researchers, DARE officers, local business partners, or a parent volunteer—needs to be a deliberate, informed decision.

❖ QUESTIONS AND SUGGESTED ACTIVITIES FOR CHAPTER 5

1. To what extent do the particulars of a situation dictate your ethical responsibilities? For example, one student may be pregnant but coping well with the problem (from all that you know), and another student may be distraught and endangered by her pregnancy. To what extent does the student's emotional state and concern dictate your ethical responsibilities (e.g., drawing in outside resources versus the problem itself)? That is, to what extent are ethical issues embedded in a social context.

2. To what extent is the teacher responsible for student development other than academic progress? Should teachers assume responsibility for developing prosocial attitudes—for example, toward cooperation and responsibility? To what extent are the relationships between teachers and students confined by the teaching role? Does this differ with student age?

3. To what extent should students be encouraged to provide information (pejorative) about other students? Under what circumstances is this justified?

4. Alternatively, are there situations in which encouraging or requiring students to share positive information about other students might also have negative ethical implications? Why do you feel this way? Provide an example or two to illustrate your point.

5. What are the ethical responsibilities involved when a teacher passes information about a student to another teacher? Does it matter whether it is academic information or social information? Are there circumstances in which a student might benefit from the exchange of information among teachers? Provide an example or two to make your point.

6. Alternatively, are there circumstances under which a student would be placed at a disadvantage (or even a severe disadvantage) because of teachers sharing negative information among themselves? Provide a couple of examples to illustrate your point. Compare your responses with those of classmates, and using this information, develop some guidelines that you feel are appropriate for differentiating when teachers should and should not exchange information. How defensible do you think your guidelines are?

7. You are disturbed because Lisa and Chuck (who sit side by side and are close friends) have scored identically on the first three chemistry tests. Chuck has only been an average student throughout high school, but he is getting the *exact* same score as Lisa (an honor student)—A's—on the first three tests. What, if anything, should you do? Would a conversation or some other technique be appropriate? Should other teachers or a parent be involved?

8. Jack was overwhelmed by performance anxiety during his first presentation in a sophomore introductory speech class. The assignment was simple—talk in front of the class about anything you wish for 5 minutes. It was clear to you, the class, and Jack that he was excessively nervous to the point of being incoherent. Should you talk privately to Jack? Is it possible that talking might worsen the problem? What can and should you do as a teacher? Under what circumstances would you be motivated to discuss Jack's problem with a school counselor or with Jack's parents?

9. In three separate writing assignments a student has brought up the topic of suicide. As a teacher, how would you approach this subject with the student? What are several questions that you would want to ask the student?

10. Can a teacher say, "I am not going to deal with issues of morality unless they are in the classroom"? To what extent can a teacher overassume his/her responsibilities and intrude on parent or guardian responsibilities? For instance, to what extent does the teacher have the right or obligation to intervene because a student is consistently very passive (and hence, being manipulated) in peer relationships?

❖ REFERENCES

Ames, C. (1992). Achievement goals and the classroom motivational climate. In D. Schunk & J. Meece (Eds.), *Student perceptions in the classroom* (pp. 327–348). Hillsdale, NJ: Erlbaum.

Doris, J. (Ed.). (1991). *The suggestibility of children's recollections*. Washington, D.C.: American Psychological Association.

Editorial. (December 27, 1993). *Arizona Daily Star*.

Garbarino, J., Dobrow, N., Kostelny, K., & Pardo, C. (1992). *Children in danger: Coping with the consequences of community violence*. San Francisco: Jossey-Bass.

Good, T. (1983). Classroom research: A decade of progress. *Educational Psychologist, 18*, 127–144.

Good, T., Biddle, B., & Brophy, J. (1975). *Teachers make a difference*. New York: Holt, Rinehart, & Winston.

Howe, K., & Cutis Dougherty, K. (1993). Ethics, institutional review boards, and the changing face of educational research. *Educational Researcher, 22*, 16–21.

Loftus, E. (1994). The repressed memory controversy. *American Psychologist, 49*(5), 443–445.

Martin, J. (1992). *The school home*. Cambridge, MA: Harvard University Press.

McCaslin, M., & Good, T. (1992). Compliant cognition: The misalliance of management and instructional goals in current school reform. *Educational Researcher, 21*, 4–17.

McCaslin, M., & Good, T. (1996). *The informal curriculum*. In R. Calfee & D. Berliner (Eds.), *Handbook of educational psychology*. New York: Macmillan.

McCaslin, M., & Murdock, T. (1991). The emergent interaction of home and school in the development of students' adaptive learning. In M. Maehr & P. Pintrich (Eds.), *Advances in motivation and achievement* (pp. 213–260). Greenwich, CT: JAI Press.

Melton, G. (1992). Respecting boundaries: Minors, privacy, and behavioral research. In B. Stanley & J. Sieber (Eds.), *Social research and children and adolescents: Ethical issues* (pp. 65–87). Newbury Park: Sage.

Moroski, E. (1986). *To ask or not to ask, that is the question*. Unpublished manuscript, sponsored by the Dana Intern Program, Bryn Mawr College, Bryn Mawr, PA.

Noddings, N. (1992). *The challenge to care in schools*. New York: Teachers College Press.

Parkay, F., & Stanford, B. (1992). *Becoming a teacher* (2nd ed.). Boston: Allyn & Bacon.

Rohrkemper, M. (1981). *Classroom perspectives study: An investigation of differential perceptions of classroom events*. Unpublished doctoral dissertation, Michigan State University, East Lansing.

Rohrkemper, M., & Corno, L. (1988). Success and failure on classroom tasks: Adaptive learning and classroom teaching. *Elementary School Journal, 88*, 299–312.

Rosenholtz, S. (1989). *Teachers' workplace: The social organization of schools*. White Plains, NY: Longman.

Schunk, D., & Meece, J. (Eds.). (1992). *Student perceptions in the classroom*. Hillsdale, NJ: Erlbaum.

Shavelson, R., & Berliner, D. (1988). Erosion of the educational research infrastructure: A reply to Finn. *Educational Researcher, 17*, 9–12.

Thompson, R. (1992). Developmental changes in research risk and benefit: A changing calculus of concerns. In B. Stanley & J. Sieber (Eds.), *Social research and children and adolescents: Ethical issues* (pp. 31–65). Newbury Park, CA: Sage.

Weinstein, C., & Mignano, A., Jr. (1993). *Elementary classroom management: Lessons from research and practice*. New York: McGraw-Hill.

Zaragoza, M. (1991). Preschool children's susceptibility to memory impairment. In J. Doris (Ed.), *The suggestibility of children's recollections* (pp. 27–39). Washington, D.C.: American Psychological Association.

Appendix A

Excerpts from the National Association of School Psychologists

Principles for Professional Ethics

Prepared by the Ethical and Professional Standards Committee and The Publications Committee, National Association of School Psychologists, approved by the Executive Board/Delegate Assembly of the Association on March 28, 1992.

❖ I. INTRODUCTION

The formal principles that guide the conduct of a professional school psychologist are known as *Ethics*. By virtue of joining the Association, each NASP member has agreed to act in a manner that shows respect for human dignity and assures a high quality of professional service. Although ethical behavior is an individual responsibility, it is in the interest of an association to adopt and enforce a code of ethics. If done properly, members will be guided towards appropriate behavior, and public confidence in the profession will be enhanced. Additionally, a code of ethics should provide due process procedures to protect members from potential abuse of the code. These *Principles* have been written to accomplish these goals.

The principles in this manual are based on the assumptions that: 1) school psychologists will act as advocates for their students/clients, and 2) at the very least, school psychologists will do no harm. These necessitate that school psychologists "speak up" for the needs and rights of their students/clients at times when it may be difficult to do so. School psychologists are also restrained to provide only those services for which they have acquired an acknowledged level of experience, training, and competency. Beyond these basic premises, judgment is required to apply the ethical principles to the fluid and expanding interactions between school and community.

❖ III. PROFESSIONAL RELATIONSHIPS AND RESPONSIBILITIES

A) General

1. School psychologists are committed to the application of their professional expertise for the purpose of promoting improvement in the quality of life for students, their families, and the school community. This objective is pursued in ways that protect the dignity and rights of those involved. School psychologists accept responsibility for the appropriateness of their treatments and professional practices.

2. School psychologists respect all persons and are sensitive to physical, mental, emotional, political, economic, social, cultural, ethnic, racial, gender, sexual preferences, and religious characteristics.

3. School psychologists are responsible for the direction and nature of their personal loyalties or objective. When these commitments may influence a professional relationship, the school psychologist informs all concerned persons of relevant issues in advance.

4. School psychologists in all settings maintain professional relationships with students, parents, the school and community. Consequently, parents and students are to be fully informed about all relevant aspects of school psychological services in advance. The explanation should take into account language and cultural differences, cognitive capabilities, developmental level, and age so that the explanation may be understood by the student, parent, or guardian.

5. School psychologists shall attempt to resolve situations in which there are divided or conflicting interests in a manner which is mutually beneficial and protects the rights of all parties involved.

6. School psychologists do not exploit clients through professional relationships nor condone these actions in their colleagues. Students, clients, employees, colleagues, and research participants will not be exposed to deliberate comments, gestures, or physical contacts of a sexual nature. School psychologists do not engage in sexual relationships with students, supervisees, trainees, or past or present clients.

7. School psychologists attempt to resolve suspected detrimental or unethical practices on an informal level. If informal efforts are not productive, the appropriate professional organization is contacted for assistance, and procedures established for questioning ethical practice are followed.

      a. The filing of an ethical complaint is a serious matter. It is intended to improve the behavior of a colleague that is harmful to the profession and/or the public.

      b. School psychologists enter into this process thoughtfully and with concern for the well-being of all parties involved. They do not file or encourage the filing of an ethics complaint that is frivolous or motivated by revenge.

8. School psychologists respect the confidentiality of information obtained during their professional work. Information is revealed only with the informed consent of the client, or the client's parent or legal guardian, except in those situations in which failure to release information would result in clear danger to the client or others.

9. School psychologists discuss confidential information only for professional purposes and only with persons who have a legitimate need to know.

10. School psychologists inform their clients of the limits of confidentiality.

◆ B) Students

1. School psychologists understand the intimate nature of consultation, assessment, and direct service. They engage only in professional practices which maintain the dignity and integrity of students and other clients.

2. School psychologists explain important aspects of their professional relationships with students and clients in a clear, understandable manner. The explanation includes the reason why services were requested, who will receive information about the services provided, and the possible outcomes.

3. School psychologists understand their obligation to respect the rights of a student or client to initiate, participate in, or discontinue services voluntarily.

4. Recommendations for program changes or additional service will be discussed, including any alternatives which may be available.

◆ E) REPORTING DATA AND CONFERENCE RESULTS

1. School psychologists ascertain that student or client information reaches only authorized persons.

      a. The information is adequately interpreted so that the recipient can better help the student or client.

      b. The school psychologist assists agency recipients to establish procedures to properly safeguard the confidential material.

2. School psychologists communicate findings and recommendations in language readily understood by the intended recipient. These communications describe potential consequences associated with the proposals.

3. School psychologists prepare written reports in such form and style that the recipient of the report will be able to assist the student or client. Reports should emphasize recommendations and interpretations; reports which present only test scores or brief narratives describing a test are seldom useful. Reports should include an appraisal of the degree of confidence which could be assigned to the information.

4. School psychologists review all of their written documents for accuracy, signing them only when correct.

5. School psychologists comply with all laws, regulations, and policies pertaining to the adequate storage and disposal of records to maintain appropriate confidentiality of information.

Appendix B

CODE OF ETHICS OF THE EDUCATION PROFESSION ADOPTED BY THE 1975 NEA REPRESENTATIVE ASSEMBLY

Preamble

The educator, believing in the worth and dignity of each human being, recognizes the supreme importance of the pursuit of truth, devotion to excellence, and the nurture of democratic principles. Essential to these goals is the protection of freedom to learn and to teach and the guarantee of equal educational opportunity for all. The educator accepts the responsibility to adhere to the highest ethical standards.

The educator recognizes the magnitude of the responsibility inherent in the teaching process. The desire for the respect and confidence of one's colleagues, of students, of parents, and of the members of the community provides the incentive to attain and maintain the highest possible degree of ethical conduct. The Code of Ethics of the Education Profession indicates the aspiration of all educators and provides standards by which to judge conduct.

The remedies specified by the NEA and/or its affiliates for the violation of any provision of this Code shall be exclusive and no such provision shall be enforceable in any form other than one specifically designated by the NEA or its affiliates.

❖ PRINCIPLE 1—COMMITMENT TO THE STUDENT

The educator strives to help each student realize his or her potential as a worthy and effective member of society. The educator therefore works to stimulate the spirit of inquiry, the acquisition of knowledge and understanding, and the thoughtful formulation of worthy goals.

In fulfillment of the obligation to the student, the educator—

1. Shall not unreasonably restrain the student from independent action in the pursuit of learning.

2. Shall not unreasonably deny the student access to varying points of view.

3. Shall not deliberately suppress or distort subject matter relevant to the student's progress.

4. Shall make reasonable effort to protect the student from conditions harmful to learning or to health and safety.

5. Shall not intentionally expose the student to embarrassment or disparagement.

6. Shall not on the basis of race, color, creed, sex, national origin, marital status, political or religious beliefs, family, social or cultural background, or sexual orientation, unfairly:

    a. Exclude any student from participation in any program;
    b. Deny benefits to any student;
    c. Grant any advantage to any student.

7. Shall not use professional relationships with students for private advantage.

8. Shall not disclose information about students obtained in the course of professional service, unless disclosure serves a compelling professional purpose or is required by law.

❖ BILL OF TEACHER RIGHTS

◆ PREAMBLE

We, the teachers of the United States of America, aware that a free society is dependent upon the education afforded its citizens, affirm the right to freely pursue truth and knowledge.

As an individual, the teacher is entitled to such fundamental rights as dignity, privacy, and respect.

As a citizen, the teacher is entitled to such basic constitutional rights as freedom of religion, speech, assembly, association, and political action and equal protection of the law.

In order to develop and preserve respect for the worth and dignity of humankind, to provide a climate in which actions develop as a consequence of rational thought, and to insure intellectual freedom, we further affirm that teachers must be free to contribute fully to an educational environment which secures the freedom to teach and the freedom to learn.

Believing that certain rights of teachers derived from these fundamental freedoms must be universally recognized and respected, we proclaim this Bill of Teacher Rights.

❖ ARTICLE I—RIGHTS AS A PROFESSIONAL

As a member of the teacher profession, the individual teacher has the right:

Section 1   To be licensed under professional and ethical standards established, maintained, and enforced by the profession.

Section 2   To maintain and improve one's professional competence.

Section 3   To exercise professional judgment in presenting, interpreting, and criticizing information and ideas, including controversial issues.

Section 4   To influence effectively the formulation of policies and procedures which affect one's professional services, including curriculum, teaching materials, methods of instruction, and school-community relations.

Section 5   To exercise professional judgment in the use of teaching methods and materials appropriate to the needs, interests, capacities, and the linguistic and cultural background of each student.

Section 6   To safeguard information obtained in the course of professional service.

Section 7   To work in an atmosphere conducive to learning, including the use of reasonable means to preserve the learning environment and to protect the health and safety of students, oneself, and others.

Section 8   To express publicly views on matters affecting education.

Section 9   To attend and address a governing body and be afforded access to its minutes when official action may affect one's professional concerns.

LISTENING TO PARENTS: UNDERSTANDING FAMILIES

Our primary goal in this chapter is to promote linkages between home and school for the purpose of better communication, if not integration, of the so-cial/instructional environments that students negotiate. We believe that improved communication between these contexts will increase the effectiveness of *each* in the co-regulation of student/child mediational processes. Both contexts benefit—and thus, the student/child benefits compoundedly—because structural supports and provision of opportunities at home and school can function interactively and compatibly, as opposed to independently (which often occurs) or antagonistically (which, however infrequent, is too often).

The idea that differing individuals and contexts enhance their own and one another's goals when in a supportive relationship is a basic premise of the bio-ecological approach to development (e.g., Bronfenbrenner & Neville, 1994). This perspective, like the Vygotskian framework that guides this book, embeds the child within multiple contexts and in progressively more complex relationships within those contexts. Bronfenbrenner and colleagues (e.g., Kagan & Weissbourd, 1994) explicitly address social issues (e.g., education, divorce, poverty, structural safety nets) as contexts for child development.

The bio-ecological perspective helps us keep mindful of how these social issues affect *parents* as well as their children. Thus, a social-issues perspective helps us address our second goal for this chapter, exploration of enactment strategies and opportunities that might promote the attainment of our primary goal: the better integration of home and school to the benefit of students/children. In our discussion of how to realize home-school integration, we will distinguish among parents' goals for their children's schooling and their enactment strategies to follow through on those goals (and/or meet the goals imposed by others). One emphasis will be on the kinds of social supports, obstacles, and opportunities that promote or impede parent goal attainment, including those that are associated with the school and the classroom teacher. A second emphasis in our discussion of parent and home is family relationships in general and parenting "managerial" styles in particular. Our expectation is that teachers might better understand first, how home learning likely affects students' understanding of school and classroom norms and events, and second, how families likely *interpret* the dynamics of schooling.

Finally, we suggest how teachers might improve their understanding of family dynamics through communication with parents so that both teacher and parents might better assess and meet the goals of home-school compatibility. We should stress at the outset that by *compatible*, we do not mean that the contexts of home and school should be homogenous—although the early family support movement did and some contemporary educators do make that claim (e.g., Epstein, 1989). We also stress at the outset that teachers cannot "fix" the family or the conditions that encompass it. Increased understanding of families, however, can improve the coordination of home and school to better promote co-regulation of student mediation and realization of enabling opportunities.

Zeigler (1994) puts it well, when he writes:

> The family support movement has come a long way from the early days, when biased scholars unflinchingly advanced the theory that families in poverty suffered from so-called cultural deprivation, a concept that made it necessary for us to direct our interventions toward making all families more closely reflect the values and behavior of the mainstream middle-class socio-economic culture. We know now that such attempts at homogenization are neither desirable nor possible, but it is still important for us to avoid hubris in the wake of the many programmatic successes that the last decade has brought to proponents of family support. In many circumstances, even the most comprehensive program cannot alter the ecology of the larger environment enough to make a significant difference for great numbers of families. Even unlimited counseling, early childhood education, and home visits cannot compensate for the absence of jobs, which in turn can provide reasonable income, affordable and safe housing, adequate health care, and access to an integrated neighborhood where children encounter positive role models (Zeigler & Muenchow, 1992). To effect these fundamental changes, we have to change the basic features of society itself. (pp. xvi–xvii)

Those who take a psychological approach to the study of families often equate *family* with *parent,* and *parent* with *mother.* Thus much of what we "know" about families is about mothers' parenting practices and their effects on children. The goal in much of this research tradition is to link child outcomes with parenting behavior patterns. Societal conditions like socioeconomic status are used to describe the parent rather than conditions of society. (See, for example, Bowman, 1994.)

We agree with Zeigler that a subtraction or deficit model of "culture deprivation" to describe families and parenting is inappropriate and hinders the work of teachers who strive to understand their students and better facilitate the relationship between home and school so that students thrive. In short, we do not adhere to a strict hierarchy of family or parenting behavior that ignores context. However, we do identify a "bottom line" under which families may not go. Children must be safe, and they must be loved—if not loved, at least cared for. If teachers identify family situations where this bottom line has been violated, they must take appropriate, legal action as discussed in Chapter 5. In this chapter, however, our emphasis is on the majority of families with whom teachers interact—those who care for and love their children.

Finally, much of what we discuss in this chapter is cast in a dichotomous language (e.g., teacher-parent; home-school) when, in practice, this is not the case. Teachers are members of families; the experiences they bring to the teacher-parent relationship is part of that context. Indeed, teacher-parent relationships are frequently relationships between two parents, one of whom is also a teacher. Ironically, much of the literature we review on extant relations and barriers between parents and schools also applies to teachers when *they* relate to schools as the advocates for their own children. We are mindful that teachers who are also parents also have difficulty in maintaining traditional relations with their children's teachers. They, too, work; they work the same hours. And they know the pay.

Teachers, like many parents, also work in places over which they have limited control and little interaction with those in control (Spencer, 1986). Indeed, The National Commission on Excellence in Education (1983) described teachers' work life as "on the whole unacceptable" (p. 22). Teacher employers also can be nonsupportive of time off to allow contact with their children's schools. Teachers, like many other employees, also have to use their own sick days when their children are ill. Teacher-parents also know the dilemma of trying to act upon information that is second-hand, contradictory, and from potentially conflicting sources of self-interest (their child and their child's teacher). Many teachers are single parents; others are members of dual-career marriages; still others are employed because the family could not survive on a single paycheck (Spencer, 1986). We believe that this shared personal experience should facilitate teacher-parent interaction in spite of larger institutional policies that at times appear to promote adversarial relations.

❖ EDUCATIONAL EXPECTATIONS AS OBSTACLES FOR PARENTS

We begin with a description of tensions in educators' conceptions of family and parent involvement in schools, which at times seem to ignore the differences—the diversity and the conflict—in our culture and the variety of forms that a "family" and "involvement" can take. Educators tend to unidimensionalize families; they also unidimensionalize what they want from them.

Educators are concerned that discrepancies between home and school values may undermine student attendance, compliance, and achievement. These are considered directly related. Educators reason that student attendance and promptness increase exposure to the curriculum. Once in school, students' adherence to school rules decreases management problems; therefore, more time is spent on instruction of the curriculum, and that instruction goes more smoothly. Thus, two major goals of educators are engaging parents in the task of getting their children to school and parental support of school and classroom discipline codes and procedures.

Policy makers also believe that student achievement is linked to achievement opportunities, which are, in turn, a function of the amount and quality of student time at school and time on task (and, we would add, quality of instruction and task). Indeed, "time" was a primary organizational construct for recommended changes in schooling outlined in *A Nation at Risk* (National

Commission on Excellence in Education, 1983). This widely read, widely acclaimed, and widely criticized (e.g., Berliner & Biddle, 1995) government-sponsored report called for immediate and sustained changes in American schools to promote student achievement and international competitiveness.

A Nation at Risk recommended: more time for school (7-hour days, and a 200- to 220-day school year), more student time in school (attendance policies with clear sanctions and incentives), more instructional time in school (through improved schoolwide management systems and more "efficient" organization of student grouping for instruction), and more school time at home (through increased amounts of homework). *A Nation at Risk* attempted to increase the role of school in the lives of students. The government sponsors seemed unaware of (or unconcerned with) the potential effects of these mandates that would shift the bulk of students' time *out of home and into school*. Neither teachers' nor parents' voices were represented in this document.

Tensions will arise between home and school when goals or the paths to meet them are not shared and misperception and miscommunication continue unchecked. Notice, for example, the intrusion on families' available time with their children and teachers' available time to be with their own families that would result if these report recommendations were implemented. A few questions about the logic of the report come to mind: From the teacher perspective, if what we are already doing is inappropriate, why would doing it more make it appropriate? From the parent perspective, whose child is this?

A Nation at Risk did not address families' diverse needs or beliefs in our country or explain how the report might impinge on them. We think their final admonishment to parents, quoted below, reflects a rather limited view of who families are, the diversity of goals they may hold for their members (of which education may only be a subset), and the considerable sacrifice it might take to support and pursue their goals—educational or otherwise. We quote from this report at length because we believe it displays: 1) an inability to recognize potential conflicts between homes and schools about the function of schooling and 2) a limited view of "home goodness," both of which simply exacerbate the conflict between homes and schools, setting the stage for escalation of adversarial rather than cooperative relations.

But your right to a proper education for children carries a double responsibility. As surely as you are your child's first and most influential teacher, your child's ideas about education and its significance begin with you. You must be a *living* example of what you expect your children to honor and to emulate. Moreover, you bear a responsibility to participate actively in your child's education. You should encourage more diligent study and discourage satisfaction with mediocrity and the attitude that says "let it slide"; monitor your child's study; encourage good study habits; encourage your child to take more demanding rather than less demanding courses; nurture your child's curiosity, creativity, and confidence; and be an active participant in the work of the schools. Above all, exhibit a commitment to continued learning in your own life. Finally, help your child understand that excellence in education cannot be achieved without intellectual and moral integrity coupled with hard work and commitment. Children will look to their parents and teachers as models of such virtues. (p. 35)

To repeat, this level of arrogance is not only ineffective, it is simply unacceptable. Unfortunately, it continues. Government thinking about educational policy does not necessarily improve upon reflection or with time. The message of *A Nation at Risk* was that students needed to work longer, educators needed to work harder, and parents needed to be educators. These prescriptions failed to get citizen support. In the sequel, *Prisoners of Time* (National Education Commission on Time and Learning, 1994), policy makers change the rhetoric and contend that educators should use time more flexibly and that schools should concentrate on what "really matters." What really matters in *Prisoners of Time* are the "basics": math, science, and history—just like schooling in France, Germany, and Japan. Notably absent from the debate about education for the year 2000 and beyond is any real parent voice (except those of a few highly organized interest groups). Citizens, even elected representatives, have not played a role in defining educational goals. It seems unreasonable to expect parents and other citizens to embrace schools and to become actively involved when they are denied any voice in curriculum goal setting (e.g., "When do priorities shift to (from) skill acquisition to (from) problem solving?"), enactment strategies (e.g., "How can we design contexts within which students are objectively, and feel psychologically, safe?"), or their evaluation (e.g., "What constitutes success?").

◆ SOURCES OF CONFLICT IN PARENTS' MEETING EXPECTATIONS

Getting one's child to school and promoting recognition of its authority seem to many to be an easy enough task—and not much to ask. Consider the following analysis, however, by Casanova (1987), who writes from the perspective of improving "cultural compatibility" between various homes and school, not duplicating the home environment in the school (as suggested by Corno, 1989) or making the home more school-like (as suggested by Epstein, 1989).

Casanova explores a variety of reasons why a child consistently may be late to school. She notes that some reasons may be cultural; for example, perhaps time is not an important construct in the student's culture. Or perhaps the student is responsible for getting a younger sibling to the babysitter. Or maybe it is practical: the family does not have an alarm clock. Or maybe it is a characteristic of the student (she is lazy). To this analysis we would add that perhaps it is a matter of family resources: finances may not allow the replacement of a broken alarm. Perhaps time or transportation is not available to shop. Perhaps the student is chronically tired due to late work hours or family crises, and "5 more minutes" extends through the first school bell. Or maybe the parent does not have time to monitor the child; maybe the parent does not care; maybe the parent is so overwhelmed with personal difficulties s/he is not able to care. Or perhaps it is the *student* who does not care and refuses to comply with parent requests and persuasion. Perhaps the student knows that nothing much happens during the first period. Maybe no matter what the quality of schooling, its "rewards" do not inform her future.

Our point is that getting students to school is not necessarily easy; why students are not in school or are late to school is not apparent. We agree with Casanova (1987): If we wish to understand, we need to: 1) *suspend judgment* and 2) *ask*, rather than assume, a parent's or child's motives, values, or goals. The first step in problem resolution is mutual understanding of the problem, problem ownership, and intervention: what is the problem, whose problem is it, and whose responsibility is it to solve it? Our position is that most, if not all, problems are *shared*. Thus, conversations are essential ingredients for their understanding and resolution.

◆ EXACERBATION OF CONFLICT BETWEEN PARENTS AND EDUCATORS

Rather than suspending judgment, however, recent actions by schools and other social institutions indicate that judgments are being made—and made within an adversarial framework. Webb, Covington, and Guthrie (1993) report that current attempts to increase school authority replace a focus on incentives ("carrots") to positively reinforce students for attendance and participation to a focus on sanctions ("sticks") meant to negatively reinforce these behaviors. That is, rather than reward a student for school performance ("positive reinforcement" to increase desired behavior), these procedures stop negative consequences if student school performance meets criteria ("negative reinforcement" to increase desired behavior [see Skinner, 1953, for other consequence strategies to modify behavior within the "behaviorist" tradition]).

Webb and colleagues provide as an example the no-pass/no-play regulations for participation in school sports and extracurricular activities which exist in at least 10 states. At first glance, such rules seem reasonable enough: if students are not passing their academic courses, they should not be spending time in extracurricular activities. Time would be better spent on study, the primary task of schooling. At second glance, however, we are not as able to justify the reason. Negative sanctions like no pass/no play often sever the only links that students in difficulty have to school by dissolving their relationships with their coaches and teammates (Women's Sports Foundation, 1989). For these students, no-pass/no-play regulations are perceived as—and are—punitive, focused on taking away rather than enabling. Rather than keeping these students in school, such policies often show them the exit.

Other societal institutions align themselves with mandatory school attendance and performance regulations through direct intrusion in the home and other nonschool domains of students' lives. For example, Webb, Covington, and Guthrie (1993) report that, in 1988, West Virginia enacted legislation to deny a driver's license to anyone under the age of 18 who could not prove either current enrollment in or graduation from high school. Subsequently, several other states have enacted "no-pass/no-drive" laws.

Ironically, those who advocate sanction programs seem to believe that students are not doing well because they *choose* not to do well; thus, it is their own fault. Students are to blame, they should be held accountable, and they should be punished. However, as Webb et al. note, students who are in the position to worry about losing extracurricular-activity privileges at school and driving privileges in their community typically have had difficulty in school for some time and often are considerably behind in their classes. Thus, sanctions at this point—even though considerably threatening and costly to students—likely do little to correct the learning failure. We might ask whether no-pass/no-play/no-drive policies have multiple purposes. First, such policies increase fade-out and drop-out for many students rather than promoting their achievement. Second, *average* high-school grades may increase under such policies because there are fewer (and more "select") students in the count.

The appropriateness of the "sticks" approach to improving school attendance and performance is even more worrisome when applied to school-aged parents. Some states have policies about school attendance that intrude directly into the financial security and safety of young parents and their children. Minnesota requires parents under the age of 18 who receive Aid to Families with Dependent Children (AFDC) to attend school once their infants are 6 weeks old. In Ohio, all custodial parents under the age of 19 who receive AFDC monies must obtain a high-school diploma or a general education diploma (GED).

Students are not the only targets of societal coercion for school attendance, compliance, and performance. Tangri and Moles (1987) report that all states have a law holding parents personally responsible for school vandalism if a case can be made that parents did not appropriately supervise their child or direct her/his behavior. Webb, Covington, and Guthrie (1993) examine state policies linking support for dependent children and schooling. One example they report is Wisconsin, where adolescents must be in school or their families lose their aid-for-dependents benefits. Consider the power and invitation to abuse it that are extended to the defiant adolescent in such households—the same child that the school is unable to influence, even with its relative expertise and clout. As we will see, there is a considerable body of research on internalization and compliance that predicts the futility of such programs (e.g., Hoffman, 1985; Lepper, 1985; McCaslin & Good, 1996).

Webb et al. note that programs that tie student behavior to parent consequences are based upon questionable motivational assumptions and are unfair in the sense of punishing an entire family for the actions of a single member, who cannot be held accountable in a fundamental sense. Such parent sanctions seem to convey a formal misunderstanding of the role of motivation in schooling, a lack of sensitivity to the difficulty involved in maintaining low income families, and a lack of respect for parents and their relationships with their children. Such policies appear based on anything but the rule, to 1) suspend judgment and 2) ask.

◆ DIVERSITY VERSUS ADVERSITY

Independent of family economic status or student success in school, attendance and endorsement of school authority are not congruent constructs in all families. And lack of congruence does not equal mindful resistance or defiance. Casanova (1987) describes a difference in family beliefs about school authority from the perspective of ethnicity. She reports that Puerto Rican parents tend to give the school control over the discipline and instruction of their children when in school; however, the decision to send (or not) a child to school on a given day remains in parents' control. Anglo parents tend to uphold the opposite: they give the school the authority to demand student attendance, but Anglo parents claim the right to be involved in curriculum and discipline decisions.

Casanova stresses that the issue is not to decide "who is right" but to understand differences that must be recognized if teachers, parents, and students are to work together effectively. Indeed, one goal of this chapter is to help teachers understand the context of family and how diversity within and among families is *part* of the schooling context, not independent of it or counter to it. As we have asserted throughout, families and schools are distinct yet overlapping and dynamic systems, that can be compatible and interactive in the life of the child/student (see also, Corno, 1989)—who also is engaged in continuous change.

How then, might we stop the monologue of no-pass/no-play and transform the dialogue between teachers and parents into an authentic conversation that enhances the development and education of the young? One step is to understand what facilitates and impedes parents' involvement in their children's schooling.

❖ PARENT INVOLVEMENT IN SCHOOLS

If we assert that parents are interested in the education of their children, indeed, share the task of education, then we need to consider why they are not more actively involved than they appear to be. If you are an experienced teacher, you probably have heard your share of excuses for unkept appointments from defensive and possibly hostile parents. Sometimes, however, excuses are real. Agreed, perhaps appointments should not have been made if they could not be kept. But let's consider both aspects of the problem: the press to promise (parent motivation) and the keeping of a promise (parent enactment strategies and structural supports).

◆ Motivation: The Press to Promise

Throughout this book, we have argued that a model of co-regulated learning (see Chapter 1, Figures 1.1–1.4) is a viable heuristic for understanding student mediational processes and teachers' role in scaffolding and supporting them. We think this model is also a useful heuristic for understanding parents' mediational processes in general and their involvement in their children's schooling in particular. Parents' motivation can be distinguished from their enactment strategies to meet their goals, and their evaluation of progress if not success.

From a parent-involvement perspective, then, the first part of the process—engaging parent interest—is a "motivational" one, which precedes actual parent participation or "enactment." The motive to participate can stem from a variety of sources. For example, parents' motivation could be a desire to co-participate in their child's education or an unwanted dependency on the teacher to "know what to do" with their child (both "intrinsic motives"). Or the parent could seek out the teacher because of a need to impress her/him or avoid loss of AFDC monies (both "extrinsic motives"). Perhaps parent motivation involves a combination of intrinsic and extrinsic motives (the parent is concerned about the child's learning, wants the teacher to believe that, and is also worried about the family finances).

Most likely, parents' motivation, like anyone's motivation, is determined by multiple influences and serves more than one goal. As we stated previously, we do not adhere to the "hierarchy of goodness" often found in research on motivation which unilaterally places intrinsic motivation above extrinsic considerations. Sometimes intrinsic motivation is a luxury that not all can afford, sometimes tasks simply must be done. Thus, it seems more helpful for teachers to consider parent motivation, like their own, as multifaceted, a matter of proportion, and contextual.

The promise to participate, then, is a motivational decision that begins with "What do I want?" The decision about *how* to participate, to set goals, the "What am I going to do?" is also a motivational decision based on a variety of factors—most notably skills, resources, efficacy, and dispositions. For example, if a parent is comfortable in the school, values reading, and knows how a library works, s/he may define participation as volunteer work in the library. Another parent may feel more efficacious interacting with the students; s/he supervises a field trip. It might not occur to another that s/he has anything to *offer* the school; by *participation* s/he means scheduling a conference with the child's teacher. In short, parent motivation is multifaceted, integrates motive with skill in the setting of goals (that likely change over time), and precedes actual participation.

In addition, parents' lives are complicated. Goals to participate in one child's schooling must be juggled—coordinated—with other family and personal goals. Bronfenbrenner and Neville (1994) describe it well:

> Recent studies revealed a second major disruptive factor in the lives of families and children: the increasing instability, inconsistency, and hectic character of daily family life. The following commentary on the American scene is evocative of this pervasive trend: In a world in which both parents usually have to work, often at a considerable distance from home, every family member, through the waking hours from morning till night, is "on the run." The need to coordinate conflicting demands of job and child care, often involving varied arrangements that shift from day to day, can produce a situation in which everyone has to be transported several times a day in different directions, usually at the same time— a state of affairs that prompted a foreign colleague to comment: "It seems to me

that in your country, most children are being brought up in moving vehicles."
(Bronfenbrenner, 1989, p. 13, in Bronfenbrenner & Neville, 1994, pp. 15–16.)

Thus, parents must not only want to be involved in their child's schooling, they also need to prioritize that goal as they coordinate multiple goals. It's not easy. It was never easy; however, it is now even more difficult as the quality of life in many American families continues to erode (Weissbourd, 1994).

◆ ENACTMENT: STRATEGIES AND SUPPORTS

We call the second part of the parent involvement "problem," *the promise unkept*, an issue of enactment. As we have discussed previously, volition is part of strategic enactment and it is in itself a skill (Corno, 1992; 1993; Heckhausen, 1991; Kuhl, 1985; McCaslin & Good, 1996). Enactment involves the strategic pursuit of a goal (e.g., arranging schedules, rearranging work commitments) and the ability to protect intentions to meet a goal (also termed *volition*)—in our example, the parent intention to participate in her/his child's schooling. Volition is an important part of seeing through and following through on motivational decisions. Thus, strategies to meet goals are better implemented when there also are effective strategies to keep the many distractions in life from getting in the way of what we set out to accomplish (see Corno, 1992 for an excellent discussion of various volitional strategies and their promotion in the classroom).

The recriminations, "The road to hell is paved with good intentions," "The best laid plans. . . . ," "But you said you would," are familiar expressions of a failed volitional task. Modern theory and research on volition conceptualizes volitional behavior as something that is *learned* rather than a character trait (Corno, 1992; 1993). In our framework of co-regulation of mediational processes, volition is acquired, can be taught, and should be structurally supported (see McCaslin & Good, 1996).

For example, some situations are more difficult than others for enabling enactment strategies because there are just too many pulls in too many directions for any one person to handle, or obstacles cannot be circumvented and simply prevent individual enactment. In our perspective, then, the educators' question changes from "Why don't parents meet their commitments (to their own or our goals)?" to "Why aren't parents more volitional in participating in their children's schooling?" to "How can we encourage parents to prioritize participation in their children's education *and* help realize that commitment through structural supports that facilitate parent enactment of their intentions?" Like multiple sources of motivation, we consider enactment strategies and supports to have multiple sources, namely parents, their children, teachers, *and* the school. Finally, just as parents need support in prioritizing their involvement, so too teachers need institutional supports to protect their intentions to involve parents. Parent involvement makes schools more authentic; however, it also can make classroom matters more complex.

In summary, as we review the data on parent involvement in school, we think it is useful to distinguish parent motivation (including goal setting and coordination) from enactment strategies and supports. Getting parents interested is an important step, but it is not especially predictive of their actual participation. Schools could do much to structurally support parent involvement by allowing them more opportunities to protect and, thus, enact their intentions (e.g., more flexible hours for meetings, maintenance of safety during nonschool hours, provision of transportation, child care during parent-teacher conferences, availability of translators). Even so, a considerable number of parents are involved in their children's schooling. We now look at who they are and the forms that involvement takes.

◆ SOME DATA ON VOLUNTEERS

Tangri and Moles (1987) report survey research by Stallworth and Williams (1983) in which parents described the type of involvement they wanted in their children's schooling. The data parallel Casanova's (1987) discussion of Anglo parents described previously. These researchers report that parents wanted to be involved in decisions about discipline procedures in the classroom and throughout the school, the amount of homework assigned, and evaluation of student learning. It is noteworthy that these parents reportedly did *not* want to support more multicultural and bilingual education in the schools. (This is a recurring problem in educational evaluations where the research base represents the cultural majority yet school participants reflect a diverse culture.) In this same study, teachers and principals did not think parents would be as helpful as parents believed themselves to be. In particular, teachers considered parents the least important decision makers in the educational process. As Wilkes (personal communication), notes, it appears that schools devalue parents in school yet expect parents to value schooling—an interesting paradox. Some schools also appear to devalue parents *at home*. Bowman (1994) notes that schools often provide wrong and inconsistent advice to parents on how to improve their "parenting skills" to better their children's achievement. Casanova (personal communication) adds that often schools assume that parents do not know their children as well as teachers do. Tangri and Moles (1987) stress, however, that both teachers and parents reportedly would like more *connections* between home and school.

Connections do not mean decisions, and they are not necessarily meaningful. When parents are involved in schools, they typically do not participate in substantive decision making. One exception to this generalization is that some parents do participate in individualized educational planning (IEP) meetings for their children. However, these meetings typically are problem driven and remediation focused, involving an array of educational and psychological "experts" who identify and design an appropriate educational response to a problem presented by the parent's child—often in language the parent does not use and may not understand. Thus, in general, when parents are involved in (or "witness") decision making, decisions are restricted to their particular child—typically framed by and in pursuit of school goals—and their job is to rubber-stamp the prescription.

In short, parents volunteer their time and their talents to help the school meet *its* goals for their children. The extent of parent volunteerism appears considerable and, we suspect, different than commonly believed. The data certainly challenge assertions of "parent apathy." Tangri and Moles (1987) report that 79 percent of public schools rely on parent volunteers; this is especially the case in elementary schools, where 88 percent report parent volunteers (compared with 60 percent of high schools). Thomas (reported in Tangri & Moles, 1987) calculated that, at the rate of $5 per volunteer hour, for every dollar spent by school districts they received $50 in volunteer services. Effective use of parent volunteers (*effective* is often defined by increased student attendance, compliance, and achievement) is enhanced by: 1) parent training in a variety of interpersonal skills, including group process, and 2) the opportunity to meet with the classroom teacher to better understand her/his goals. So, some parents connect with schools and help them meet their goals; other parents' connections with schools (those about whom teachers are typically concerned) tend to consist of contact *by* schools—usually when something is wrong.

◆ Some Considerations in School–Home Contacts

Parents report that they both want and have contact with the school: 87 percent of parents report having some form of contact with their child's school; 70 percent report attending a teacher conference or writing to their child's teacher within the previous two years (in Tangri & Moles, 1987). The issue, then, does not appear to be contact *per se*, but the nature of the contact and the role it affords parents.

Parents are often in a reactive mode when in contact with the school. The very mechanisms that often are used to relay information to busy parents—report cards, newsletters, and telephone calls—in effect systematically restrict the parents' role in their child's schooling. In our experience with report cards across the grade levels, for example, there is an ever-decreasing space for parent comment, and eventually the signature of a parent is not required. We suggest that through such changes in reporting on student progress, schools systematically devolve parent participation in the evaluation of their child's schooling. We include the following parent account because we suspect her experience and feelings of alienation represent that of many parents. As you read this, be mindful that this parent had instituted a no-pass/no-play policy with her son, based upon previous semester performance and school suggestions, and wrote to his teachers asking for advice on the usefulness of this strategy to improve his work as it appeared to be counterproductive:

> Parents seem to come in third when discussing the needs among students, teachers (institutions) and parents. . . . Sometimes it feels we are never approached for our opinion on anything. . . . Last semester I wrote a letter to all of my son's teachers when mid-period progress reports came out. . . . My son's grades were extremely varied [mid-period reports in 4 of the 7 classes indicated failing or "D" grades, missing work, etc.]. . . . Bottom line, I never heard from any teacher. I

never knew if the teachers had even received the letters. [Final period report card included three "F" grades, one "C-", and two "A" grades]. . . . Teachers can tell students, teachers can tell parents, but who tells teachers? (Anonymous, 1994, with permission)

Newsletters home are a bit more consistent and neutral, but their primary purpose (and effectiveness criterion) is to facilitate housekeeping matters (e.g., lunch fees, bus schedules, permission deadlines) rather than meaningfully engage the parent in classroom processes.

And we all know what it's like to receive a phone call requiring a decision without sufficient time to think through the task—especially while making dinner or monitoring multiple activities. Simply recall your response to the last phone solicitor who caught you in the middle of several tasks: "Hello, Mr. Gonzalez! My name is Mary! How are you this evening?!" Consider that all Mary was trying to do was sell you aluminum siding or perhaps a family photo session. Mary was not pressing for a solution to a problem she believed your child was facing. Consider as well that the phone solicitor likely just came on the evening shift; the teacher has already put in a very full (and perhaps difficult) day, and s/he is still not finished. Her/his personal life is still on hold.

In short, many of the home-school contact mechanisms that exist promote harried, if not adversarial, relationships for *all involved*. This does not serve the parent, the teacher, or the child about whom they share concern. Like an increasingly perfunctory report card, the evening phone call certainly doesn't help motivate parents to seek or to prioritize proactive participation in their child's schooling. Nor do these mechanisms help teachers consider parents as coparticipants in their child's education.

◆ SOME CONSTRAINTS ON PARENT PARTICIPATION

The National Education Association (1982) points out that parents have no obligation to communicate with schools. The NEA concludes that it is the school's responsibility to "contact the parents as needed and to minimize barriers that tend to overwhelm parents, such as inflexible time schedules, use of status symbols, and the presence of more school staff than parents at conferences" (in Tangri & Moles, 1987, p. 524). Sarason (1993) also notes attitudinal obstacles to parent participation, "because parents tend to view teachers with a strange and inhibiting mixture of respect, fear, and ambivalence. And teachers tend to view parents as uninterested or hypersensitive and judgmental" (p. 59).

Schools also tend to be isolated from the community; to some extent, the constraints on parent motivation to participate and their strategies to follow through on their intentions are products of this isolation. (Fortunately, in some cases, more school integration with various social agencies is beginning to occur.) Let's consider some of the motivational constraints that parents bring to the task of deciding to participate in their child's school.

Motivational Constraints   First, there is the issue of prior experience. Not surprisingly, parents who themselves did not particularly succeed in or enjoy school are less likely to be comfortable in the school setting or seek out school contact because of their own feelings and prior history (see, for example, Lightfoot, 1978). Schools may have changed in the interim, but these parents wouldn't know that: their avoidance has promoted (and likely reified) old images and hurts (see Bandura, 1986, for more complete discussion of avoidance and phobic processes).

Second, as Casanova (1987) notes, cultural differences in perception about the appropriate role of parents in schools can influence parent motivation to *not* participate. Some parents may even believe that the best way they can support the schools is to "let them get on with their business," a belief that might have originated with the parent or been perceived at the school.

Third, language differences in the home can impede communication with teachers. Romero, Mercado, and Vàzquez-Faría (1987, p. 349) report that, among school-aged children, an estimated 2.5 million speak a language other than English or live in homes that do not speak English. Projection data indicate that the non-English-language-background population in the United States will have grown from 30 million in 1980 to 39.5 million by the year 2000. Independent of the sheer magnitude of the task, language differences between home and school can result in lack of communication and miscommunication, and decrease parent motivation to participate.

Fourth, as Tangri and Moles (1987) explain, perceptions by parents of school personnel as apathetic, indifferent, or hostile to parent participation, and the reciprocal beliefs of school staff that parents are apathetic or lack skills for meaningful participation result in a self-fulfilling cycle of parental noninvolvement (and, we add, teacher lack of interest).

Fifth, some authors (e.g., Lightfoot, 1978) argue that motivational problems are the inevitable product of the emotionally laden conflict between teachers and parents over the education and ownership of "their" student/child. Reports like *A Nation at Risk* can only exacerbate the problem.

Enactment Constraints   Even when parent motivation to participate does emerge, there can be impediments to parent ability to follow through on intentions and actually participate. Often these impediments are due to a lack of structural supports, which schools need to address and rectify in any serious effort to increase parents' participation in the schooling of their children. Schools need to consider as well the changing worlds of their employees (Spencer, 1986). Schools cannot assume that teachers readily are available for evening phone conferences, breakfast meetings, and after-hours presentations. Teachers' lives are complicated; the solution to increased support for parent accessibility to the school does not simply translate into increased teacher responsibilities and an expanded definition and length of the work day. In brief, the constraints on parent participation we describe here likely apply to constraints on teachers as well.

First, social conditions are changing. The rise of single-parent families and two-employed-parent families are well known. Thus, the logistics of participating in schools through the traditional means are waning. Current evidence, however, suggests that there are no differences between employed and nonemployed parents in time spent *at home* monitoring and helping with homework (Tangri & Moles, 1987). We have already noted that evening phone contacts are not a panacea; employers and schools could facilitate school participation through more flexible schedules and media (e.g., a "parent hotline" staffed for most of the waking day; videotapes of classroom lessons for parents to borrow). At a minimum, schools need to involve parents *early* in any school concerns.

Second, as we have noted, most parents lead incredibly complicated lives. Multiple children, aging parents, illness, and other responsibilities can overwhelm parent resolve. Families divorcing or recently divorced especially benefit from supportive teachers and predictable schedules and structures in school. Children benefit when both custodial and noncustodial parents are kept informed of child progress and difficulties.

Third, some parents believe that they have increasingly limited influence as their children grow up. By the time their children reach high school, many parents believe that their desire to participate in their child's education is a moot point. And by the time they are in high school, adolescents have multiple teachers who know students less intimately than do teachers in other educational structures (e.g., the contained classrooms of elementary school). Thus, adolescents' teachers are less apt to seek and support parent involvement of a particular student in the first place. As we discuss in Chapter 2, these changes in parent efficacy, school structure, and teacher knowledge converge at an unfortunate time in student development (Eccles, Midgley, Wigfield, Buchanan, Reuman, Flanagan, & MacIver, 1993; Tangri & Moles, 1987).

Fourth, safety concerns are rising. Many parents live in transient neighborhoods; schools are not always in safe settings. It is not unusual, for example, for urban schools to lock their buildings to personnel by 4:00 P.M. Schools can appear forbidding; they also are not necessarily accessible places—either physically or temporally. At minimum, schools need to be safe places for employees, students, and parents during the day and in the dark.

Fifth, neither parents nor teachers know how to create roles for parents that are meaningful and efficacious for parent, teacher, and child/student (Tangri & Moles, 1987). Much work needs to be done to create school structures and opportunities to support meaningful parent participation in their child's education. The definition of *meaningful parent participation* is apt to be a source of vigorous discussion and debate, and we do not claim to have an answer. We do believe, however, that the dichotomies that typically frame the debate need to be more insightful than the current prevailing ones of:

a. "Blame the parent for students not achieving the goals we set for them" (e.g., Tomlinson, 1993), and

b. Parents' claims that schools have no role in health promotion and individual precaution in an era of AIDS, increased student sexual activity, and interest in drugs (e.g., Quindlen, January 12, 1994).

Surely we are capable of more subtle and incisive analyses of the function of parents in schools and schools in families so that we may better design supportive structures between them, for the betterment of children.

Evaluation Constraints   When parents do set and enact goals to participate in their child's schooling, they do not always receive feedback that their participation has made a difference. Indeed, the narrow definition of successful parent involvement typically used by schools (attendance, compliance, achievement) leaves little support for the parent to assess his/her own criteria for participation (e.g., child comfort in class, improved peer relations, decreased parent isolation from the everydayness of the child). Ironically, self-evaluating parents might actually undermine their own motivation. Like their children, parents may well learn that their own goals are not relevant—if they do not make progress toward school goals, they are not welcome; if they criticize school goals, they are not welcome.

◆ Summary

We have described a relationship between home and school that is not particularly efficacious for its participants. It appears that educators associate parent involvement (through whatever means) with student attendance, compliance, and achievement, which are linked. Schools apparently define, and prefer, the parent to be an enforcer of school goals and procedures, not a co-participating decision maker. We maintain, however, that if parents can only be instrumental or obstructive to the school's attainment of its goals, a conflicted if not adversarial relationship is apt to pervade. It appears that this is often the case.

Thus far, we have attempted to debunk prevailing myths of parent apathy by examining data on when and how parents do participate in their children's schooling and the motivational and enactment obstacles that may limit that participation. Our analysis of motivational and enactment factors that might inhibit parent participation is meant to help increase understanding of potential barriers so that schools become: 1) more willing to consider how to involve parents in *meaningful*, authentic ways in the schooling of their children (see also Newmann, 1992), and 2) more effective in their attempts to support that involvement.

We believe that blaming parents or limiting their role to "school enforcers" is futile if our goal is to enhance the education and development of their children. Similarly, blaming schools is simplistic and unhelpful. Parents and schools need not be in adversarial relationships; indeed, we believe they cannot be in such relationships if education of children is to occur. Our position is similar to Bowman (1994) and others (e.g., Spodek & Saracho, 1990) who argue that educators must be sensitive to the family context that inhibits or facilitates students' achievement, learn how to develop closer home and school relationships, and become aware of possible differences in how learning occurs at home and at school.

We turn now to the second theme in our discussion of family: family relationships and parenting "managerial" styles. One goal is to alert teachers to the potential family dynamics, through which any school communication about children is filtered and through which students likely interpret the events of school—especially if the events are ambiguous. We then present strategies for listening to and talking with parents that promote shared understandings of student difficulties *and* progress—and inform collaborative support. Another goal is to help teachers design settings within which parents want and know how to participate and are able to *prioritize* commitments to promote the education of their children. We consider the parent-teacher relationship an important vehicle to create this setting.

❖ FAMILY DYNAMICS

In this section we discuss how research on parents and families attempts to understand family dynamics, in particular how one family member can influence another. We examine student family life from multiple and, we believe, mutually informative perspectives: expert-novice, family systems, and parenting styles. First, we briefly discuss two interrelated positions that attend to fundamental *relationships* within families and which are recent developments in the family (vs. "parenting") literature. These approaches are more focused on process than on outcome and conceptualize parents as "facilitating" rather than causal. The first of these relational perspectives, termed *dependent-independence* (Winegar, Renninger, & Valsiner, 1989) is a conception of expert-novice relationships that the authors apply to understanding parent-child and teacher-student relationships.

The second relational approach to the study of families we briefly discuss is termed *family systems theory* (e.g., Emery, 1992). Family systems theory considers families to be systems of multiple, interconnected, and dynamic relationships. Unlike the more traditional parenting-styles approach and the dependent-independence conception, which attend primarily (but not exclusively) to parent (expert) effects on the child (novice), family systems theory attempts to actively consider reciprocal and interconnected events and conflicts within families. (Our analysis is limited to school-related dynamics; the interested reader is referred to Minuchin [1974] for fuller analysis.)

Third, our primary discussion is of the best known and most-traditional perspective on family life within child psychology, called the "parenting-styles" or "patterns of parental behavior" literature (e.g., Baumrind, 1971; 1987). Our purpose in describing this work is to provide teachers one perspective on global family-management beliefs and control strategies to help them consider both the extent of the match between classroom and home discipline and the context through which parents likely interpret reports by or about their child. We think teachers will also find this discussion useful as they consider their own classroom-management strategies and their relationship to school-level policies. Before we discuss each of these perspectives in depth, however, we first caution the reader about the inherent vulnerability of research on families.

◆ SOME RESEARCH DILEMMAS

Each of these three approaches to understanding families—dependent-independence, family systems, and parenting styles—differs in theoretical constructs but shares the difficulties encountered when trying to research them. Families are left "unto themselves" in our society unless there is concern that they have gone beneath the bottom line of safety and care for their children. Thus, in our culture, the study of family is often believed intrusive and a violation of basic rights to privacy. Families who volunteer to participate in research are likely different in important ways from those who do not; families who are "required" to participate are different from those who are not. This is an issue of *sample representation* that plagues the study of family. Even so, we think that, in aggregation, important constructs emerge for our consideration of how parents in general might mediate school communications about their children.

Identifying participants is difficult; defining *family* is difficult (e.g., Just what is a family? How do members differ across families?); so is conducting the actual research. Not only are there the usual measurement problems of defining variables carefully and measuring them reliably; there also are access problems and *event representation* difficulties, in the sense of ecological validity. For example, how do dinners in your family change when there is "company"? Event-representation difficulties are also present in terms of construct validity.

Consider the construct, *curiosity*, which is often considered one of our most primitive adaptive mechanisms for mastering the world. What does curiosity mean in a family with "secrets"? What happens when curiosity shuts down? How might this play out in school? What about when a parent is angry? Is parent anger a discrete psychological event? What does it cue to the child? How does the parent model coping with anger? What comes next? Shantz (1993) reports that some children (approximately 10 percent) report sadness over events that normally elicit anger. How might parent coping be involved in their child's atypical emotional responses?

For our purposes, we attend to those features of family research that present compelling arguments that help organize the variation in what families *do*. We assume that family behavior is best understood within a biological/psychological/social ("bio-psycho-social" in the jargon) framework. It should be clear, however, that the considerable constraints on research on parents and families underscores the powerful role of theory and decision making in the design, implementation, and interpretation of this research.

◆ SOME BASIC PARENTING CONSTRUCTS

The role of theory in understanding research design and data interpretation cannot be overstated. Before discussing the "meta" lens of each approach to understanding family, it is helpful to identify some basic parenting constructs that are used throughout the literature and to which each theory attends, at least to some degree.

Hess and Holloway (1984) note that the subject of family and achievement has been studied at least since Galton's work (1874). Hess and Holloway reviewed the extensive literature on the types of parent behavior that have been linked to their children's achievement. Their review illustrates the kinds of variables that are usually identified as predictive of school achievement. Maccoby and Martin (1983) also identify these variables as important considerations in child mental health. Thus, in research on families, the following usually are considered essential:

1. Verbal interaction between mother and child.
2. Affective relationship between parent and child.
3. Discipline and control strategies.
4. Expectations for achievement.
5. (Most recently) affects of parent beliefs and attributions about their children.

We will examine each of these variables (to varying degrees) within each of the three theoretical perspectives. We call attention to one characteristic that they all share: they focus on the *form* of the parent-child relationship, not on the *content*. Thus, even though the form of discipline may be studied across ethnic groups (e.g., whether parents exert control over their children), the content may be ignored. In some cultures (and within different cultures), for example, parents expect eye-contact from their child when he/she is being disciplined; in others, parents interpret eye-contact as defiance (Romero, Mercado, & Vàzquez-Faría, 1987). As is so often the case in psychological research, however, the assumed "content" is typically defined by a middle-class standard. Hence, little is known about cultural or economic diversity (cf. Philips, 1983) unless a deficit model (A does less of *x* than does B) is adopted (recall Zeigler's [1994] analysis presented at the beginning of this chapter).

One potential exception to this state of affairs is the recent research on parent beliefs. (Recall the research by Casanova [1987] on ethnic differences in beliefs about school authority; see also, Brantlinger [1993]; McCaslin & Murdock [1991]; and Miller [1982] for research on differences in parenting beliefs within working class families.) It is important to remember, however, that even when cultural differences are identified, little is known about the individual variation within a particular cultural or economic group: all members of a group are not alike. Nor are all members of a family.

◆ RELATIONAL APPROACHES TO THE STUDY OF FAMILIES

We briefly describe two interrelated approaches to understanding families. The first, dependent-independence, focuses primarily on the reciprocal relationships among expert, novice, and context; the second attends to the multiple dynamic relationships and underlying conflicts that contribute to a family "system." Our purpose is to provide teachers with a broad lens for understanding families before we restrict our focus to parent management styles.

Dependent-Independence Winegar, Renninger, and Valsiner (1989) emphasize the importance of *context* in understanding relationships—particularly those that involve an expert (e.g., parent, teacher) and a novice (e.g., child, student). In this perspective (consistent with Vygotskian theory, 1962; 1978), the expert is an active designer of contexts (and, we would add, creator of opportunities) within which the child develops. Thus, the child is not so much developing toward *independence* as developing an *interdependence* with a specific context. In the authors' language, the child is developing through differing states of "dependent-independence."

Expert-novice relationships are facilitating, not causal. That is, the expert does not directly affect the novice, but instead creates conditions within which the novice learns. Two ways that experts support novices are of special interest here. First, experts have the knowledge and skills to design and reorganize the environment that provides for child growth and development. The authors describe three domains of child learning that experts might seek to influence: a) expected child behavior and adoption of goals they wish the child to seek (termed *zone of free movement*); b) child interests and behavior they simply would like to encourage but cannot require (termed *zone of promoted action*); and c) skills that are within the child's reach with their supportive assistance (*zone of proximal development*—a Vygotskian term with which you may be familiar).

Second, the actions of the expert and novice are complementary. We are used to considering this relationship when we design supports for children: children are less skilled and need our help. We place alphabet, multiplication tables, the periodic table, and classroom-rule reminders on our bulletin boards to support the beginning, reluctant, or forgetful learner. Winegar et al. are careful to remind us that, just as we increase supports when they are needed, experts also *remove* them when they are not. They state, "Specifically, with experience, experts increasingly relinquish control over novices' actions, and novices take increasing responsibility for their own performance" (p. 162). Experts adjust to the novice's emerging competence; thus, just as the novice's behavior is dependent upon the actions of the expert, so too, is the expert's behavior dependent on the novice. They are in an interdependent relationship. Novices must be allowed their emergent capabilities if they are to make progress.

Our purpose in briefly noting this perspective is twofold. First, we want (again) to sensitize teachers to the functional role of context in students' relationships at home and at school. Changes in context likely affect children's ability to cope. We stress that student "independence" is not independent of the context. Thus, it is unrealistic (and not helpful for students) to expect student apparent competence to transfer across contexts—especially when these changes are abrupt and contexts are not compatible. The importance of this analysis for the daily home-school transitions that students make comes readily to mind. Consider also, for example, the transition to junior high. Work by Eccles and colleagues (1993) suggests that with the transition out of elementary school, students change from exhibiting what Baumrind (1970) terms *instrumental dependence,* which indicates competent use of resources, to display of *expressive dependence,* which indicates lack of coping. This does not have to be the case but likely will with such nonsupportive and abrupt changes in context.

Second, Winegar and colleagues remind us to *remove* supports when they are *no longer needed*: Removal of superfluous supports is supportive. In many ways this form of support is consistent with the authoritative parent (subsequently described at length) who is sensitive to changing child expertise and ability to assume responsibility for *self*-regulation rather than *other*-regulation. This perspective also reminds us of the costs of keeping a novice in a subordinate role (as happens with authoritarian parents and many school management systems, which we will discuss later at length). Failing to recognize and support the growing expertise of the novice effects: 1) the sheer quality of trust in the expert-novice relationship (e.g, "You don't think I'm competent so you do it for me to be sure it's right.") and 2) the emergent capabilities of the novice (i.e., the child who is not allowed to do the task because the expert takes over does not learn how to do the task, fail, and recover from failure; that is, his/her mediation of the task has been thwarted).

Family Systems The systems approach to understanding family locates meaningful family dynamics—and conflict—in the interconnections among its members. Here we briefly present just four premises from this tradition that seem especially helpful for building better home-school alliances for the benefit of students.

First, conflicts are considered necessary, interpersonal, and with two levels of meaning (Emery, 1992): surface level and deep level. These two levels of meaning are similar to our analysis of questions as simultaneously addressing two levels: the apparent content under discussion and the deeper scaffolding of student mediational processes (see Chapter 1). That is, surface-level meaning of conflict is fairly straightforward as it deals with specific issues and its purpose is to resolve the disagreement. The deep level of conflict is structured by the need to assert or change the existing structure or rules of a relationship. Relationships, in turn, are understood by their intimacy and power.

Second, family systems can be understood by alliances and loyalties and by their permeability to "others." *Permeability* is defined by where and when boundaries are imposed, their degree of rigidity, and under what conditions (if any) they may be crossed. Third, family conflicts are developmentally related. From the family systems perspective, increases in child autonomy trigger power struggles that require renegotiation of parent-child boundaries. Emery puts it this way: "Parents are not expected to dominate children, but they are expected to remain dominant" (p. 278). Fourth, conflicts among members of a family affect the entire family (we will return to this point later).

We think these constructs are extremely useful for consideration of home-school conflict as well as family conflicts. Indeed, we suspect that much home-school conflict is understood and dealt with at the surface level, when the real issue is deeper: "Who has the power over my child and in what domains?" Working with differences in permeability of family boundaries is part of the teaching experience: while some families are perhaps too open to the school (e.g., some limited-English-language families place enormous faith and belief in the school to bring their child and family a better life, and they give the school complete access—recall Julio and his father in Chapter 2), others are completely closed, family secrets remain at home (e.g., situations of abuse—see Chapter 5).

With development comes an increasing area of child autonomy that can be viewed by parents as a subtraction model:

More child autonomy = Less parent authority

Not *different*, simply *less*. Emery notes that conflict between parent and child escalates during developmental transitions like the "terrible twos" and early and late adolescence because these are times of rapidly increasing demands by the child for independence. He maintains that these markers inform the content, frequency, and intensity of parent-child conflict. He explains:

> The content of the most frequent conflicts should follow a pattern of age-graded autonomy issues, such as preschoolers' selection of clothes, school-aged children's homework, and adolescents' curfews. . . . More frequent and intense conflicts are expected when the boundaries depart significantly from developmental norms (restrictiveness or permissiveness is great), when boundaries are deeply penetrated (parents attempt to regulate behavior that has long been in the child's control or the converse), when boundaries are unclear (discipline is inconsistent), when parental dominance is in doubt (parents hold little authority), and during developmental transitions (because of sudden jumps in children's struggles for autonomy). (p. 279)

These developmental changes are considered within a power struggle, although Emery notes that sometimes they can be confused as a threat to intimacy. Indeed, this is a common misperception of adolescence: the anger that often accompanies the constraints placed on adolescent striving for independence is seen by parents (and, we would add, by teachers) as a desire for less intimacy, when in reality the opposite may be true.

Intimacy struggles can also be mistaken for power struggles. Consider the child who always seeks "negative attention," who tests each and every limit, each and every rule. We've all taught (or will teach) such children. Consider how your attitude and approach might change if this child were seen not so much as testing your authority as seeking more affection. Responding to an intimacy struggle is certainly different from responding to power assertion—certainly less threatening.

Finally, an important contribution of a systems approach to our understanding of families is that conflict between members affects other family members as well. How other members intervene (or not) has important implications for alliances (power) and loyalties (intimacy) within the family. The normative structure of Western families is that parents, in general, remain considerably more powerful than children. Difference in power between spouses or between siblings is supposed to be small compared to the difference in power between parents and children. Similarly, predictable patterns of normative family intimacy prevail. The love between spouses and between the parents and all of their children *as a group* is the normative pattern. Parents are not expected to love a child more than a spouse, nor are they to have favorites among their children.

Insert *schools* for *families*, *educators* for *parents*, *colleague* for *spouse*, *students* for *children*, and *regard* for *love* in the above:

> The normative structure of Western *schools* is that *educators*, in general, remain considerably more powerful than *students*. Differences in power between *colleagues* or between *students* is supposed to be small compared to differences in power between *educators* and *students*. . . . The regard between *colleagues* and between *educators* and all of their *students as a group* is the normative pattern. *Educators* are not expected to regard a *student* more than a *colleague*, nor are they to have favorites among their *students*.

The basic rules of school alliances and loyalties emerge. School systems, by design, do not appear all that different from family systems. We suspect experienced teachers are gaining insights into families and schools, parenting and teaching, as they read this chapter. We also suggest that directly addressing the structural similarities between homes and schools is one important step in designing proactive, interactive, and compatible relations between them.

Implications for Teachers   Clearly, this approach is also rich in its potential to help teachers predict when family conflicts might be especially frequent and intense for students at home—and when teachers may experience more conflicts at school. Conflict—particularly conflict based in struggles for autonomy and power—seems an important lens for reflecting upon family and school relationships with developmental changes in children. Once again, we can consider the mismatch between children's emerging capacity for self-regulation and parents' (schools') need for control that is insensitive to the child's increasing capabilities. To this we now add, "and increasing needs for autonomy," although we recognize that the independence for which the child strives is in a fundamental sense dependent upon the context that supports it. Family systems theory also allows more insight into the intimacy aspects of human relationships that are part of "context." For example, much of the expressive dependency of the student in middle-school transition may be due to an intimacy struggle as much as a crisis in competence: teachers are psychologically distant, the number of peers has just increased geometrically, and the older students are so remote.

A systems theory allows us to identify the many potential sources and meanings of conflict, so that when a parent complains that her daughter "simply won't do her homework," we might better understand and help parent and child resolve the conflict *both* at the surface ("I don't like doing homework") and deep ("You always try to control me.") levels of meaning. Teachers of middle- and high-school students may also want to reconsider their plans for increasing parent involvement in their adolescents' homework. A systems approach also provides clues when a family may be under considerable stress. In some perspectives, a "parentified child" (i.e., a child with disproportionate power and parental intimacy) might be seen as self-regulatory and of little concern (indeed, we can imagine wishing there were more such students in our classroom). Systems theory reminds us, however, that such behavior indicates a problem: even though presently adaptive, it is not unilaterally good for the child. Finally, a systems approach reminds us that families differ in the placement and rigidity of boundaries that admit schools. Teachers need to be sensitive to the limits families place on school in their home and teacher access to their children. As we will discuss in the final section of this chapter, one way to be included *in* families' boundaries is to *include families* in the definition of problems, determination of problem ownership, and responsibility for resolution.

◆ PARENTING–STYLES LITERATURE

Our third approach to understanding families, parenting styles, assumes the parent-child conflict that is one aspect of the family systems perspective. A parenting-styles approach also assumes the expert-novice distinction of the dependent-independence perspective. The parenting-styles perspective does not negotiate these dynamics—they are basic premises: parents are the authorities whose task it is to manage their children. The parenting-styles literature adheres to a psychological model that recognizes reciprocal causality (Bandura, 1986) between parents and children (i.e., a child also influences the parent who influences her/him). Typically, however, the parenting-styles literature locates parent and child outcomes along a broad, unidirectional causal path: parents' influence *on* and control *over* their children (e.g., Baumrind, 1971; 1987). Parenting styles are as likely to be discussed in terms of their "outcome" (i.e., type of child behavior) as they are by the processes (e.g., control) they engage (e.g., Steinberg, Elmer, & Mounts, 1989).

The parenting-styles literature is less likely to explore systematically reciprocal interactions in parent-parent, parent-child, parent-sibling, or sibling relationships. (Why does Anna defy her supportive mother but not her passive father? Why does her brother, who admires Anna tremendously, always comply with both parents? How does this change the relationship between father and mother? These are not questions in this literature.) Nor does the parenting-styles approach attend to context. We do want to stress, however, that current research on parenting styles is no longer a strictly unidimensional model (i.e., parent behavior x produces child characteristic y). Thus, simple conceptions of parenting that seek to link causally parent behavior and student achievement are less sophisticated than current working theory.

Parenting-styles research typically has lacked an ethnic lens. Although this literature may eventually evolve to better understand the family in a culturally diverse society (see Maccoby & Martin, 1983), it is not yet there. At present, parenting-style models are fairly simple extensions of dimensional analyses of stable parent (and coparent) behavior; yet their very simplicity makes them useful tools for interpreting parent-child dynamics that may help teachers understand, predict, and, thus, influence how a student's schooling experience might be mediated at home.

We consider "parenting style" to be more aptly named "managerial style," because that is the primary concern of this literature: how do parents manage their children, and how do management strategies promote parents' goals for their children? The parenting literature has long been influenced by studies that used factor analyses to organize the vast array of behavior that parents either were observed or reported to engage. Early analyses by Schaefer (1959) identified two *independent* dimensions of parent behavior: affect and control. The "Schaefer circumplex" continues to organize the parenting literature.

It is important to note that parents' control of their children and parents' love of their children are independent of each other, because in lay experience we often assume that they are correlated. And we can be sure that children—especially young children—are even more apt to believe they are correlated, so that if a parent punishes them, the parent does not like or love them. (Parental reassurances that this punishment "hurts me more than it hurts you" lack a certain credibility!). Even in situations of "love-withdrawal" (Hoffman, 1985) as a managerial technique, parent affect remains constant; it is the child's *belief* in the relationship between affect and control that the parent exploits. One major contribution of the parenting-styles literature is the finding that control and affect are not correlated: how one manages a child is not related to one's love for her/him.

Control   The recent elaborations of type of parent control owe much to the early work of Baumrind (1971) (see McCaslin & Murdock, 1991, for extended examples and discussion). Typically, the parent control dimension is anchored on one extreme by "laissez-faire" or "permissive" management. In this managerial style, parents exert little control over, structure for, or instruction to their child. Parents function as resources that their child may choose to use or not—either is fine. Laissez-faire parenting is a management policy of noninterference.

At the other extreme is the "authoritarian" control anchor. Authoritarian parents exert considerable control over their children. Control can seem to be a goal in and of itself, because these parents control decision making and their child—independent of the child's present or emerging capabilities. Authoritarian parents tend to not discuss the reasons for their expectations and demands on their child: *might* makes *right*. They have a right to order, and they do. Authoritarian control is dogmatic and obedience-focused. When a child errs, the parent is more apt to understand the behavior as an act of willfulness rather than due to a lack of understanding or knowledge. And intentional misbehavior is more apt to result in punishment than instruction. Coercive authority, in turn, interferes with the development of "moral agency" (Hoffman, 1983; Lepper, 1981). By *moral agency* we mean a sense of oneself as an individual whose acts are based upon one's principles and values rather than the perceived threat (or reward) from another. Ironically, authoritarian parenting is a management policy that creates the conditions for its continued coercive presence.

A third control profile, which Baumrind (1971; 1987) termed *authoritative*, lies between the control anchors. Authoritative control is the most reciprocal of the three, in that the parent actively recognizes the influence of the emerging child on the appropriateness, degree, and arena of parental control. Authoritative parents provide rationales for their "firm yet flexible" limits on child behavior. They *discuss* their standards, *teach* their children how to meet them, and *expect* their standards to be met. Self-control rather than parent control is the goal of the authoritative parent; self-control is seen as an ever-increasing capability that is learned. Authoritative control, then, is a structural and instructional scaffold that is interactive with the child's emergent self-regulation. External supports are fluid and meant both to influence and to support the child's self-constructions so that eventually external sources are not needed: both skill and disposition become part of the child's "tool kit." In short, authoritative management is co-regulation of child mediational processes and action between parent and child for the purpose of emergent child self-regulation.

Finally, a fourth control profile, identified in Baumrind's more recent (1987) work, is termed *traditional*. Traditional management involves a specific integration of authoritarian and authoritative control to support the continuity of family world view and values. Traditional parenting seeks to instill in the child the values that have defined the family in the past so that these values continue to define the family in the future. Traditional management is based in a strong belief system that typically values order above risk-taking. It differs from both authoritarian and authoritative management in that the considerable exertion of control in childhood is meant to serve later self-discipline. Unlike authoritarian management, traditional management does not *keep* the child in a subordinate role; as the child reaches certain "markers" (e.g., ability to drive), power is shared. Unlike authoritative management, traditional management does not consider the child a reciprocal participant in power early on, and parental instruction is not for the purpose of the child constructing her/his *own* perspective and value system. Thus, traditional parenting is likely more "authoritarian" in control with young children and more "authoritative" in control as the child's age earns her/him increasing privileges and as family values have been internalized.

Affect We provide relatively little discussion of parent affect—the second dimension of parent behavior—because, as we stated at the outset, parents must care for, if not love, their children. Thus, while some may argue the relative merits of different parent management styles *per se* (although, we would argue, and data support [Baumrind, 1987; Steinberg, Elmer, & Mounts, 1989] that permissive parenting is not healthy for children), there is little debate about the importance of parental affection (see also Doane & Diamond, 1994).

We do want to emphasize the independence of affect and control in parenting styles, however. When reading the descriptions of managerial control, readers likely envisioned parental affect as well. Did you assume, for example, that authoritarian parents do not care for their child? authoritative parents do? It is important to be mindful of the possible positive and negative affective characteristics of each management approach. For example, some parents may be permissive because they can't be bothered (negative affect—"rejection"), because they respect and value their child's inner goodness (positive affection based in humanistic beliefs), or because they simply are overwhelmed and cannot cope (affect toward child unknown).

Consider that some authoritarian parents may wish to protect their child from a world they believe to be threatening and unsafe; other authoritarian parents may enjoy controlling a disliked child or displacing their frustrations and hostility onto one who is (believed) not able to strike back. This last scenario, the authoritarian, hostile, and harsh parent has more recently been termed *punitive* by Baumrind (1987), to better distinguish this pattern from parents who are authoritarian and who love their child.

Similarly, authoritative parenting can be based upon love for the child; indeed, Baumrind (1971; 1987) and others (Maccoby & Martin, 1983) assume that it is. However, we can imagine and McCaslin (in progress) has interviewed authoritative parents who are engaged in a cool, legalistic enterprise: they know the most effective way to raise tomorrow's entrepreneur and that's the parenting business they are in. Finally, some traditional parents may seek to inculcate family values because they welcome their child to that family; others may not have enough confidence in their own beliefs to allow a child to "test" them; other traditional parents may evoke family values because they do not value or trust the child as an individual, and "family" is meant to coerce or at least suppress the disliked individual.

Implications for Teachers In short, parent management style does not equal parent affection. It is important that teachers distinguish these features, both when thinking about parents' approach to their children and children's interpretation of their parents' behavior. The same parent behavior can be interpreted in quite different ways by children who believe it to be based ultimately in parental concern or rejection. Consider, for example, how a child's interpretation of parent denial of phone privileges may differ by perceived parent affect. How about being given a second chance? Does the child believe s/he is being supported or set up? Upon reflection, it should be clear that how the child perceives parent behavior is, in part, dependent upon the affect the child believes is behind it. The same holds true for just about any action between an "expert" and a "novice." We know of one former professional athlete, for example, who claims that as long as his coach was yelling at him, he (the athlete) knew he was doing all right. But if his coach was silent, he worried.

We also believe that how families control their children has important implications for teachers. Consider the differences in how you have felt or would feel about sending notification of a student's low grade to a home when you know that one of the following styles prevails. (Examples are from McCaslin, 1990, in progress; McCaslin & Murdock, 1991).

1. *The parents are permissive managers.* They simply do not pay much attention to school matters and likely will not respond. Their child knows this and doesn't much care that you are contacting the home. There is likely to be no change in student performance and possibly a decline in student attitude.

2. *The parents are authoritarian managers.* They will assume that if the child is not achieving, s/he is not paying attention and possibly misbehaving. Low grades are punishable, and the parents will likely respond with restrictions rather than help. Their child knows this, dreads taking the grade home, and sees the school as punitive in its outreach.

3. *The parents are authoritative.* They will likely discuss with the child whether s/he feels unsure of her/his learning and why this might be. If the work is too difficult, these parents might provide tips on how the child can recognize when s/he does not understand something, generate strategies for getting help, and practice them. If low grades are due to lack of motivation, these parents might discuss ways to make work more interesting and palatable, but nonetheless stress student responsibility. In either case, the parent is likely to contact the teacher; their child's adaptive learning requires classroom structures and supports in addition to those at home. Their child knows this and knows this low grade is not apt to be a small event in her/his family. But s/he also knows that even if parent response is long and potentially tedious, it will not be punitive.

4. *The parents are traditional in management style.* A note home will result in the parent reminding the child, "In our family, we always try our best, set priorities, see it through, and follow it through. Is this your best? Do it over again, carefully." Their child knows that her/his parents will assume the teacher gave work s/he should be able to do, and they will "give a lecture." The child may be resigned about how s/he will be spending the evening (no television tonight!) and really wish this weren't happening on the day of a favorite program, but s/he will not worry that the event will get too big.

Review these scenarios as you consider as well whether or not you believe the parent cares for the child. Considering parent management style allowed you to diagnose to some extent how effectively sending the low grade home will further your instructional goals for the student. Management and affect go hand in hand, however. Parental affect mediates the effectiveness of their management. Lamborn, Brown, Mounts, and Steinberg (1992) studied how adolescents' engagement in schoolwork was influenced by family, extracurricular activities, part-time jobs, and peers. They found that parental "monitoring without warmth or affection without limit setting is much less effective" in influencing adolescents (p. 175). Consideration of parent affect as well allows you to consider how it might be for the student—beyond potential instructional gain—and how it might affect your relationship with that student. We believe that many teachers who suspect punitive parents (i.e., authoritarian and hostile) have lost more than a little sleep and risked their relationship with students, because they sent home notices of failed achievement. These are important considerations in any communication with families (see Chapter 5 for extended discussion). As we have stated elsewhere, we envision the teacher as the student's advocate; in alliance with parents, if possible. We believe that understanding potential home interpretations of school events will help teachers better meet that role.

Finally, we briefly note that parent management style informs more than the *parent* mediation of school communications. It also informs how *students* might mediate school management systems. Schools want compliance from students (McCaslin & Good, 1992, 1993); so, too, do most nonlenient parents. (Even some permissive parents may want compliance but not know how to get it.) How parents approach that compliance differs in at least the three nonlenient ways we have described (authoritarian, authoritative, traditional). Consider the confusions a student may experience whose authoritarian upbringing (i.e., reliance on authority) works just fine for getting along with authority in school—in the early grades, anyway. Suddenly, in fourth grade the student is expected to be self-reliant and not to need teacher directives, sanctions, or approval—but to adhere to them nonetheless. The student is expected to have internalized these goals and strategies, yet the management systems at home and school do not teach them—indeed, they may even *obviate* the development of internalized self-control (see McCaslin & Good, 1992, 1993). In effect, then, the student is left behind *because* s/he accepted the management programs of home and school. We suspect this is not an unusual scenario. Indeed, much of adolescents' "risky" behavior may be due to the sudden changes in home management from "Do as I say" to "You're on your own."

What about the student from the authoritative home who has been taught to think through expectations, to focus on the reasons and intentions beneath a given behavior or rule? How does this student make sense of Cantor-like management systems with their rigid adherence to narrow conceptions of obedience? How can teacher behavior be seen as caring and supportive when her/his punishment does not account for student intention and effort? When her/his rewards for compliance make the student feel controlled or used rather than self-determining (e.g., Deci & Ryan 1985)?

Students from traditional homes likely end up in a similar dilemma. At a time when their family ("finally") recognizes their capability for self-control and sense of values, the school still adheres to impositions of external control—as if the student somehow did not value what the school was about. If all these external controls are required, the reasoning might follow, "Maybe I don't/shouldn't value what school is about." Thus—in contrast to the student from an authoritarian home, who tends to learn that external consequences are part of any reason for behavior—the high-school student from a traditional family is more apt to learn that external constraints are required in the *absence* of personal value. Attention must be paid to the implication of that reversal: the presence of external incentives speaks volumes about the believed absence of internal value and self-regulation (e.g., Lepper, 1985).

Our point is that students mediate their schooling experience; family approaches to management are likely to be a fundamental part of that mediation. We have illustrated how students whose parents engage each of four management styles might interpret student failure. How might these parents interpret student success? curiosity? Family mediation is not just tied to interpretations of school management strategies; more recent approaches to instruction that are based on a constructivist view of the learner (e.g., Delpit, 1992) are also open to varied interpretation. Although authoritative parents can likely absorb curricular innovations into their general management style because of its parallel instructional (and reciprocal) components, authoritarian and traditional parents likely have more difficulty.

Authoritarian parents are often nonplussed by their children writing their own and reading classmates' stories rather than learning from a text. Innovative spelling is not necessarily appreciated or helpful. The authors recall one authoritarian parent who prided herself on teaching her preschooler how to spell and write the name of her favorite animal, *horse*, underneath the child's numerous drawings. The two spent many an afternoon drawing and labeling pictures for friends and relatives. The mother treasured these moments and was already worried about losing similar times when her daughter went to first grade. Her worries were well-founded: in a few months she would be informed by her now-upset first-grader that mother did it all wrong: in class, teacher said it was spelled h-o-r-s. Teacher is right; Mom is wrong. Mother cannot imagine her daughter is telling the truth. Not an unusual, but certainly an unfortunate, beginning for home-school relationships—one that is not apt to encourage school within home boundaries.

Consider as well the child of traditional parents who is told in class not to worry about grammar, that the only thing that matters in today's assignment is the content. As McCaslin (1990) recounts the dilemma for a sixth-grade student, "Nora" (whom you met in Chapter 2):

> Nora's mother may well look poorly on an assigned essay that comes home with errors in punctuation and spelling, yet boasts a "good thinking!" message from the teacher. Nora is apt to get a "mom talk," as she calls her mother's sermons, and made to do it over until it is "right." Nora's teacher's credibility is likely on the line, certainly by Nora's mother, and now perhaps by Nora as well. Both Nora and her mother are getting messages from the popular culture that the form and

physical attractiveness of the messages are what is important—not its accuracy or level of critical comment (p. 47).

Unfortunately, the curricular "innovation," like the popular culture, appears to define form and content as independent features of composition. This definition inevitably leads to "taking sides." And when home and school are on different sides of a false choice, it is the child who loses. We maintain that both parent and teacher are "right," in a specific context. The issue is not to be "right," however, but to acknowledge and deal with the conflict. It begins with conversation.

In short, student home life mediates classroom experience and classroom communication with home. To ignore this mediation is to risk miscommunication and misperception, a state of affairs with which we are all too familiar. Teachers will do well to consider how parents and students mediate schooling in addition to how teachers might actively influence these perceptions.

◆ CONCLUDING COMMENTS

We would be remiss if we did not directly address the putative advantages of authoritative management and its relation to emergent dependent-independence and normative family conflict. Clearly, these three constructs are related: authoritative management is, in the moment, all about the adjustment of support and the creation of affording contexts for children. Conflict between individuals that involves discussion and mutual resolution is healthy for all system participants.

Data based upon *outcomes* of authoritative parenting (which is mostly associated with the middle class) appear to support the efficacy of this approach. Children of authoritative parents, more than children of any other parenting style, show the most-advanced levels of autonomy and independence for their ages, have greater confidence and healthier self-concepts, and exhibit "instrumental" rather than "emotional" dependence (Baumrind, 1971, 1987). Apparently this is especially true for young girls (Baumrind, 1970). Children of authoritative parents also achieve more in high school (Steinberg, Elmer, & Mounts, 1989) and engage in more appropriate, "healthy," types of risk taking as adolescents (Baumrind, 1987). Thus, authoritative parents apparently are more effective in building cognitive structures and self-control skills in their children which help them become both more independent and more responsible *within the contexts of school and middle-class society, which these parents help design.*

As we have discussed elsewhere (McCaslin & Good, 1992, 1993), we hypothesize that authoritative management is more apt to successfully inculcate self-regulation and the internalization of values because it keeps the child focused on internal rationales as opposed to external reasons for behavior. In addition, we note that authoritative parents are mostly found in racial/ethnic-majority, middle-class families. Thus, the world within which they function—and within which they have ample resources—is the same world that schools aspire to influence. A reasonable hypothesis is that the supportive contexts of home and school overlap more for these children than they might for children of other parent management systems *and/or* other socioeconomic or cultural contexts.

Finally, just as there are "optimal amounts" in nearly every construct that describes human phenomena, we maintain that the very virtues of authoritative parenting can be overextended; authoritative parenting is not a panacea within or across contexts. In an edited volume meant to underscore how to promote talent development in children (Bloom, 1985), Sloane describes parent influences on children's talent development. The chapter chronicles the reports of parents and families of variously talented individuals (e.g., pianists, swimmers, tennis players).

General patterns of reported parent behavior across families indicate authoritative parenting (and, in some accounts, authoritative management of older children within a more traditional family). Parents consistently modeled and stated their expectations, provided guidance and instruction, created contexts and opportunities for their child to demonstrate competence and independence, and monitored their child's progress—in school, in the talent area, and in other recreation. The motivation that tended to pervade these families was "mastery-oriented" and "individualistic" (e.g., Ames, 1992). That is, the parents of the talented individuals stressed quality of achievement ("If it is worth doing it is worth doing well" [p. 440]) and self-striving for excellence ("No matter how many times you do something, you always try to do it as well or better than the time before" [p. 441]). Importantly, parents set and modeled goals for their child that were short-term, set in the everydayness of the activity, and *not* focused on some distant and large aspiration (e.g., win the Olympics), consistent with modern efficacy theory (e.g., Bandura, 1986).

We think that the most critical feature of these individuals' talent development is that it all began in the *parents' interest area*. Initially, parent goals were simply to encourage the child to participate with their parents around a parent interest, in the hope that it would evolve into a shared interest of mutual enjoyment. As the child's skills developed (through maturation and intentional exposure to activities appropriate for his/her age and abilities), the parents *transferred achievement values* to child progress in the interest area.

Parents supported their child by attending performances, displaying ribbons, and the like. With the child's increased expertise also came a change in family life: the family became organized around the child (e.g., lessons, meals, transportation, vacations). The talented child became the *definition of the family* as "the child's lessons, practice, and competition in the field dominated the family's routine. . . . other family interests were gradually eliminated" (p. 462). The talented child's other interests were also eliminated as parents channeled their child's energies and replaced "interest" with "achievement striving" ("You can only excel in one thing at a time. . . . defining a task and staying with it is the only way to excel" [p. 465]).

In some ways this process is similar to the self-fulfilling-prophecy research (Brophy & Good, 1970; Good & Brophy, 1994) that has been used to explore how teachers might communicate performance expectations to students. What is instructive here, however, is that these parents do not start with the expectation to create a "superstar." In contrast, the process is more subtle and indirect in its initial expression but certainly just as consuming in its result.

We explore these dynamics at length because we suspect that, to a considerable extent, these parents represent society's "dream parents." As teachers, you may have thought how great it would be if parents like this had a passion for literature or science that they wished to share with their child. There are costs to this level of parental commitment, however, and we want to suggest that *more* is not always *better*. Consider, for example, the pressure (and personal limitations) of being the "favored" child, who defines and provides the cohesion for "our family." How can this child change? try something else? explore other identities? fail? be forgiven by her/his siblings?

Imagine being the talented child's sibling, who simply doesn't measure up and consequently feels ignored. As one sibling charged, her parents were never home for her birthday; they were always at a competition with her brother. Interestingly, parents of these "special" children did not believe that the talented child was the most talented of their children in that particular area. What distinguished the talented children was their persistence, their "willingness to work and their desire to excel." In other words, these children were known by their motivation and enactment strategies—especially volitional "staying with it"—as much as, if not more than, their aptitude. Their achievements, however, were not cost-free for themselves, their siblings, or their parents.

❖ CONCLUSION: TALKING WITH PARENTS

We began this chapter by examining extant home-school relationships, specifically some supports and constraints on parents' involvement in educational decisions, their child's schooling experiences, and their child's actual attendance and performance in school. We then provided a different perspective on parents—namely, their life at home. Using three different approaches, we examined how family dynamics might affect parent mediation of communications from and about school and their child's mediation of school. In this final section, we consider how teachers might frame: 1) parents' concerns to better understand them, and 2) their own concerns so that parents can better understand teachers within the context of parent-teacher conferences.

◆ FRAMING PARENTS' AND TEACHER CONCERNS

First, we think it is important to be mindful of the possible constraints to parental involvement. Parents may well enter a teacher conference feeling defensive, misunderstood, and wrong before they even start. This is because, as Tangri and Moles (1987) note, conferences often occur when students are in trouble, and as we discussed, parents are often stressed for good reason. So parents are defensive; teachers are not trained in how to discuss and handle conflict. No wonder parent-teacher conferences are described in terms of their "potential" rather than their actual accomplishments!

We think it is useful to consider two layers in the parent-teacher conference: the first is the expectations the parents bring, their possible discomfort, defensiveness, and resistance; the second is the problem, issue, or simply routine procedure that the conference is to be about. Simple recognition of the parents' discomfort seems an important start. Teachers would do well to consult texts on interpersonal communication skills (e.g., Gordon, 1970) to help them develop a vocabulary that does not trigger defensiveness ("Why don't you monitor Brad's homework?") or unintentionally patronize ("Now I assume you want what is best for your child."). We suggest that you review the chapter on interviewing students: how might you use these skills in questioning and interview design to talk with parents?

Our purpose here is to provide two additional frameworks that we think might be useful in talking with parents. The first concerns what type of problem the child is presenting ("problem ownership"); the second is what type of goal you wish to engage parent and child in pursuing.

Problem Ownership   Gordon's (1970, 1974) concept of problem ownership is especially helpful for understanding student behavior at home and at school. Indeed, Gordon's 1970 work is aimed at parents; the 1974 volume targets teachers. Gordon hypothesized that conflicts between adults and children can be categorized to represent three different kinds of need frustration, constituting three "levels" of problem ownership. We accept the usefulness of this general framework, although we would argue that problem "levels" are best considered on a continuum, because adults have some degree of responsibility in all child/student problem presentations (see Rohrkemper, 1982, 1984, 1985 for more complete discussion).

The first of Gordon's levels is a *self-owned* problem, which occurs when another interferes with our ability or our needs. For parents ("parent-owned") and teachers ("teacher-owned"), these occur when children/students make us feel frustrated, upset, irritated, or angry—usually because they are perceived as challenging our authority. *Other-owned* ("child"- or "student"-owned) problems exist separately from the adult and do not concretely affect her/him. For example, perhaps the child is disappointed because the school canceled the field trip because of inclement weather. The third category, *"shared"* problems, occur when adult and child (parent-child, teacher-student) interfere with each other's need satisfaction: parent likes a quiet evening, child likes heavy-metal music; teacher likes to see all the students' faces, student hairstyles interfere. Gordon predicts, and research has found (Brophy & McCaslin, 1992; Brophy & Rohrkemper, 1981; Rohrkemper, 1984, 1985; Rohrkemper & Brophy, 1983; Stollak, Scholom, Kallman, & Saturansky, 1973) that these levels of problem ownership are associated with interpersonal understanding, attributional patterns (e.g., Weiner, 1986), and reported behavior—in adults and in children.

Adults and children interpret self-owned problems as intentional and controllable behavior by others, whose purpose is to thwart the perceiver's own needs. They respond to this attribution with anger and punishment. In contrast, other-owned problems that do not directly affect the perceiver are attributionally understood as unintentional and uncontrollable behavior. The perceiver feels empathy/pity and the behavioral response is supportive. Finally, in shared problems—where both parties have legitimate needs—the behavior may or may not be seen as ultimately controllable; however, in the given situation it is believed unintentional. Specific plans for compromise (often within a certain level of irritation) are established. In classrooms, this often means behavior modification contracts.

Problem ownership seems a powerful tool for organizing conflict and understanding why some behavior can "get to you"; whereas other, seemingly similar, behavior does not arouse you in the same way. It is especially useful to consider how different managerial approaches may inform interpretations of the "same" child behavior. Consider how you would reframe problem ownership from the dependent-independence and family systems perspectives. We think problem ownership emerges as a useful tool for organizing experience and the discussion of conflict from each of these theoretical perspectives. It certainly informs us about those occasions when our behavior is apt to be unthinking, reactive, self-defeating, and perhaps self-fulfilling: harshly criticizing a child who has problems with authority (a common response by parents and teachers who feel threatened); overly nurturing and supporting a child who displays expressive, emotional dependency, or immediately simplifying work and reducing performance expectations for a student having difficulty (common responses by parents and teachers who feel pity).

Identifying the problem, and recognizing the attributional interpretations and helping/rejecting behavioral scenarios it likely elicits, seem to be the first steps in altering problem behavior. The next step is identifying what you wish to achieve.

Socialization Goals Kelman (1951, 1958) distinguishes among three goals of any management attempt (see also McCaslin & Good, 1992, 1993, for more complete discussion). One can attempt to promote *compliance*, which occurs when an attitude or behavior is expressed only when the person expects to get a reward or avoid a punishment. Another goal might be *identification*, in which the attitude and appropriate behavior exist as long as the model the person wishes to be like is present. A third goal is termed *internalization*, which, like moral agency (Hoffman, 1985), is indicated when the attitude and behavior occur in a variety of settings without the presence of external consequences. These three types of management/socialization goals should be the source of many hypotheses for you as you consider them in relation to our discussion of parent management styles, dependent-independence, and family systems. How might you consider your own behavior with students as well as parents' behavior with their children? Can you imagine certain problems that students present in your classroom for which you would be satisfied with "compliance" goals? We know that in our classrooms, we do not much care if students have *internalized* the reason for the behavior of not calling out; we just don't want them to do it. Our attitude toward student tolerance for frustration and learning from failure is a different story, different goal, however.

Determining the socialization goals that we aspire to instill is one part of the puzzle. The second is to consider what motivational state the child may be in. Lepper (1983) distinguishes among instilling, maintaining, and inhibiting attitudes and behavior. Instilling behavior is all about careful use of rewards that are then carefully faded. Maintaining behavior calls for very subtle, if any, external rewards; indeed, attention must be paid not to undermine extant motivation. Recall the child of the authoritative parents who felt *controlled* rather than *reinforced* by rewards. Finally, Lepper's work reminds us not to confuse inhibiting behavior with instilling attitudes. Teachers and parents cannot assume that because the child no longer skips school s/he is motivated to learn.

In short, teachers and parents need to agree upon the socialization goals they will pursue. We allow that some "problems"—for example, a penchant for loud, clashing colors in clothing—are simply not worth the considerable investment required for an internalization goal (of harmony in nature!). Other problems are worth that effort: prevention of drug abuse, promiscuous sexual activity, passivity in girls, gang memberships. We could go on. The point, and it certainly is not new with us: don't sweat the small stuff. Sometimes compliance is good enough.

Make a Plan   Third, after the problem has been identified and goals set, strategies to attain them need to be explored and likely will involve parent, teacher, and student in their implementation. We have already described the guidelines for a co-regulated, problem-solving interview with students (see Chapter 3), which has some relevance to our vision of a successful parent-teacher (-student) conference. Like the interview guidelines with students, our parent-teacher conference guidelines are meant to serve as a thoughtful heuristic to help teachers better plan their goals for the session. We offer these guidelines:

1. Schedule an initial conference about positive, or at least neutral, topics to set a nondefensive tone. If that is not possible, begin the problem-focused conference with a positive or neutral topic.

2. Explore the perceptions of each participant (both parents, student). State your perceptions. Give the parents credit for knowing/understanding their child.

3. Make the interview a cooperative one. Establish mutual agreement about why the conference is scheduled, definition of the problem, and acceptance of problem ownership.

4. Maintain a professional demeanor at all times.

5. Accept the parent's (and student's) anger, but not necessarily the behavior.

6. Distinguish emotion from behavior but recognize their relationship.

7. Work to understand the perceptions of each participant (both parents, student) throughout the conference.

8. Cooperatively generate possible alternative strategies, assess their feasibility, and determine how they might be implemented and how progress might be known and evaluated.

9. Encourage parent (and student) ownership of whatever plan is adopted.

10. Clarify your own and others' responsibility in making the plan work.

11. Encourage follow-up conversations and conferences; maintain open communication.

12. Remember: The parent is *more than* the parent of a "problem" child.

◆ CONCLUDING COMMENTS

We believe that teachers can do much to create a supportive environment within which students thrive and their families feel welcomed. We have attempted to provide a framework for thinking about parent-teacher relationships and how these might be organized to promote co-regulation by teachers and parents as they design supportive contexts to enhance student self-regulation and adaptive learning.

❖ QUESTIONS AND SUGGESTED ACTIVITIES FOR CHAPTER 6

1. Given the growing diversity in U.S. schools, it is likely that at some point during your teaching career you will have students with limited English proficiency (perhaps a student from Viet Nam or Cambodia). How can you have productive communication with parents who have limited English-speaking proficiency? What strategies could you use to be sure that effective communication is taking place?

2. Think about your own SES background. Compared to your classmates, how has it influenced your development by determining the type of experiences that you have had? Is it possible that your SES background might affect your interactions with parents who come from a different background? If, for example, you are from a middle-class background, is it possible that you might resent affluent parents (who pay tutors, take "credit" for their child's learning, etc.)? Similarly, if you come from a middle-class background, might you be likely to undervalue the parenting skills and dispositions of parents who come from lower-income circumstances?

3. There are considerable clinical data to indicate that people sometimes treat other individuals on the basis of their background. For example, doctors might ask more questions of high-SES patients because they

think that these individuals are articulate and are capable of expressing relevant hypotheses about their present conditions. There are also data to suggest physicians may ask fewer questions of low-income individuals, assuming that they are less capable of understanding themselves and their environment. How might your perceptions of successful and less-successful parents determine the type of questions that you ask and the general rapport and communication style that you develop with parents?

4. There is some literature to indicate that reports of physical abuse go up following the distribution of report cards. How can we as educators do a better job of preventing this from happening? Think about the particular grade that you will teach and the type of community that you are most likely to be in—specifically, what will you do to attempt to reduce this problem?

5. In working with parents, it is possible that a teacher might create difficulties (for the student) by sharing certain information with the parent or custodial guardian. Identify three or four situations where it might be risky to share information with parents. Share your list and discuss your concerns with other classmates. In what ways are they different, and in what ways are they similar? Drawing upon this information, what general statements can you make about the type of information that is more and less desirable to communicate to parents. How defensible are your conclusions?

6. In working with parents, how would you deal with a situation in which a female student characteristically assumes a passive role during class discussion and during small-group work? You are concerned about the student's passivity. In Chapter 5, we asked you to consider your role with this student *within* the classroom. Now, consider how you might attempt to communicate this concern with parents. Would your strategy differ for parents who differed in some marked way (e.g., an authoritative versus a traditional home)?

7. The authors note that typically it is constructive to allow students to assume more responsibility as they show increased skill or maturity. How might this apply in a high school? For example, if teachers believe in increasing student autonomy, how might instruction and accountability vary between 10th- and 12th-grade classrooms? Similarly, in an elementary school, how might instruction and management vary in 3rd- and 6th-grade classrooms?

8. Recall the earlier distinction between *average* and *range* of ability with regard to a particular skill. Given that some seniors may have less skills for coping as autonomous learners than do some 10th-graders (or 6th-graders versus 3rd graders), how can the 12th-grade teacher (or 6th-grade teacher) have a classroom that on average demands more self-regulation than the typical 10th-grade classroom (or 3rd-grade classroom), but still recognize that some older students need at least as much teacher scaffolding as do younger students?

9. A parent who has a sophomore son and a senior daughter expresses concern about how to deal with the son's anger that his sister has more privileges than he does. The parent wants to know how to represent the legitimacy of extending more privileges to the daughter (later curfew hour, etc.) as a result of her advanced maturity, especially her advanced coping skills for dealing with diverse social situations. How would you respond? Would it make a difference if the male were the older student?

10. On page 208 in this chapter, the authors describe four types of home environments. Which type best describes your experience? What else would you add to the "best-fit" scenario that would make it more descriptive for you? How might your home environment experiences influence how you manage students in the classroom?

11. The authors make the point that some behavior can "get to you," whereas other seemingly irritating behavior does not arouse you in the same way. Given your previous experiences (i.e., the management style you experienced at home and in schools) and your teaching goals, what student behaviors are most likely to upset you the most? the least? Why?

12. In what ways might involving parents in students' homework be beneficial? detrimental? Would it vary in terms of student age? If so, why? What other factors would be relevant to the efficacy of involving parents in students' school work?

❖ REFERENCES

Ames, C. (1992). Classrooms: Goals, structures, and student motivation. *Journal of Educational Psychology, 84,* 261–271.

Bandura, A. (1986). *Social foundations of thought and action: A social cognitive theory.* Englewood Cliffs, NJ: Prentice-Hall.

Baumrind, D. (1970) Socialization and instrumental competence in young children. *Young Children, 26,* 104–119.

Baumrind, D. (1971). Current patterns of parental authority. *Developmental Psychology Monographs, 4,* 1–103.

Baumrind, D. (1987). A developmental perspective on adolescent risk-taking in contemporary America. In C. Irwin, Jr. (Ed.), *Adolescent social behavior and health* (pp. 93–125). San Franscisco: Jossey-Bass.

Berliner, D., & Biddle, B. (1995). *The manufactured crisis.* New York: Longman and Addison-Wesley.

Bloom, B. (Ed.). (1985). *Developing talent in young people.* New York: Ballantine.

Bowman, D. (1994). Home and school: The unresolved relationship. In S. Kagan & B. Weissbourd (Eds.), *Putting families first* (pp. 51–72). San Francisco: Jossey-Bass.

Brantlinger, E. (1993). *The politics of social class in secondary school: Views of affluent and impoverished youth.* New York: Teachers College Press.

Bronfenbrenner, U., & Neville, P. (1994). America's children and families: An international perspective. In S. Kagan & B. Weissbourd (Eds.), *Putting families first* (pp. 3–27). San Francisco: Jossey-Bass.

Brophy, J., & Good, T. (1970). Teachers' communication of differential expectations for children's classroom performance: Some behavioral data. *Journal of Educational Psychology, 61,* 365–374.

Brophy, J., & McCaslin, M. (1992). Teachers' reports of how they perceive and cope with problem students. *Elementary School Journal, 93,* 3–68.

Brophy, J., & Rohrkemper, M. (1981). The influence of problem ownership on teachers' perceptions of and strategies for coping with problem students. *Journal of Educational Psychology, 73,* 295–311.

Casanova, U. (1987). Ethnic and cultural differences. In V. Richardson-Koehler (Ed.), *Educators' handbook: A research perspective* (pp. 370–393). White Plains, NY: Longman.

Corno, L. (1989). What it means to be literate about classrooms. In D. Bloome (Ed.), *Learning to use literacy in educational settings* (pp. 29–52). New York: Ablex.

Corno, L. (1992). Encouraging students to take responsibility for learning and performance. *Elementary School Journal, 93,* 69–83.

Corno, L. (1993). The best-laid plans: Modern conceptions of volition and educational research. *Educational Researcher, 22,* 14–22.

Corno L., & Kanfer, R. (1993). The role of volition in learning and performance. In L. Darling-Hammond (Ed.), *Review of research in education* (vol. 19, pp. 3–43). Washington, DC: American Educational Research Association.

Covington, M. (1992). *Making the grade: A self-worth perspective on motivation and school reform.* New York: Cambridge University Press.

Deci, E., & Ryan, R. (1985). *Intrinsic motivation in self-determination in human behavior.* New York: Plenum.

Delpit, L. (1992). Acquisition of literate discourse: Bowing before the master? *Theory Into Practice, 31,* 296–302.

Doane, J., & Diamond, D. (1994). *Affect and attachment in the family: A family-based treatment of major psychiatric disorder.* New York: Basic Books.

Eccles, J. S., Midgley, C., Wigfield, A., Buchanan, C., Reuman, D., Flanagan, C., & MacIver, D. (1993). Development during adolescence: The impact of stage-environment fit on young adolescents' experiences in schools and in families. *American Psychologist, 48,* 90–102.

Emery, R. (1992). Family conflicts and their developmental implications: A conceptual analysis of meaning for the structure of relationships. In C. U. Shantz & W. W. Hartup (Eds.), *Conflict in child and adolescent development: Cambridge studies in social and emotional development* (pp. 270–298). New York: Cambridge University Press.

Epstein, J. (1989). Family structures and student motivation: A developmental perspective. In C. Ames & R. Ames (Eds.), *Research on motivation in education: Goals and cognitions* (vol. 3). San Diego, CA: Academic Press.

Good, T., & Brophy, J. (1994). *Looking in Classrooms* (6th ed.). New York: HarperCollins.

Gordon, T. (1970). *P.E.T. Parent effectiveness training: The tested new way to raise responsible children*. New York: P. H. Widen.

Gordon, T. (1974). *T.E.T.: Teacher effectiveness training*. New York: McKay.

Heckhausen, H. (1991). *Motivation and action*. (P. Leppmann, Trans.). Berlin Heidelberg, Germany: Springer-Verlag.

Hess, R., & Holloway, S. (1984). Family and school as educational institutions. In R. D. Parker (Ed.), *Review of child development research, Vol. 7: The family* (pp. 179–222). Chicago: University of Chicago Press.

Hoffman, M. (1985). Affective and cognitive processes in moral internalization. In E. Higgins, D. Ruble, & W. Hartup (Eds.), *Social cognition and social development: A sociological perspective* (pp. 236–274). Cambridge: Cambridge University Press.

Kagan, S., & Weissbourd, B. (Eds.). (1994). *Putting families first*. San Francisco: Jossey-Bass.

Kelman, H. (1951). Processes of attitude change. *Public Opinion Quarterly, 25*, 57–78.

Kelman, H. (1958). Compliance, identification, and internalization: Three processes of opinion change. *Journal of Conflict Resolution, 2*, 51–60.

Kuhl, J. (1985). Volitional mediators of cognition-behavior consistency: Self-regulatory processes and action versus state orientation. In J. Kuhl & Beckmann (Eds.), *Action control: From cognition to behavior* (pp. 101–128). Berlin: Springer-Verlag.

Lamborn, S., Brown, B., Mounts, N., & Steinberg, L. (1992). Putting in school perspective: The influence of family, peers, extracurricular participation, and part-time work on academic engagement. In F. Newmann (Ed.), *Student engagement and achievement in American secondary schools* (pp. 153–181). New York: Teachers College Press.

Lepper, M. (1981). Intrinsic and extrinsic motivation in children: Detrimental effects of superfluous social controls. In W. Collins (Ed.), *Minnesota Symposium on Child Psychology* (Vol. 14). Hillsdale, NJ: Erlbaum.

Lepper, M. (1983). Extrinsic reward and intrinsic motivation: Implications for the classroom. In J. Levine & M. Wang (Eds.), *Teacher and student perspectives: Implications for learning* (pp. 281–317). Hillsdale, NJ: Erlbaum.

Lepper, M. (1985). Social-control processes and the internalization of social values: An attributional perspective. In E. Higgins, D. Ruble, & W. Hartup (Eds.), *Social cognition and social development: A sociocultural perspective*. (pp. 294–330). New York: Cambridge University Press.

Lightfoot, S. (1978). *Worlds apart: Relationships between families and schools*. New York: Basic Books.

Maccoby, E., & Martin, J. (1983). Socialization in the context of the family: Parent-child interaction. In P. H. Mussen (Ed.), *Handbook of child psychology (4th ed.): Vol. 4. E. Hetherington, Ed. Socialization, personality, and social development* (pp. 1–101). New York: John Wiley & Sons.

McCaslin, M. (1990). Motivated literacy. In J. Zutell &. McCormick (Eds.), *Literacy theory and research: Analysis for multiple paradigms* (39th yearbook, pp. 35–50). Rochester, NY: National Reading Conference, Inc.

McCaslin, M. (in progress). *Adaptive learning: A co-regulation perspective*.

McCaslin, M., & Good, T. (1992). Compliant cognition: The misalliance of management and instructional goals in current school reform. *Educational Researcher, 21,* 4–17.

McCaslin, M., & Good, T. (1993). Classroom management and motivated student learning. In T. M. Tomlinson (Ed.), *Motivating students to learn: Overcoming barriers to high achievement* (pp. 245–261). Berkeley, CA: McCutchan.

McCaslin, M., & Good, T. (1996). The informal curriculum. In D. Berliner and R. Calfee (Eds.), *The handbook of educational psychology.* New York: Macmillan.

McCaslin, M., & Murdock, T. (1991). The emergent interaction of home and school in the development of students' adaptive learning. In M. Maehr & P. Pintrich (Eds.), *Advances in motivation and achievement* (Vol. 7, pp. 213–259). Greenwich, CT: JAI Press.

Miller, P. (1982). *Amy, Wendy, and Beth: Learning language in South Baltimore.* Austin: University of Texas Press.

Minuchin, S. (1974). *Families and family therapy.* Cambridge, MA: Harvard University Press.

National Commission for Excellence in Education. (1983, April). *A nation at risk: The imperatives for educational reform.* Washington, DC: U.S. Department of Education, National Commission for Excellence in Education.

National Education Association. (1982). *Productive relationships: Parent-school-teacher.* Washington, DC: National Education Association.

National Education Commission on Time and Learning. (1994, April). *Prisoners of time.* Washington, DC: U.S. Government Printing Office.

Newmann, F. (1992). *Student engagement and achievement in American secondary schools.* New York: Teachers College Press.

Philips, S. (1983). *The invisible culture: Communication in classroom and community on the Warm Springs Indian reservation.* White Plains, NY: Longman.

Quindlen, A. (January 12, 1994). Parental "victory" in condom case could turn out costly and tragic. *The Arizona Daily Star,* p. A12.

Rohrkemper, M. (1982). Teachers' self-assessment. In D. Duke (Ed.), *Helping teachers manage classrooms* (pp. 77–96). Alexandria, VA: Association of Supervision and Curriculum Development.

Rohrkemper, M. (1984). Influence of teacher's socialization style on students' social cognition and reported interpersonal classroom behavior. *Elementary School Journal, 85,* 245–275.

Rohrkemper, M. (1985). Individual differences in students' perceptions of routine classroom events. *Journal of Educational Psychology, 77,* 29–44.

Rohrkemper, M., & Brophy, J. (1983). Teachers' thinking about problem students. In J. Levine & M. C. Wang (Eds.), *Teacher and student perceptions: Implications for learning* (pp. 75–104). Hillsdale, NJ: Erlbaum.

Romero, M., Mercado, C., & Vàzquez-Faría, J. (1987). Students of limited English proficiency. In V. Richardson-Koehler (Ed.), *Educators' handbook: A research perspective* (pp. 348–369). White Plains, NY: Longman.

Sarason, S. (1993). *You are thinking of teaching?: Opportunities, problems, realities.* San Francisco: Jossey-Bass.

Schaefer, E. (1959). A circumplex model for maternal behavior. *Journal of Abnormal and Social Psychology, 59,* 226–235.

Shantz, C. (1993). Children's conflicts: Representations and lessons learned. In R. Cocking and K. Renninger (Eds.), *The development and meaning of psychological distance* (pp. 185–202). Hillsdale, NJ: Lawrence Erlbaum Associates.

Skinner, B. (1953). *Science and human behavior.* New York: Macmillan.

Sloane, K. (1985). Home influences on talent development. In B. Bloom (Ed.), *Developing talent in young people* (pp. 439–476). New York: Ballantine.

Spencer, D. (1986). *Contemporary women teachers: Balancing school and home.* White Plains, NY: Longman.

Spodek, B., & Saracho, O. (1990). Preparing early childhood teachers for the 21st Century. In B. Spodek & O. Saracho (Eds.), *Early childhood teacher preparation* (pp. 23–44). New York: Teachers College Press.

Stallworth, J., & Williams, D., Jr. (1983). *Executive summary of the final report: A survey of school administrators and policymakers.* Austin, TX: Southwest Educational Development Laboratory.

Steinberg, L., Elmer, J., & Mounts, N. (1989). Authoritative parenting, psychosocial maturity, and academic success among adolescents. *Child Development, 60,* 1424–1436.

Stollak, G., Scholom, A., Kallman, J., & Saturansky, C. (1973). Insensitivity to children: Responses of undergraduates to children in problem situations. *Journal of Abnormal Child Psychology, 1,* 169–180.

Tangri, S., & Moles, O. (1987). Parents and the community. In V. Richardson-Koehler (Ed.), *Educators' handbook: A research perspective* (pp. 519–550). White Plains, NY: Longman.

Tomlinson, T. (1993). Educational reform: The ups and downs of good intentions. In T. Tomlinson (Ed.), *Motivating students to learn: Overcoming barriers to high achievement* (pp. 3–20). Berkeley, CA: McCutchan.

Vygotsky, L. (1962). *Thought and language.* Cambridge, MA: MIT Press.

Vygotsky, L. (1978). *Mind and society: The development of higher psychological processes.* Cambridge, MA: Harvard University Press.

Webb, F., Covington, M. V., & Guthrie, J. W. (1993). Carrots and sticks: Can school policy influence student motivation? In T. M. Tomlinson (Ed.), *Motivating students to learn: Overcoming barriers to high achievement* (pp. 99–123). Berkeley, CA: McCutchan.

Weiner, B. (1986). *An attributional theory of motivation and emotion.* New York: Springer-Verlag.

Weissbourd, B. (1994). The evolution of the family resource movement. In Kagan, S., & Weissbourd, B. (Eds.), *Putting families first* (pp. 28–48). San Francisco: Jossey-Bass.

Winegar, L., Renninger, K., & Valsiner, J. (1989). Dependent-independence in adult-child relationships. In D. Kramer & M. Bopp (Eds.), *Transformation in clinical and developmental psychology* (pp. 157–168). New York: Springer-Verlag.

Women's Sports Foundation. (1989). *High school athletics prove boon.* New York: Women's Sports Foundation.

Zeigler, E. (1994). Foreword. In S. Kagan & B. Weissbourd (Eds.), *Putting families first: America's family support movement and the challenge of change* (pp. xi–xix). San Francisco: Jossey-Bass.

Zeigler, E., & Muenchow, S. (1992). Headstart: The inside story of America's most successful educational experiment. New York: Basic Books.

NAME INDEX

SUBJECT INDEX